Library of
Davidson College

A Guide to Romantic Poetry in Germany

Miroslav John Hanak

A Guide to Romantic Poetry in Germany

PETER LANG
New York · Bern · Frankfurt am Main · Paris

Library of Congress Cataloging-in-Publication Data

Hanak, Miroslav John.
A guide to romantic poetry in Germany.

Includes index.
1. German poetry–18th century–History and criticism. 2.German poetry–19th century–History and criticism. 3. Romanticism–Germany.
I. Title. II. Series
PT535.H36 1988   831'.6'09145   87-3515
ISBN 0-8204-0629-5

CIP-Kurztitelaufnahme der Deutschen Bibliothek

Hanak, Miroslav John:
A guide to romantic poetry in Germany / Miroslav John Hanak. – New York; Bern; Frankfurt am Main; Paris: Lang, 1987.
ISBN 0-8204-0629-5

© Peter Lang Publishing, Inc., New York 1987

All rights reserved.
Reprint or reproduction, even partially, in all forms such as microfilm, xerography, microfiche, microcard, offset strictly prohibited.

Printed by Weihert-Druck GmbH, Darmstadt, West Germany

DEDICATION

To my wife Peggy and daughter Jennifer for their efforts to keep the working environment reasonably quiet, orderly, and free from interruptions. I should also like to mention the inspiration provided by the monumental work and erudition of Eric Voegelin to which I owe many of the insights set down in this volume. To my wife goes my gratitude for having done most of the indexing, a thankless effort without which, however, this volume would lose much of its practicality. Her assistance in repeated proofreadings of the MS was equally invaluable. Finally, my deepest appreciation goes to Mmes Susan Willbern and Louise Birdwell, my typists, for the endless hours of drudgery that went into the typing of the MS.

ACKNOWLEDGMENTS

I should like to express my thanks to the following publishers and authors for the granting of copyright-related permissions to quote them in this book:

1. George Allen and Unwin, in connection with J. B. Baillie's translation of Hegel's *Phenomenology of Mind* (London: George Allen and Unwin, 1955). Acknowledgment is hereby also extended to J. B. Baillie, translator.

2. Walter de Gruyter and Co., in connection with Raimund Belgardt's *Romantische Poesie, Begriffe und Bedeutung bei Friedrich Schlegel* (The Hague: Mouton, 1969). Acknowledgment is hereby also extended to Raimund Belgardt, author.

3. G. K. Hall and Co., Publishers, in connection with John Neubauer's *Novalis* (Boston: Twayne Publishers, 1980). Acknowledgment is hereby also extended to John Neubauer, author.

4. Kohlhammer GmbH Verlag, in connection with *Hölderlin. Sämtliche Werke*. Kleine Stuttgarter Ausgabe (Stuttgart: Kohlhammer, 1961), edited by Friedrich Beissner. Acknowledgment is hereby also extended to Friedrich Beissner, editor.

5. Oxford University Press, in connection with R. C. Collingwood's *The Idea of History* (Oxford: Oxford University Press, 1946). Acknowledgment is hereby also extended to R. C. Collingwood, author.

6. Verlag Philipp Reclam, in connection with *Hölderlin. Gedichte* (Stuttgart: Reclam, 1963), edited by Konrad Nussbächer. Acknowledgment is hereby also extended to Konrad Nussbächer, editor.

7. George Weidenfeld and Nicolson, Ltd., in connection with *Romantic Period in Germany*, edited by Siegbert Prawer (New York: Shocken Books, 1970). Acknowledgment is hereby also extended to Siegbert Prawer, editor, and the contributors to his book: Raymond Immerwahr, Roger Paulin, Gillian Rodger, Paul Roubiczek, Brian Rowly, and James Trainer.

A special thanks is due to Professors Keith McFarland, Dean of Graduate Studies, and James McFeeley, Assistant Dean of Graduate Studies, East Texas State University for their aid and encouragement that eased the task of writing this book. It was once again an ETSU grant (and minigrant) that provided a portion of the funds necessary for the completion of this second volume of ROMANTIC POETRY ON THE EUROPEAN CONTINENT. Likewise I should like to commend Ms. Susan Willbern for her dedicated loyalty and exemplary execution of the technical aspect of collating, editing, and typing the MS.

DEDICATION	v
ACKNOWLEDGMENTS	vii
BILINGUAL INDEX OF POEMS COMMENTED	xiii
PREFACE TO THE SECOND VOLUME	xxix

TABLE OF CONTENTS

PART ONE.	GERMAN ROMANTICISM		1
CHAPTER I.	GERMAN IDEALISM IN THE ROMANTIC ERA. NOTES		5 29
CHAPTER II.	FRIEDRICH SCHLEGEL'S VISION OF PROGRESSIVE PERFECTIBILITY THROUGH ROMANTIC CULTURE. NOTES		34 55
CHAPTER III.	PERIODIZATION OF THE ROMANTIC MOVEMENT IN THE GERMAN-SPEAKING WORLD. NOTES		63 69
CHAPTER IV.	TRANSITION FROM CLASSICISM TO ROMANTICISM. HÖLDERLIN'S MYTHIC POETRY AND DIALOGUE WITH A MUTE TRANSCENDENCE. NOTES		71 88
CHAPTER V.	EARLY ROMANTICISM. THE BERLIN-JENA GROUP.		
	1.	Tieck, Master of the _Kunstmärchen_ and the Tale of Horror. NOTES	92 101
	2.	The Magic Idealism of Novalis, Poet of Self-transcendence Through Death. NOTES	104 119
	3.	Brentano's Manifesto of the Romantic Ethos: Sublimation of Meaning into Music and Legend. NOTES	123 138

	4. Achim von Arnim: Reformer of Society Through the Revival of German Ethnic Consciousness. NOTES	142 149
CHAPTER VI.	CULMINATION AND LEVELLING OF THE ROMANTIC PATHOS.	
	1. Chamisso, Uhland, and Eichendorff. Reconciliation of Romantic Yearning with Nature and Reality. NOTES	151 174
	2. Wilhelm Müller, Rückert and von Platen. Stirrings of Realist and Classical Elements in the Romantic Mood. NOTES	182 190
CHAPTER VII.	THE CYCLICAL PATTERN OF CULTURAL EVOLUTION AND THE THREE PHASES OF LITERARY GENESIS. THE PRINCIPLES OF REGENERATIVE RESILIENCY IN WESTERN CULTURE. NOTES	195 200
CHAPTER VIII.	EXISTENTIAL COMPROMISE OF DECLINING ROMANTICISM WITH REALITY IN THE AGE OF EMPIRICAL SCIENCE. HEINE AND LENAU.	
	1. Heine the Exasperating Proteus of Elitist Revolutionism.	
	a. The Lyrical Sufferer. Adolescent Worship of the Ghost Nymph. The Book of Songs.	201
	b. Heine's Lyrical Maturity and Some Levelling of the Affective Turmoil. "Lyrical Intermezzo," Dramas, "Homecoming" and the North-Sea Cycles.	210

- c. Heine the Paris Emigré.
   Maturing Political Thought.
   <u>New Poems</u>, <u>Germany, A Winter's Tale</u>. <u>Atta Troll</u>. 223

- d. Heine the Hesitant Rediscoverer of Transcendence. Tension Between Nazarenism and Hellenism Unresolved. 238
   NOTES 248

2. Lenau, the Terminal Figure of German Romanticism. 265
   NOTES 275

BILINGUAL INDEX OF POEMS COMMENTED

I. Hölderlin:
- "Hyperion's Song of Destiny" ("Hyperions Schicksalslied") — 74-75
- "To the Fates" ("An die Parzen") — 75-76
- "The Poet's Calling" ("Dichterberuf") — 77-78
- "Menon's Laments for Diotima" ("Menons Klagen um Diotima") — 74; 78-81; 88-89
- "Bread and Wine" ("Brot und Wein") — 80-81
- "The Rhine" ("Der Rhein") — 81-86
- "Half of Life" ("Die Hälfte des Lebens") — 87

II. Tieck:
- "Music Speaks" ("Die Musik spricht") — 96-97
- "Boccaccio" ("Boccaz") — 97
- "San Lorenzo and Bolsena" ("San Lorenzo und Bolsena") — 97
- "The Apparition" ("Die Erscheinung") — 98; 102-103
- "Christmas" ("Weinachten") — 98
- "Penitential Sermons" ("Die Busspredigten") — 99
- "Life" ("Leben") — 99
- "Through Shining Love Lament to Song is Turning" ("Durch lichte Liebe wird das Leid zu Liede") — 99-100

	"The New Spring" ("Der neue Frühling")	100
III.	Novalis (Friedrich von Hardenberg):	

        <u>Hymns to the Night</u> (<u>Hymnen an die Nacht</u>):

Hymn No. 1 ("Hymne No. 1")	114-15
"Yearning for Death" ("Sehnsucht nach dem Tode")	115-16

        <u>Devotional Songs</u> (<u>Geistliche Lieder</u>):

"Song VII," "Hymn" ("Hymne")	117
"Song XV" ("Lied XV")	117

        Songs from <u>Heinrich von Ofterdingen</u> (Lieder aus <u>Heinrich von Ofterdingen</u>):

"Song of the Hermit" ("Das Lied des Einsiedlers")	117-18

        <u>Miscellaneous Poems</u> (<u>Verschiedenes</u>):

	"Eyes on Living Men I'm Training" ("Alle Menschen seh' ich leben")	118
Brentano:	"On the Rhine" ("Auf dem Rhein")	131-32
	"Lore Lay"	132-33
	"The Cradle Tune" ("Wiegenlied")	133-34 <u>140</u>
	"The Song of the Spinning Woman" ("Der Spinnerin Lied")	134-35
	"Echoes of Beethoven's Music" ("Nachklänge Beethovenscher Musik")	135-36

Romances of the Rosary (<u>Romanzen vom Rosenkranz</u>):

    "Eighth Romance," "Peace to Every Chore Decreeing " ("Allem Tagewerk sei Frieden!")   136-37

Achim von Arnim:

    "Too Light It Is for Sleeping" ("Mir ist zu licht zum Schlafen")   147

    "Keep Beckoning Trees, You That Listen" ("Ja winkt nur, ihr lauschende Baume")   147

    "It Feels Sultry on the Earth" ("Auf der Erde ist es schwül")   147-48; <u>150</u>

Chamisso: "The Women of Weinsberg" ("Die Weiber von Weinsberg")   155; <u>174-175</u>

    "Boncourt Castle" ("Das Schloss Boncourt")   155-56

    "The Cross Review" ("Die Kreuzschau")   156-57

Uhland: "The Minstrel's Curse" ("Des Sängers Fluch")   158-59

    "A Castle on the Sea" ("Das Schloss am Meere")   159-60

    "The Landlady's Daughter" ("Der Wirtin Töchterlein")   160

    "The Blacksmith" ("Der Schmied")   160

    "Siegfried's Sword" ("Siegfrieds Schwert")   160-61

    "Swabian Lore: ("Schwäbische Kunde")   161

"Bertran de Born" 161-<u>178</u>

Eichendorff:

"Echoes" ("Nachklänge")	167
"Yearning" ("Sehnsucht")	167-68
"The Broken Ring" ("Das zerbrochene Ringlein")	168
"The Evening" ("Der Abend")	168
"Moon Night" ("Mondnacht")	168
"The Hermit" ("Der Einsiedler")	168-69
"The Night Flower" ("Die Nachtblume")	169
"Beautiful Strange One" ("Schöne Fremde")	169
"In the Forest" ("Im Walde")	169
"Twilight" ("Zwielicht")	169
"The Forest Discourse" ("Waldgespräch")	169-70
"Night Song" ("Nachtlied")	170
"The Merry Wanderer" ("Der fromme Wandersmann")	170
"Sea Calm" ("Meeresstille")	170-171
"Divining Rod" ("Wünschelrute")	171
"On the Death of My Child" ("Auf meines Kindes Tod")	171
"Abroad" ("In der Fremde")	172
"On a Castle" ("Auf einer Burg")	173

Wilhelm Müller:

    "Vineta"   182-83

Rückert: "Barbarossa"   183

    Songs of Children Dead (Kindertotenlieder):

    "As Shade in Daytime Arriving" ("Du bist ein Schatten am Tage")   185

    "Midnight" ("Mitternacht")   186

von Platen:

    "The Pilgrim Before San Yuste" ("Der Pilgrim vor Sankt Yust")   188

    "The Grave in the Busento" ("Der Grab im Busento")   188-89

    Ghazels:

    "The Pain One Single Person Feels" ("Es liegt an eines Menschen Schmerz")   189;<u>190</u>; <u>192</u>,<u>194</u>

Heine: Book of Songs ("Youthful Sorrows--Dream Images") (Buch der Lieder, "Junge Leiden--Traumbilder"):

Song No. 2   "She Snapped: Be Still, A cold Grave I" ("Da sprach sie schnell: Sei still, ich hab")   203

Song No. 4   "Thus Spoke the Dream God, Slyly Showing Me" ("So sprach der Traumgott, und er zeigt' mir schlau")   204;<u>248</u>

Song No. 5   "Why Raves My Blood and Rushes So?" ("Was treibt und tobt mein tolles Blut?")   204

Song No. 6	"She Strangely Stared At Me and Sat" ("Da staunt' mich an gar seltzamlich")	207
Song No. 7	"You Now Have the Ransom, Why Do You Delay?" ("Nun hast du das Kaufgeld, nun zögerst du doch?")	207
Song No. 8	"That Ancient Song, Do You Still Know" ("Ei, kennt ihr noch das alte Lied")	207
Song No. 9	"Her Pallor Could With Marble Vie" ("Sie war wie Marmelstein so bleich")	205-06
Song No.10	"Good Many Pale Corpses Stalking" ("Da hab ich viel blasse Leichen")	207

"Youthful Sorrows--Romances" ("Junge Leiden--Romanzen"):

Song No. 2	"The Mountain Voice" ("Bergstimme")	208; <u>251</u>
Song No. 4	"Poor Peter" ("Der arme Peter")	208
Song No. 5	"The Song of the Prisoner" ("Lied des Gefangenen")	208
Song No. 6	"The Grenadiers" ("Die Grenadiere")	208, <u>251</u>
Song No. 9	"Don Ramiro"	208-209; <u>251</u>
Song No.10	"Belshazzar" ("Belsatzar")	209; <u>252</u>
Song No.11	"The Minnesingers" ("Die Minnesänger")	209
Song No.15	"The Ditty of Remorse" ("Das Liedchen von der Reue")	209

<u>A Lyrical Intermezzo</u>
(<u>Lyrisches Intermezzo</u>):

"The Prologue" ("Prolog") 210

Song No. 1 "During the Splendid Month of May" ("Im wunderschönen Monat Mai") 210

Song No. 10 "The Lotus Flower" ("Die Lotusblume") 210

Song No. 31 "The World Is So Fair and the Sky Is So Blue" ("Die Welt ist so schön und der Himmel so blau") 210

Song No. 33 "Up North a Fir Tree Lonely" ("Der Fichtenbaum steht einsam") 210

Song No. 43 "From Ancient Tales It's Waving" ("Aus alten Märchen winkt es") 210

Song No. 47 "They Tormented Me Sorely" ("Sie haben mich gequälet") 211

Song No. 51 "My Songs, So They're Full of Poison" ("Vergiftet sind meine Lieder") 211

Song No. 58 "The Trees in Autumn Wind Shaking" ("Der Herbstwind rüttelt die Bäume") 211; <u>252-53</u>

Song No. 59 "A Star Is Yonder Falling" ("Es fällt ein Stern herunter") 211

Song No. 65 "The Evil, Ancient Ditties" ("Die alten, bösen Lieder") 211

<u>The Book of Songs</u>. "Homecoming" (<u>Das Buch der Lieder</u>. Heimkehr):

Song No. 2 "I cannot Come Up With a Reason" ("Ich weiss nicht was soll es bedeuten") 214

Song No. 3	"My Heart, My Heart Is Heavy" ("Mein Herz, mein Herz ist traurig")	214
Song No. 5	"The Sightless Grandmother Sitting" ("Die blinde Grossmutter sitzt ja")	214-15
Song No.14	"Far Out Still Gleamed the Evening Sea" (Das Meer erglänzte weit hinaus")	215
Song No.21	"How Can You Sleep So Soundly" ("Wie kannst du ruhig schlafen")	215
Song No.22	"The Maiden Sleeps in Her Bedroom" ("Die Jungfrau schläft in ihrer Kammer")	215
Song No.24	"Oh, What a Wretched Atlas I, a World" ("Ich unglückselger Atlas! Eine Welt")	215-16
Song No.25	"The Years Are Coming and Going" ("Die Jahre kommen und gehen")	216
Song No.39	"My Heart Grows Heavy and I'm Yearning" ("Das Herz ist mir bedrückt, und sehnlich")	216
Song No.42	"Friend, Why Are You Still Repeating" ("Teuerer Freund! Was soll es nutzen")	216
Song No.44	"It's High Time Now That With Common Sense" ("Nun ist es Zeit, dass ich mit Verstand")	216
Song No.45	"The Good King Visvamitra" ("Der König Wiswamitra")	216,<u>254</u>
Song No.47	"You Are Just Like a Flower" ("Du bist wie eine Blume")	216
Song No.79	"The Castrates, Though, Were Complaining" ("Doch die Kastraten klagten")	216

Song No.87	"Death--That's Nighttime's Frigid Chill" ("Der Tod, das ist die kühle Nacht")	216
Song No.88	"Tell Me, Where's Your Pretty Sweetheart" ("Sag, wo ist dein schönes Liebchen")	217
	"Twilight of the Gods" ("Götterdammerung")	217
	"Doña Clara" ("Donna Clara")	217
	"Almanzor" ("Almansor")	217

North Sea, First Cyclus (Die Nordsee, Erster Zyklus):

No. 3	"Sunset" ("Sonnenuntergang")	218-19; 255
No. 8	"Storm" ("Sturm")	219
No. 9	"Calm at Sea" (Meeresstille")	219
No. 10	"Marine Specter" ("Seegespenst")	220
No. 11	"Purification" ("Reinigung")	220-21

North Sea, Second Cyclus (Die Nordsee, Zweiter Zyklus):

No. 6	"The Gods of Greece" ("Die Götter Griechenlands")	221
No. 7	"The Waves Go on Rumbling Their Rumble Eternal" ("Es murmeln die Wogen ihr ewges Gemurmel")	221-22

Germany, A Winter's Tale (Deutschland, ein Wintermärchen):

Head 2	"The Customs Union" ("Der Zollverein")	225, 256-57

Head 4	"The Flame of the Bonfire in These Parts" ("Die Flamme des Scheiterhaufens hat hier")	225
Head 7	"To Frenchmen and Russians Belongs the Land" ("Franzosen und Russen gehört das Land")	225
Head 11	"This Is the Wood Called Teutoburg" ("Das ist der Teutoburger Wald")	225
Head 13	"Poor Cousin, Whenever Your Face I View" ("Mit Wehmut erfüllt mich jedesmal")	225
Head 17	"The Middle Ages Anyway" ("Das Mittelalter immerhin")	225
Head 23	"Dried Up, Without Leaves, Trod Down by the Feet" ("Verwelkt, entblättert, zertreten sogar")	225

New Poems, I "New Spring" (Neue Gedichte; I "Neuer Frühling"):

No. 6	"Through My Mind Soft Accords Wind" ("Leise zieht durch mein Gemüt")	226
No. 15	"The Slender Water Lily" ("Die schlanke Wasserlilje")	226
No. 29	"There Once Was an Old Ruler" ("Es war ein alter König")	226
No. 35	"Never Fear, the Love I Bear You" ("Sorge nie dass ich verrate")	226-27
No. 40	"Those Noble Wishes Flower" ("Die holden Wünsche blühen")	227

II "Miscellaneous"--"Seraphine"
("Verschiedenes--Seraphine"):

No. 7 "Upon This Rock We're Going to Build" ("Auf diesem Felsen bauen wir") 227,<u>257</u>

No. 10 "A Young Miss Faced the Sea Coast" ("Das Fräulein stand am Meere") 227-228

"Clarissa" ("Clarisse"):

No. 5 "Too Late Has Come What You're Now Smiling" ("Es kommt zu spät was du mir lächelst") 228

"Catherine" ("Katharina"):

No. 7 "I Dreamt Lately I Went Strolling" ("Jüngstens träumte mir") 228

"Tannhäuser" (Der Tannhäuser") 228-29

III. "Abroad" ("In der Fremde"):

No. 3 "Once I did Have a Lovely Fatherland" ("Ich hatte einst ein schönes Vaterland") 229

"Occasional Poems" ("Zeitgedichte")

"An Assurance" ("Zur Beruhigung") 230,232

"Night Thoughts" ("Nachtgedanken") 229-30, 232

IV. "Romances" ("Romanzen"):

No. 4 "Conjuration" ("Die Beschwörung") 230

"The Underworld" ("Unterwelt")

No. 23 "King Harald Harfagar" ("König Harald Harfagar") 230-31 xxiv

    V. "To Ollea" ("Zur Ollea"):

No. 8 "Helen" ("Helena") 231; 258

    VI. "Supplement" ("Nachlese"):

    "Silesian Weavers" ("Die
    schlesischen Weber") 232, 258-59

    "The New Alexander" ("Der
    neue Alexander") 242

    Atta Troll:

Head IV. "Ronceval, You Noble Dale"
    ("Ronzeval, du edles Tal!") 232-33

Head V. "And They Think They are
    Entitled" ("Und sie glauben
    sich berechtigt") 233

Head VI. "What By Law of Nature Always"
    ("Was naturgeschichtlich
    immer") 234, 259

Head VIII. "Up There, On the Stars'
    Pavilion" ("Droben im dem
    Sternenzelte") 234

Head IX. "Yes, I Am a Bear, a Bear I"
    ("Ja, ich bin ein Bär, Ich
    bin es") 234

Head X. "Property! Right of Possession"
    ("Eigentum! Recht des
    Besitzers") 234

Head XI. "To the Land of West Barbarians"
    ("Nach dem Land der Westbar-
    baren") 234-35

Head XIX. "If a Devil or an Angel"
    ("Ob's ein Teufel oder
    Engel") 235

Head XX. "You I love More Than the Others"
    ("Denn ich liebe dich am
    meisten") 236

Head XXII.   "Spirit Other Poets Boast"
              ("Andre Dichter haben Geist")   236

Head XXVII.   "Of Youthful Dreams the Echoes"
              ("Klang das nicht wie
              Jugendträume")   236-37

              Paralipomena to "Atta Troll"
              (Paralipomena zu "Atta Troll"):

Head XXIII.   "And Instead of Singing Praises"
              ("Und anstatt von einem Bären")   237

              Romancero (Romanzero):

              "First Book--Stories"
              ("Erstes Buch--Historien"):

              "The Apollonian God" ("Der
              Apollogott")   238

              "Two Knights" ("Zwei Ritter")   238,260

              "Witzliputzli"
              ("Vitzliputzli")   238-39

              "Third Book--Hebrew Melodies"
              ("Drittes Buch--Hebräische
              Melodien"):

              "Princess Sabbath" ("Prinzessin
              Sabbath")   240

              "Jehuda Ben Halevy"   240;
                                                     260-61

              "Disputation" ("Disputation")   242

              "To Edom" ("An Edom")   242,261

              Poems 1853 and 1854
              (Gedichte 1853 und 1854):

    No. 7   "Castle Affront" ("Affrontenburg")   242

    No. 8   "To Lazarus" ("Zum Lazarus")

		"The Sable Lady Against Her Breast" ("Es hatte mein Haupt die schwarze Frau")	243-44
		"How Tediously, Step By Step" ("Wie langsam kriechet sie dahin")	244
	No. 9	"What the Sphinx Is Deep Inside" ("Die Gestalt der wahren Sphnix")	245

From the Mattress Grave (Aus der Mattrazengruft):

	No. 7	"My Day Was Pleasant, Happy Was My Night" ("Mein Tag war heiter, glücklich meine Nacht")	244
	No. 19	"Morphia" ("Morphine")	244;263
		"To Mouche" ("Für die Mouche")	245;263
	No. 28	"About a Summer Night I Lately Dreamed" ("Es träumte mir von einer Sommernacht")	245-46
	No. 29	"Your Hands You Wring Now Even Sadly" ("Du ringst sogar die schönen Hände")	247

Lenau:

| | | "Ahasuerus, the Wandering Jew" ("Ahasver, der ewige Jude") | 268 |
| | | "The Wandering Jew" ("Der ewige Jude") | 268 |

Voices (Stimmen):

| | | "The Voice of the Rain" ("Die Stimme des Regens") | 269 |

Reed Songs (Schilflieder):

| | | "Home the Sun Its Way Is Wending" ("Drüben geht die Sonne scheiden") | 269-70 |

"Where the Pond in Peace Reposes" ("Auf dem Teich, dem regungslosen") — 270

"Lake and Waterfall" ("See und Wasserfall") — 270

"Supplication" ("Bitte") — 270

"Autumn Lament" ("Herbstklage") — 270-71

"Winter Night" ("Winternacht") — 271

"Question" ("Frage") — 271

"Calm at Sea" ("Meeresstile") — 271

Figures (Gestalten):

"The Three Gypsies" ("Die drei Zigeuner") — 271-72

"The Distant One" ("Die Entfernte") — 272

"Arrival and Parting" ("Kommen und Scheiden") — 272

PREFACE

The analysis of the poems offered in this Guide follows, although not exclusively, the selections that constitute my English-language anthology entitled Romantic Poetry on the European Continent which appeared in 1983. I find little to add here to my interpretation of the poetic experience associated with the Romantic era.

Once I have laid down the general principles of this experience in Germany, I attempted to avoid generalizing abstractions which tend to lead to sweeping conclusions seldom fitting explicit and implicit a priori assumptions. I subjected each poem of the above-mentioned anthology to a detailed scrutiny; after a biographical sketch of the author and a historical mise-en-scène, both of varied length depending on the sociopolitical involvement of each author, I proceeded to outline also the rest of his non-poetic work.

The analyses refer to both form, i.e., to each poem's prosody, and to content, such as ideological concerns, as well as the poet's aesthetic intent. I do not believe in theses postulated by proponents of affective or intentional fallacies, nor those of cultural or aesthetic relativists. Hence my analyses tend to suggest a more or less definitive world view on the part of each poet, an identifiable underpinning of the specific creative process that clearly precedes it, but just as often is formulated, openly or by indirection, as a result of that process. Hence author, his historical setting, his involvement (or lack of it) with his world, and his poetic expression form one whole, interpretable, and difficult to separate. Given its historical setting, the purpose of the art of the Romantic was a clearly understandable communication with, and often, education and regeneration of the human race.

Expert and layman alike should be thus led to recognize Romanticism as a clearly identifiable, distinct, and unique movement in the history of art. No one denies that Romantic attitudes, emotions, and aesthetic components are a historically recurring constant; this does not change the fact that Romanticism proper was a universal movement developing in the last decade of the eighteenth and in the first decades of the nineteenth century. Only an exhaustive number of examples concretizing the climate of opinion which gave the Romantic era its typical cast will make fully comprehensible its unique way of being; it might silence cultural relativists who, without the courtesy of seeking a clear definition of its features, would find Romanticism everywhere and anytime that star-crossed lovers pine for and fail to attain the absolute.

GERMAN ROMANTICISM.

AN OVERVIEW

Some literary historians set the span of German Romanticism at exactly four decades from 1795 to 1835.[1] In 1795, Hölderlin, the first great poet of the transition from Neo-classicism to Romanticism, spent some time with Schiller in Jena. Little if anything of Schiller's ripening classicism in the purest "Greek" sense of the word seems to have rubbed off on Hölderlin who was destined to become one of the first poètes maudits, "haunted poets" of the modern era. In that year Schiller produced his epoch-making treatise in aesthetics On Naive and Sentimental Poetry and a lengthy poem in praise of nature and progress entitled The Outing. At the time Schiller pursued earnestly the aesthetic principles of Goethe's Classicism, "noble simplicity and quiet greatness," thus drawing farther away from Romantic sensibility which was beginning to assert itself in Germany in the mid-Nineties.

As for Hölderlin, he took a position of tutor in the family of the banker Gontard in Frankfurt. An ostensibly Platonic involvement with the lady of the house led to emotional complications which in turn spurred a brief period of feverish and fruitful poetic activity; after 1798, Hölderlin leads the life of an itinerant tutor, ending, eventually, in mental derangement and a death long overdue after four decades of gradual decay and benightedness.

The only publications that could make the year 1795 less arbitrary as inception date of German Romanticism are Ludwig Tieck's The Story of Mr. William Lovell and Jean Paul Richter's Hesperus. The two novels herald the advent of morbid solipsism and unbridled self-indulgence in the erotic and fantastic, typical of the hero of the new era plagued by a tendency to schizophrenic

Doppelgängerei. The full impact of Tieck's <u>Lovell</u> was not felt, however, until publicized as an "absolutely new character" in Friedrich Schlegel's <u>Athenäum</u> (Fragment 418) some three years later.

The <u>terminus ad quem</u> set for Romanticism's demise after 1835 seems equally arbitrary: Eduard Mörike, one of the transitional figures from Romanticism to realism, was still pastoring in Cleversulzbach, hardly a Jena or Weimar in terms of culture centers of the changing literary climate and mores; Heinrich Heine, another disaffected Romantic, a German Jew turned questionable Protestant and even less convincing Parisian, saw his writings put on the index in Germany in that year, which again hardly represents a decisive literary feat. Goethe, the father and one full half of German classicism, had been dead for three years, after having flirted briefly, almost two decades earlier, with the Romantic mode. The great "realist" genre writer Gottfried Keller and the realist idealizer of salient moments in the apocalypse of mankind Friedrich Hebbel, didn't make their literary debuts until the eighteen-forties. Heinrich Kleist, the poet of magical demonism and life-threatening unconscious drives, had surpassed the frivolous games of Romantic irony as early as 1808; he was dead three years later, twenty-four years before the alleged terminal date of a movement with which he had never fully identified. Obviously, the four decades between 1785-1835 are a pat, arbitrary approximation, unattended by any meaningful breakthroughs or downfalls of the movement, and must be revised in the light of specific trend-setting manifestoes and masterpieces which, rather than reflecting changes in the aesthetic climate, are its primary molding forces.

As indicated earlier, the "German Lands," and Switzerland foremost among them, seconded the expansion of the British phenomenon known as "Romantic,[2]" contributing their own unique sensibilities to its full unfolding on the Continent.

Immerwahr summarizes the opinions of various Germanists who agree that Romanticism in Germany "is characterized by the striving to synthetize opposites." Immerwahr credits German Romanticism with

> a highly sophisticated examination of its own creative process... [aiming] ultimately at a restoration of poetic intuition. The recipient of German Romantic literature, in turn, experiences a self-conscious enjoyment of the workings of this whole process.... These characteristics...are precisely what Friedrich Schlegel and his contemporaries termed irony.

Immerwahr proceeds to identify the forces generally cited as causing "these characteristics" as

> the influence of the critical approach to metaphysics and epistemology developed by Kant and his followers, or that of Hamann's and Herder's ideas on language and cultural history; the interplay of such tendencies as philosophical rationalism and religious pietism, or of Storm and Stress and German Classicism....[3]

It is evident that among the most forceful influences on the "romantische Geist," the Romantic spirit, was German idealist philosophy, as it was evolving, <u>pari passu</u> with literature from Neoclassical order to Romantic "rational" freedom or free "rationality," and further, inevitably, into hardly rational, but intuitive, often pseudomystical flights toward a secularized beyond, created by Fichte, Schelling and Hegel. Together with the critical writings of the Schlegel brothers, German post-Kantian idealism was largely responsible for the molding of the climate of Romantic aestheticism in or about the year 1798. In that year appears Schelling's second monumental work dealing with the World Soul; Fichte finishes his Doctrine of Science, Hegel outlines his dialectic system during his stay in Frankfurt (1798-1800), and the Schlegel brothers begin to publish their pace-setting journal Athenäum. Even in England, 1798 is Romanticism's banner year: Coleridge and Wordsworth publish their Lyrical Ballads, not the least important of which is the programmatic Preface, called in the first edition "Advertisement." It is no coincidence that the previous year 1797 is known as the Balladenjahr, the Year of the Ballad, marking the zenith of German Classicism, when the collaboration between Goethe and Schiller produced some of the finest gems of German lyrical poetry.

In the light of this, it becomes necessary to outline the birth and flowering of German Romanticism out of enlightened rationalism via post-Kantian idealism, showing how both end up in a pantheist-mystical gnosis where the boundaries of philosophy and poetry all but disappear. Even the great system builders like Kant, the enlightened classicist, and Hegel, the Romantic pantheist, draw closer, each in their own way, to the asystematical subjectivism of the artist, while poets like Novalis, and poet-essayists like the Schlegel brothers gravitate to a systematic exposition of their intuitive insights. In this respect, the "Romantic" philosophers and poets tend to be, ironically, more "regular" thinkers than the full-fledged enlighteners of Fontenelle's and Voltaire's ilk who generally couched their thought in more or less frivolous occasion pieces. Though intuitive and deductive, rather than inductive and empirical, the Romantic systematizers of critical insights led, at least in Germany, poetry along paths previously explored through the impassive medium of philosophic and critical prose.

"During its first period,... Romanticism was not only a literary, but also very consciously a philosophical movement," comments Paul Roubiczek.[4] He adduces the testimony of Friedrich Schlegel who anticipates Victor Hugo's mélange des genres beyond the latter's coalescence of strictly literary forms.

> The whole history of modern poetry is a continuous commentary on a short text of philosophy...poetry and philosophy should be united.[5]

CHAPTER I

GERMAN IDEALISM IN THE ROMANTIC ERA

It is difficult to consider Johann Gottfried Herder a systematic philosopher, but he definitely has a method. His Ideas for the Philosophy of History of Mankind (1784-91) developed a philosophy of history and ethnic psychology that inspired his teacher Kant -- mostly negatively -- to write his own interpretation of the historic process in An Idea for a Universal History from the Cosmopolitan Point of View (1784).

Herder, and his other teacher, Johann Georg Hamann, became the chief proponents of the cognitive value of emotions; Hamann argued in Socratic Memorabilia (1759) that the archrationalist Socrates (in his Platonic representation) realized that conceptual knowledge cannot penetrate the ultimate questions of being; in this he fundamentally agreed with Kant's view that the necessarily existing noumena were, qua underlying principles of objective knowledge, unapproachable through discursive reasoning. The noumenal Ding an sich, thing-in-itself, though beyond human grasp, had to be assumed as Ultimate Reality beyond the unstable phenomena of time and space; only the noumena made possible a limited scientific knowledge. Hamann and Herder went beyond Kant's admission of sentiment and emotion to the exclusive club of cognitive faculties. Kant the classicist, respectful of measure in all things, was satisfied to claim that he "had to deny absolute conceptual knowledge of any substance, in order to make room[6] for faith," for

> we have no concepts of understanding, and consequently no elements for the knowledge of things, save in so far as intuition...and that we can therefore have no knowledge of any object as thing-in-itself, but only in so far as it is an object of sensible intuition, that is, an appearance...[this insight] has limited all that we can theoretically know to mere appearances.... [It is consequently evident that] even the assumption...[of the three fundamental substances of] God, freedom and immortality is not permissible unless at the same time speculative reason be deprived of its pretensions to transcendent insight. For in order to arrive at such insight, [reason] must make use of principles which...extend only to objects of possible experience, ...thus rendering all practical extension of pure reason impossible.[7]

Hamann and Herder sought the Kantian "something more," i.e., absolute knowledge, declared approachable only through the "practical sources of knowledge.[8]" Impelled by their overreaching subjectivism, they sought to possess the Absolute not through "practical reason," i.e., enlightened faith, but exclusively through man's affective faculties.

In this, Hamann and Herder not only radicalized Kantian intersubjectivity, an approach developed in Kant's Third Critique (Critique of Judgment, 1791) that pretended to bring about general knowledge approaching the universal and absolute without objectification; they glorified as unique the bias toward <u>sensibility</u>, that paralleled along generally mystic paths the vaunted rationalism of eighteenth century Enlightenment. Hamann and Herder thus legitimized the nobility and cognitive force of the affects, bringing about an era which Rousseau and Voltaire had helped to prepare: the age of Revolution, of emotional, moral and aesthetic liberalism, and of Romantic Utopias.

    Building on Rousseau's condemnation of society and progress as corruptors of "natural man," Herder reinforced the Genevan's ambiguous enthusiasm for imagination by declaring it the most original and unerring source of cognition. Rousseau's awe before "wild," untamed nature and his praise of "naive" insights of children and untutored folk into the Ground of Being, Herder embodied in a system of sorts. He introduced a number of catchy aphorisms about language, poetry, the "folk mind" and primitive, an unconsciously self-creating art that quickly became programmatic slogans for the forthcoming renaissance of the affects in the European West. In Germany, this rehabilitation of preterrational enthusiasm and sentiments was to manifest itself first as the iconoclastic <u>Storm and Stress</u>, also known as <u>die Geniezeit</u>, the Age of Genius; gestating for about two decades, it eventually evolved into the first phase of the Romantic movement proper.

    Herder elaborated the concept of poetic naiveté into a theory of aesthetic genesis, an ethnic sociology and a philosophy of language and history, all based on vague flashes of intuition rather than on empirical research. In his essay <u>On Later German Literature</u> (1766-67) he postulated poetry as "the mother tongue of humankind," an idea he owed to Hamann. Language in its more rudimentary stages strives to communicate primarily the universal "feelings, passions, affects;" while still "in this infantile stage," language is more "music of the soul than a communication of thoughts;" it is at this point that "poetry comes into being.[9]" Herder outlined the maturation process of language from this unconscious but direct transfer of feeling to a progressively more conscious formulating of logical thought; in this, he simultaneously abandoned Kant's "aesthetic ideas" as an intersubjective compromise between concepts and feeling,[10] and pioneered the triumph of emotionalism for Storm and Stress as well as the Romantic movement. He saw language in its later "life forms" alienating itself from "true poetry," as it strove, "ever more consciously, after artificial beauty and regularity;" finally, fully conceptualized language becomes

> the merely correct language of scientific thinking, i.e., philosophy, losing all its youthfully poetic charm.[11]

The only true poetry is, by definition, folk poetry in which Herder included what Schiller was to call three decades later "naive" poetry. According to Herder, such poetry represents directly, clearly and with graphic liveliness the "natural" folk feelings and sentiments. As such immediate and natural poetry qualifies the Old Testament, the Homeric epics, Shakespeare, the poems of Ossian, as well as Thomas Percy's Reliques of Ancient English Poetry. This partial catalogue indicates the partiality for the heroic past so essential to European Romantics, and particularly to those in Germany and in Spain. More than the French, the latter believed to have found the aesthetic concerns of the present in the great poetic achievements of Greek antiquity and their own idealized Middle Ages.

Herder proceeded to demonstrate the superior genius of folk poetry in a vast collection of Folk Songs (1778-79). It was an anthology of fine poems whose folk origins were often rather questionable. Aside from German, Serbian and Danish ballads, Spanish romances and poems from the Eddas, it included songs from Shakespeare's dramas, from Ossian and Bishop Percy's Reliques.

Herder sought the origins of a nation's poetry in the "spirit of its language;" both language and poetry were manifestations of "folk spirit," which was in turn determined by

> race, soil, climate, by the history and traditions of any given nation.[12]

In this Herder anticipated Hippolyte Taine's theory of race, moment, milieu, coined almost a century later; ironically, Taine's determinants of literary genesis were to serve the doctrine of deterministic positivism, the archenemy of creative spontaneity worshipped by the Romantics. Herder's identification of environmental and genetic factors pretended to explain ethnic differences between nations and, eventually, "the human soul per se and in its appearance on this earth." This knowledge he believed would lead in turn to the "awakening of mankind" and a "harmonious development of all human inclinations," resulting in a "mature humanity."[13]

Herder synthetized his ideas on language, poetry and history of the earth and mankind in the earlier-mentioned Ideas for the Philosophy of History of Mankind. This magnum opus brought up to date the principle of Aristotelian entelechy, the embodiment of the highest potentiality of a species, postulating a progressive ontology of all existence toward the production of ever more perfect specimens.

Like Plato, Herder conceived the world as an organism; but rather than a static zoon empsychon ennoun, a creature endowed with soul and mind,[14] Herder's universe was actually a dynamic evolutionary process from inanimate to animate nature, culminating in a graduated scale of cultures and individuals. According to R. G. Collingwood, Herder envisioned the universe as

> a kind of matrix, within which,

> at a specially favored region
> which... may be regarded as
> its center, there crystallizes
> out a peculiar structure, the
> solar system. This again is a
> matrix within which its special
> conditions give rise to the
> earth... peculiar among the
> planets in being a fit theater
> for life, as the seat of the
> next stage in evolution....

The chain of Herderian entelechies continues to narrow down inorganic genera and species (continents, geographic areas, etc.) to ever-more specialized avatars of organic life, plants, animals, the human species, races and nations.

> In each case new specialization
> exists in an environment consist-
> ing of the unspecialized matrix
> [Aristotelian potentiality] from
> which it has emerged, and is it-
> self nothing but a focal point
> at which the inner nature of this
> matrix emerges into complete
> realization [of the actualized
> entelechy].

In man, who is "an end in himself," the process reaches its culmination, since "rational and moral life" alone justifies his existence.[15]

The same as man is privileged among animals -- being the perfect animal by transcending mere animality -- so some continents, lands, races and genial individuals are privileged over others, enjoying a meaningfully higher, i.e., "historical" life.

> The favored center in which this
> historical life arises is Europe,
> owing to its geographical and
> climatic peculiarities...in
> Europe alone human life is

> genuinely historical..., Europe
> [being] a privileged region of
> human life, as man is privileged
> among the animals....[16]

The frightening implications for racial postulates dividing races into superior and inferior, and, commensurately, historic rights to privilege and survival are obvious: Herder prepared the ground not only for the deterministic positivism of the almighty fact in the nineteenth century, but also for the superior race mania and genocide of the twentieth. The epilogue, in which Herder declares as goal of this racial evolution a

> universally pervasive cultural
> development [Bildung] of all
> social strata and nations through
> education, laws and constitution
> of the [individual] lands[17]

does not alter the fact that, precisely because of his theories' appeal to the emotions, rather than to reason, it was his speculative ontology of race that influenced future thinking rather than his genial insights into the genesis of aesthetic ideas and their embodiment in the folk soul.

In terms of impact on his immediate followers and further development of German idealism and Romanticism, Herder's most influential heritage was his conception of man as

> a link between two worlds, the
> natural world out of which he
> has grown, and the spiritual
> world... realizing itself on
> the earth.[18]

The monumental metaphysical systems of Fichte, Schelling and Hegel owe much to the "marvellous quantity of fertile and valuable thought"[19] supplied by Herder's rudimentary anthropology, rightly considered the precursor of its modern empirical variety. Less felicitous among these insights proved to be his identification of "various physical types of human beings" and the analysis of

> the manners and customs of these various types as expressions of psychological peculiarities going with physical ones.[20]

Kant, the last and greatest survivor of the Enlightenment, reacted vigorously against his student's radically affective interpretation of the genesis of antropological traits and racial types. His own version of the historical progress of mankind's self-consciousness appeared just months after Herder's *Ideas* under the title *An Idea for a Universal History from the Cosmopolitan Point of View*. According to Collingwood,

> In the true style of the Enlightenment [Kant] regards past history as a spectacle of human irrationality, and looks forward to a Utopia of rational life [combining] the Enlightenment point of view with the Romanticist, very much as his theory of knowledge combines rationalism and empiricism.[21]

The most genial insight offered by this work that otherwise hardly ranks with Kant's three monumental *Critiques* is the vindication of irrationality as a gadfly of life exuberance, a proposition one would expect to find -- and in fact does -- in Hegel and Nietzsche. By stating that

> Everything is *really* [in terms of the unapproachable noumena] and in itself mind; everything is *phenomenally*, or seen from the spectator's point of view, nature. Thus human action, as we experience it in our own inner life, is mind [Geist],...

> free, self-determining moral activity; but human action as seen from outside, as the historian sees it, is just as much nature,... namely, because it is being looked at, and thus converted into phenomenon.[22]

Here Kant anticipates the triumvirate of master-metaphysicians of the Romantic period Fichte-Schelling-Hegel. By recognizing history "as a progress toward rationality, which is at the same time an advance *in* rationality,[23]" and identifying the moving force of irrationality, "pride, ambition, greed" as its opposite, "the evil in human nature," a "purley selfish discontent" opposing "the happiness of a stagnant life,"[24] Kant shows Hegel the way to the principle of double negation as core of the dialectic progress of mind, mediating its own self-consciousness through thought *qua* power of negation. The entire Hegelian system with its salient points is embryonically contained in Kant's recognition of the enlivening virtue of discord: "the Cunning of Reason," a "diremption" of the potentially self-reconciled ego from the world which it repeatedly fails to recognize as itself, as long as the world fails to recognize consciousness as its reciprocal object, the "distinction without difference," the mutual hate-love relationship of master and bondsman, and most important of all, the "material logic" that postulates A equaling A only in so far as non-A opposes A, with the rational revealing itself in the world as *already* the real. Kant's view of history as noumenally grounded reason progressing towards free self-embodiment in the world of the phenomena is already more of a Hegelian and hence, Romantic vision, than a Kantian principle of progress according to enlightened and enlightening reason. A reformulation of nature running by immutable laws given it by an uninvolved clockmaker, the rationalist master-builder of the universe, that makes it a compelling force driving man

> to leave ease and inactive
> contentment [i.e., order and
> measure] behind, and throw him-
> self into toils... in order that
> these may drive him... in the
> discovery of means to rise
> above them

reflects already the Romantic hybris demanding what is humanly unattainable in this world. Kant's view of fundamentally anti-rational nature that

> does not care for human happiness,
> [implanting in man] propensities
> to sacrifice his own happiness
> and destroy that of others,

is an admirably clear definition of the Storm and Stress, as well as of the Romantic syndrome. Finally, Kant's conception of man as following "blindly" destructive propensities called forth by nature in order to make himself

> the tool of nature in her plan,
> which is certainly not his[25]

is an unequivocal precedent of Hegel's philosophy of history which substitues Reason for Nature in his famous doctrine of the Cunning of Reason.

The mutually permeating and contradictory ideas of Herder and Kant concerning human existence-in-history inspired first the dialectic syntheticism of Fichte, and later, more or less simultaneously, the dualistic monism of Schelling and Hegel.

The first systematic dialectician of metaphysics and philosophy of history was Johann Gottlieb Fichte (1764-1814). He departs from Kant's fundamental premise that universal history is an unfolding of a plan, in the manner of a world drama, an idea that goes back to Calderón's El gran teatro del mundo, and, even farther back, to Marcus Aurelius' Stoicism. Like Herder's endeavors to identify the Folk Spirit of each nation and race, Fichte sought to define the exact spirit of his own age in his Doctrine of Science (1796-98) and in The Characteristics of the Present Age: the latter was published in 1806, when Hegel was finishing his Phenomenology of the Spirit.

Fichte starts with the assumption that every historic occurrence is an embodiment of a definite concept which is the essence of a particular age. Thus the historic process is a sequence of events embodying a sequence of identifiable ideas. Each concept, in turn, is a product or synthesis of a thesis, contradicted by an antithesis; the static construct of a merely valid syllogism is thus energized into a dynamic, living process of events that occur as true. The pure abstraction of an idea provokes its own concrete negation and becomes real, i.e., lives, moves, through the mutual tension between two extremes.

The essence and goal of history according to Fichte and his mentor Kant is rational freedom; this principle was incorporated virtually unchanged by Hegel who applied it to all reality as progress toward the freeing of potential rationality everywhere; hence the term panlogism, applied to Hegelian idealism, a system of gradually more self-conscious concretizations of Spirit, culminating in Absolute Spirit or Knowledge.

The Fichtean metaphysics of becoming reads like a blueprint for Hegel's Phenomenology, Logic and Encyclopedia: rational freedom evolves from a virtually unconscious and irrational abstraction, hardly more than a "blind instinct" reminiscent of Plato's "City of Healthy Pigs"[26] ruled by appetite, toward its logical opposite, individual freedom to self-imposed authority. Put in the words of classical and enlightened political theory, for Fichte reason begins to take shape as man abandons the freedom of the "State of Nature" and enters the sphere of freely accepted laws not of his making, i.e., he embraces the strictures of authority.

Viewed statically, freedom seems to have disappeared at this stage; but conceived in terms of a self-fulfilling dynamic plan, this antithesis of freedom does not lead to tyranny, but to a voluntary suspension of personal rights for the sake of a higher synthesis. The principle of double negation, so crucial to the dialectics of Hegel and Marx, is Fichte's invention: the thesis of instinctual, mindless license is negated by a self-imposed government authority which in turn is negated by the essential residue of freedom that had survived the first negation. This second negation has thus already become the synthesis of Freedom and Authority: a higher, conscious freedom of the citizen, compared by Collingwood to Rousseau's "civil freedom,[27]" and, as such, viewed as revolutionary.

The final synthesis between the still revolutionary "civil" mind and the impassive Laws of Nature comes into being at an even higher level of rational freedom, that of Art, in which

> mind and nature are reunited, mind recognizing in nature its own counterpart and related to it not by way of obedience but by way of sympathy and love.[28]

At this point, Fichte's idealist absolutism attains the category of Romantic self-gratification, updating Kant's categoric imperative. While Kant expected of man to become a self-legislator, a member of a "_possible_ kingdom of ends,[29]" Fichte sees the "characteristic feature of his age" in an _actual_

> free devotion of the individual to an end which, though objective, he regards as his own end.[30]

Fichte's metaphysics had an even more powerful impact on German Romanticism than his philosophy of history. Paralleling his synthetic view of an "authoritarian" and again, of a "revolutionary" stage as, respectively, more than freedom-crushing and authority-cancelling, Fichte's concept of the ego goes beyond "haughty self-obsession " to include some limitation imposed on it by the "acceptance of the transcendental" and of "morality" as checks on "complete arbitariness." In his essay entitled "Some Aspects of German Philosophy in the Romantic Period," Paul Roubiczek argues that, in spite of these inbuilt safeguards, Fichte opened for the German Romantic the way "toward complete arbitrariness.[31]"

If the embodiment of every age is that of a definite concept, by the same token, "orginally nothing is given but the Ego; and only the Ego is absolutely given." The ego is the first and absolute postulate of all intelligent and intelligible existence.

>   I am absolutely because I am;
>   and I am absolutly what I am.[32]

Roubiczek points out that these propositions are more than mere tautological patterns along the lines of "I am I;" by making the Ego absolute, Fichte, in a way, comes to terms with the empirical sphere of the non-I, what Ortega y Gasset was to call in our century "the I and my circumstance." The Fichtean "circumstance," the world beyond my me, is obviously posited, conditioned, by the Unconditional Ego of my Self. But, notes Roubiczek, Fichte also acknowledges the existence of the transcendental; consequently, the fundamental ontological triad is set as "Absolute Ego-Non-Ego-Original Ego (Ursubjektivität)," a secularized stand-in for what used to be <u>transcendental apperception or pure ego in Kant</u>.[33]

Roubiczek argues that many of the less structured and philosophically-minded Romantics neglected to follow through the subtleties of this rudimentary dialectic, simplifying it to mean a <u>carte blanche</u> for untrammeled "individuality and subjectivity." Fichte's declaration of the Ego's function as exclusive determinant of itself and of the world convinced them that the Ego (their own, not Fichte's Transcendental Self) was in each case "the creator of the world.[34]" The fact that Fichte contradicted his own ego absolutism by ascribing an additional determining force to morality, was lost on most Romantic writers. What they did, however, grasp rather well was his secularization of Eternity and the Absolute.

> The voice of conscience which imposes upon everyone his <u>special duty</u>,... the beam by which we emanate from infinity and are made single, particular beings[35]

made little impact because of its relativizing qualification; the Romantics tended to interpret each their respective duty rather broadly and vaguely. Paramount and "infallible" in its moral and existential judgments, Fichte's Ego becomes a perversion of Kant's categorical imperative and of man's membership in the kingdom of individually posited ends. Roubiczek argues convincingly that Fichte

> provides the foundations, not only for the other Romantic systems, but also for... [a so-called] "basic Romantic philosophy.[36]"

Thus the stage has been set for Hegel's more sophisticated if esoteric secularization of Divine Transcendence that will not shy back from a veiled deicide as it proudly proclaims the identity of the World with the phenomenologically clairvoyant Ego of the philosopher-Magus.

But one more dialectician intervenes in the programming of the Romantic psyche before it receives its most ambitious and sweeping conceptualization by the great systematizer of paradoxes Hegel. Friedrich Wilhelm Joseph Schelling (1775-1854), a disciple of Fichte and through him, remotely, of Kant, is simultaneously the empiricist and the great mystic among the prophets of the emerging Romantic creed. Collingwood indicates that it has never been clearly established

> whether the doctrines which Hegel shared with [the younger] Schelling were reached by independent thinking or under Schelling's influence.[37]

Schelling's <u>Ideas for a Philosophy of Nature</u>, <u>On the World Soul</u> and <u>System of Transcendental Idealism</u> were published, respectively, in 1797, 1798 and 1800, predating all of Hegel's major works; terms like "movement of nature," and "history," "rational process" of the world developing toward an "Ultimate Truth" which is complete self-consciousness, and the "Universal Mind" (Spirit) as process of reality developing toward an "absolute identity" between Ego and World have currency in Schelling's system prior to or at least at the same time as in Hegel's. On the other hand, the very principle of "esthetical," i.e., naturalist idealism, as opposed to the spiritual or rationalist idealism of Hegel, is Schelling's own, as is his existential dialectics or "metaphysical empiricism," grounded in objects of sense, rather than in Hegel's unconscious Spirit <u>qua</u> Pure Being. But, most of all, the two differ in their attitude to the mystical and transcendent: old Schelling's turn to Jakob Boehme's theosophist mysticism differs greatly from Hegel's "magic" which would convert theology into a this-worldly and absolutely logical (panlogist) ideology. All differences and similarities considered, Schelling's thought was every bit as influential in the shaping of Romantic emotionalism as was Fichte's and Hegel's.

   Schelling's metaphysics starts from a concept of Being <u>qua</u> Nature as a transcendental universal World Ground; from this aprioristic Absolute evolves the world of phenomena, culminating, the same as in Herder, in man. These at first distinct manifestations of the Absolute gradually become a knowable One. Hence, in a fashion paralleling Hegel's dictum "what is rational is already real,[38]" Schelling postulates, in an inverse order to Hegel, that what is radically "real," i.e., Nature, is all, eventually, knowable. Though operating with basically identical concepts, the two master dialecticians differ again in their view of ultimate realities. While Hegel starts from a potentially free, as yet not conscious Spirit as moving force of the dialectic process of empirical reality, Schelling identifies this process of empirical becoming as sensible Nature, the prime mover from which evolves, as a sort of a secondary absolute, History, variously conceived as Spirit, Thought, Idea, Consciousness. The goal of phenomenal becoming, according to Schelling, is the same as Hegel's: both see it as a dialectic process progressing toward the Absolute, the last and high synthesis qua Identity, in which all distinctions lose their difference. In Identity, Schelling unifies the two fundamental attributes of Being, Nature and Spirit, in a synthesis of the idea of God, terminally reconciling the Ego with the World. This "divine" Identity is the "in-difference" point between the real and the ideal.

As an aspect of this Absolute Beginning and End, Nature is made up of objects distributed according to "determinate" spatial relations, i.e., physical laws; this makes the world of fact merely intelligible; contrariwise, History or Spirit (Ego) consists of "thoughts and actions of minds"

> which are not only intelligible, but intelligent [i.e., both understandable and self-understanding]... hence they are a more adequate [if derivative!] embodiment of the Absolute [than Nature], because they contain in themselves both sides of the knowledge relation... [being] subject as well as object.[39]

Evidently the final synthesis of Hegel's Science of Logic, as Idea-Nature-Spirit, hardly differs from Schelling's: both are systematized versions of the Romantic striving for perfection in this world through an act of secular Ego divinization. Ulrich Weisstein and Arthur Henkel trace the origins of the Romantic syndrome to an attempt to surmount the "split between subject and object.[40]"

Schelling's thesis, or first level of comprehension of the Absolute, is a conception of Nature

> where reality is conceived as broken up and dispersed into separate realities (polytheism) and where political forms come into existence and perish like natural organisms.[41]

In terms of structure, Schelling's dialectic starts with a thesis corresponding to Hegel's antithesis. Hegel, too, starts from the concept of pure, immediate and virtually unconscious Being, but, precisely because it is abstract and unmediated, this Being is not articulated but a singular, opaque universal. For Hegel, the externalization and objectification of the Ego occurs out of and in opposition to this pure Being-in-itself. Only as an objectified and hence alienated ego, potential self-consciousness becomes an articulated Being-for-itself.

This difference between Hegel's spiritual-rationalist point of departure and the aesthetical-naturalist starting point of Schelling is largely a matter of emphasis. For both, the Ground of Being is unconscious and universal, only for Schelling it is the Absolute as Nature, and for Hegel, the Absolute as Spirit; both agree that the real evolves through a process of reason. Hegel's inarticulate Being-in-itself is viewed by Schelling as articulated Nature "broken up into separate realities" of perishable and perishing forms of religious and political "nature." Schelling's dialectic progresses to a stage akin to the Hegelian mirroring of the World in the Ego and vice versa. Schelling's Absolute must rise above Mind, knowing qua knower, the simply knowable, i.e., Nature, to a higher stage in which "mind knows itself." Such a higher stage is History as a

> temporal process in which both knowledge and the knowable are progressively coming into existence...[i.e., in History qua] self-realization of the Absolute where the Absolute means both reason as the knowable and reason as the knower.[42]

In spite of the different emphases on Spirit and Nature resulting in two opposing views of the inception of the dialectic process of becoming, and the difference in viewing the metaphysical structure of these two aspects of the Absolute, Schelling and Hegel are agreed on the intelligibility as well as the knowledgeable intellect of the World-become-Reason. The world qua intellect knows and becomes intelligible as well as an aesthetically (i.e., sensorily) justifiable organism, similar to Plato's ensouled, logically endowed zoon (organism), except for the latter's paradigmatic nature that only reflects, but is per se not the ultimate physical Absolute, not even dialectically. In this most radical difference between Platonic and German idealism resides the essentially Romantic nature of the latter.

It is in Hegel's Phenomenology of the Spirit (1807) that transcendental idealism made the most ambitious bid for spiritual concretization in an "eternity now." The very frustration of the human ego over its finitude accounts for this triumph of Reason in the process of self-liberation from spacial and temporal limitations which become gradually aufgehoben in all three, contradictory meanings of the word: cancelled, preserved and raised to an ever higher level of self-consciousness.

For Hegel, Spirit at the lowermost of its six principal levels (Consciousness, Self-Consciousness, Reason, Spirit, Religion, Absolute Knowledge) is simple consciousness as Understanding; but as it understands itself as such, it has already, thanks to the power of negation, i.e., concretizing thought, risen beyond mere understanding; in "merely experiencing itself," such consciousness

> reveals itself united and bound up with the supersensible world through the mediating agency of the realm of Appearance, through which it gazes into this background that lies behind appearance.

In this one, pregnant phrase, the Kantian dualism between phenomena and noumena is aufgehoben, overcome in the broadest sense of the word. The finite ego, "dirempt" by the ever-present intuition of Otherness, is momentarily reconciled with the non-I, in an attempt to cancel otherness or difference as distinction per se. The "curtain" of appearance that has veiled the "inner world" is thus withdrawn; the royal We used by Hegel repeatedly to describe his phenomenologically initiated visions[43] glimpses

> the inner being [i.e., the Ego] gazing into the inner realm -- the vision of the undistinguished self-same reality, which repels itself from itself, affirms itself as a divided and distinguished inner reality, but as one for which at the same time the two factors have immediately no distinction; what we have here is Self-consciousness.[44]

By this magic operation,[45] Hegel achieves self-mirroring at the first, lowermost, as yet hardly at all concrete -- read: spiritual -- plateau, for

> It is manifest that behind the

> so-called curtain [of mere
> appearances], which is to hide
> the inner world, there is nothing
> to be seen, unless we ourselves
> go behind there, as much in
> order that we may thereby see,
> as that there may be something
> behind there which can be seen.[46]

In this second fundamental sentence, Hegel <u>reveals</u> the thought-conretizing faculty of the "initiated," i.e., <u>Hegelian</u> Ego. What only just became aware of itself as Understanding, reproduces itself concretely already as Self-consciousness; the erstwhile dirempt self comes to terms with Infinitude as an infinitely washing mirror of the Self.

Hegel's <u>Phenomenology</u> is a magic book, a <u>grimoire</u>. Hegel himself speaks of <u>Zauberworte</u>, a magic formula[47] that pretends, much like some latter-day gnostic text, to heal modern man's existential <u>diremption</u>, effecting "a new wholeness" between World Ground and creation. Hegel the gnostic sorcerer in possession of this healing formula, i.e., his phenomenology, is for the philosopher Voegelin an "imaginator" who

> can shift the meaning of
> existence from life in the
> presence under God,... to the
> role of a functionary of history;
> the reality of existence will be
> eclipsed and replaced by the Second Reality of the imaginative
> project.[48]

In some five hundred and fifty pages that remain in Baillie's version of the <u>Phenomenology</u> Hegel does just that.

Self-consciousness is repeatedly promised this "new wholeness;" failing, also repeatedly, at the task of concretizing itself as a difference from the world without distinction, it reaches the third major plateau of self-representation as

Reason.

> The process of its own activity, i.e., of consciousness has in its [sic] case brought out the truth that individuality... [as] an actual consciousness, is... the negative of itself, i.e.,... [its own] objective extreme. [This process]... has forced [individual consciousness] to make explicit its self-existence and turned [it] into an objective fact.[49]

In a unique manipulation of the existential dread before the finite condition of man, Hegel manages to convert consciousness into a "real" object for the self, by driving it farther back into itself, into an ever-deeper alienation from empirical reality (Otherness) by simply pretending that it "stands to Reason" that such an operation, according to the dialectical principle of self-negation, must turn into its opposite, i.e., explicitness and exteriorization.

> From the fact that self-consciousness is Reason, its hitherto negative attitude towards otherness turns round into a positive attitude.[50]

This new self-realization, too, proves to be rather ephemeral. As soon as "Rational Self-consciousness" _realizes_ itself "through itself," it blunders into yet another frustrating self-representation, appropriately identified by Hegel as "the Law of the Heart and the Frenzy of Self-conceit.[51]"

A disastrous disintegration of a _potentially_ concretized universal and of self-conscious individuality recurs regularly each time Hegel's self-consciousness rises to newer heights of allegedly more "concrete" and certainly more frustrated "inwardness," i.e., of more inward

<u>rationality</u> and broader, more universally expanded <u>freedom</u>, the two fundamental constituents of spiritual absolutism. "Independent self-existence[52]" and "Concrete individuality,[53]" sought by the alienated Being-for-itself of the Romantic, are variants of the same bid for the Absolute.

At the fourth major plateau of self-cognition, consciousness rises for Hegel from the level of Reason to that of Spirit

> when its certainty of being all reality has been raised to the level of truth, and reason is <u>consciously</u> aware of itself as its own world, and of the world itself.[54]

Following the now well established pattern, Spirit in turn degenerates through independent, revolutionary self-expression into "Absolute Freedom and Terror." "Spirit in the form of absolute freedom"

> is the mode of self-consciousness which clearly comprehends that in its certainty of self lies the essence of all the component spiritual spheres <u>of the concrete sensible as well as of the supersensible world</u>, or conversely, that <u>essential being and concrete actuality consist in the knowledge consciousness has of itself</u>.

For this "pure personality" all reality "is solely spirituality;" embodied in the rationalist despot, it considers the world to be "absolutely its own will, and this will is universal will.[55]" Eventually, through the continuous process of all-negating self-disintegration, despotic will dissolves itself and

> absolute freedom leaves its self-destructive sphere of reality

> and <u>passes over into another land of self-conscious spirit</u>, where... freedom is... accepted as the truth. In the thought of this truth spirit... revives itself... and knows this being which self-consciousness involves [viz. thought] to be the complete and entire essence of everything.[56]

In a letter to Niethammer of April 29, 1814, Hegel explains this passage (written before 1806) as a prediction of the decline of French republicanism and its demise through the phenomenon of Napoleon.

> The freedom... [as the] abstract, formal freedom of the French Republic as it emerged, as I have shown, from Enlightenment, goes over from its self-destructive reality into <u>another land</u>... of the self-conscious <u>Geist</u>, where in its non-reality it is accepted as true....[57]

The universal but abstract -- and hence necessarily murderous -- freedom concept of the French finds, according to Hegel, its concretion in Germany, being accepted "in its non-reality as true" by German Romanticists. The new form and mode of experience that now arises primarily in the Germany of the Romantics is that of the "Moral Life of Spirit.[58]" Eventually, this self conscious Spirit <u>qua</u> Morality reaches the fifth and next-to-the-last plateau of consciousness as Religion, which is "consciousness of Absolute Being in general.[59]"

At this point Hegel claims Spirit begins to manifest itself for the first time truly as Absolute.

> Spirit in its own world and
> spirit conscious of itself as
> spirit, i.e., spirit in the
> sphere of religion, are the
> same.

Religion becomes "complete" when these two forms of spirit "become identical," not merely being "embraced by religion," but, conversely, as spirit becomes "a real object of its own consciousness." Spirit objectified for itself, i.e., for consciousness, cannot be but absolute, for it

> is as much aware of being a free
> and independent reality as it
> remains therein conscious of
> itself.[60]

In the concluding pages of the Phenomenology that deal with the last Aufhebung of consciousness to its sixth and last plane, the realm of Absolute Knowledge, Hegel's self at last completes its transfiguration into Pure Ego. This ego recognizes itself simultaneously as nothing but itself, and no less than the entire sum of existence.

Inevitably the Absolute Spirit undergoes its last sublation to the only "higher" level left, i.e., Nothingness (!!), all along the goal and motor force qua nihilation of objective reality, which is the same as pure thought. Spirit "sets forth its process of becoming pure and absolute" as "sacrifice" and "self-abandonment.[61]" Annihilated as a Self, Spirit intuits "outside itself" its Self as Time, "and likewise, its existence, as Space." A secularized version of Passion and Resurrection is here staged as the last act of the Phenomenology, the Gospel according to Hegel.

NOTES

[1] Walter Clauss, <u>Deutsche Literatur</u> (Zürich: Schulthess, 1966), 202.

[2] Raymond Immerwahr traces the English word "romantic" back in time, past the tetrad Macpherson-Percy-Young-Gray, the immediate inspirers of the German phenomenon, to mid-seventeenth century England. According to Logan Pearsall Smith, "around 1650, Englishmen were becoming aware of certain qualities in [chivalric] romances for which they needed a name.., their falseness and unreality, all that was imaginary and impossible in them, all that was contrary to the more rational view of life." Cf. "Four Romantic Words, <u>Words and Idioms</u> (Boston, 1925), 70. Immerwahr in turn traces the British term to the Latin "Romanus," which, according to Ernst Robert Curtius "extended first to the peoples of the Roman Empire, then, to their various dialects of Vulgar Latin, and in the Middle Ages to those literary forms which were most commonly written in the popular dialects instead of literary Latin, that is, intended for entertainment rather than for instruction or edification." Cf. <u>European Literature and the Latin Middle Ages</u>, trans. W. R. Trask, Bollinger Series XXXVI (New York: 1953), 30 ff. Cf. Immerwahr, "The Word <u>Romantisch</u> and Its History," <u>The Romantic Period in Germany</u>, ed. Siegbert Prawer (New York: Shocken Books, 1970), 35.

[3] <u>Op. cit.</u>, <u>loc. cit</u>.

[4] "Some Aspects of German Philosophy in the Romantic Period," Prawer, <u>op. cit</u>., 305.

[5] "Kritische Fragmente," 115. Cf. Roubiczek, <u>ibid</u>.

[6] My italics.

[7] *Critique of Pure Reason*, trans. N. Kemp Smith (London: Macmillan, 1929), B xxiv-xxx. Author's italics.

[8] *Ibid.*, XXVI.

[9] Clauss, *Deutsche Literatur*, 128.

[10] Immanuel Kant, *The Critique of Aesthetic Judgment*, III, Art and Artist, 49. Of the Faculties of the Mind that Constitute Genius.

[11] Clauss, *ibid.*

[12] *Ibid.*, 129.

[13] *Ibid.*, 130.

[14] *Timaeus*, 30 b-c.

[15] *The Idea of History* (New York: Oxford University Press, 1976), 89.

[16] *Ibid.*, 90.

[17] Clauss, *op. cit.*, 131.

[18] Collingwood, *op. cit.*, 89.

[19] *Op. cit.*, 90.

[20] *Ibid.*, 91.

[21] *Ibid.*, 93.

[22] *Ibid.*, 96. My italics.

[23] *Ibid.*, 99. My italics.

[24] *Ibid.*, 100-01.

[25] *Ibid.*

26 The Republic, 369C.

27 The Idea of History, 107.

28 Ibid., 108.

29 Fundamental Principles of the Metaphysic of Morals, trans. T. K. Abbot (London: Longmans Green, 1927) par. 2, 52-59. My italics.

30 Op. cit. 107-58.

31 Cf. Prawer, The Romantic Period in Germany, 309-10.

32 Grundriss der Wissenschaftslehre, par. 1 and 2. Cf. Roubiczek, op. cit., loc. cit., 311.

33 Critique of Pure Reason, trans. N. Kemp Smith (London: Macmillan, 1929), A 107-08.

34 Roubiczek "Some Aspects of German Philosophy," Cf. Prawer, 310.

35 Die Bestimmung des Menschen (1800), 292-05 of the original edition. My italics. Cf. Roubiczek, op cit., 311.

36 Roubiczek, op. cit., 311.

37 The Idea of History, 111.

38 Cf. Preface to Hegel's Philosophy of Right.

39 System des transzendentalen Idealismus, 1800. Werke (Stuttgart and Augsburg, 1858), part I, vol. iii, 587-604. My italics. Cf. Collingwood, 112.

40 Immerwahr, "The Word Romantisch," Cf. Prawer, The Romantic Period, 34.

41 System des transzendentalen Idealismus, op.cit., loc. cit. Cf. Collingwood, 112.

[42] Schelling, *System*, *ibid*. Cf. Collingwood 113. My italics.

[43] For a summary evaluation of this "we" see Kenley Royce Dove's "Hegel's Phenomenological Method," *New Studies in Hegel's Philosophy*, ed. Warren E. Steinkraus (New York: Holt, Rinehart and Winston, 1971), 44 ff.

[44] Georg Wilhelm Friedrich Hegel, *The Phenomenology of Mind*, trans. J. B. Baillie (New York: Macmillan, 1955), 212. A. Consciousness, III. Force and Understanding: Appearance and the Supersensible World, 2. Infinitude. My italics.

[45] Eric Voegelin, "On Hegel, a Study in Sorcery," *Studium Generale* 24 (1971), 335-68.

[46] Hegel, *op. cit.*, *loc. cit.* Mv italics.

[47] G. W. F. Hegel, *Fortsetzung des "Systems der Sittlichkeit*," ed. Johannes Hoffmeister, *Dokumente zu Hegels Entwicklung* (Stuttgart, 1936), 314. Cf. Voegelin, "On Hegel," *loc. cit.*

[48] *Op. cit.*, 318. Cf. Voegelin, 337. My italics.

[49] Hegel, *Phenomenology*, 272. C. [Free Concrete Mind], AA. Reason, V. Certainty and Truth of Reason. My italics.

[50] *Ibid.*

[51] *Op. cit.*, 390-400.

[52] *Ibid.*, 399.

[53] *Op. cit.*, 414-16.

[54] *Op. cit.*, 457 ff. Author's italics.

[55] *Op cit.*, 600 B. Spirit in Self-estrangement: The Discipline of Culture and Civilization.

III. Absolute Freedom and Terror. My italics.

⁵⁶ *Ibid.*, 610. My italics.

⁵⁷ Cf. Voegelin, "On Hegel," 364. Author's italics.

⁵⁸ Hegel, *Phenomenology*, *loc. cit*.

⁵⁹ *Op. cit.*, 685, VII. Religion in General.

⁶⁰ *Op. cit.*, 688, A. Natural Religion. My italics.

⁶¹ *Ibid.*, 806. My italics.

CHAPTER II

FRIEDRICH SCHLEGEL'S VISION OF
PROGRESSIVE PERFECTIBILITY THROUGH ROMANTIC CULTURE.

The decidedly more controversial half of the fraternal Schlegel team, Friedrich (1772-29) was a self-styled prophet, defender, theoretician and program director of the Romantic movement in the German-speaking world. Surpassed by his older brother August Wilhelm (1767-45) in academic prestige and worldly success, it was nevertheless Friedrich who left a stronger imprint on the movement's programmatic postulates.[1] At the same time, August Wilhelm gave full support to his brother's interpretation of literature and literary criticism as one, complementary phenomenon.[2] Thanks to the universalist bent of their minds and capacious imagination, the two acquired such breadth of learning and depth in aesthetic intuition that a renaissance of European letters out of the spirit of the Romantic urge for the Absolute became more than just a possibility.

The Schlegels' bravura in aesthetic speculation overshadowed their own rather indifferent talents as original poets,[3] playwrights and novelists, but their impact on their more creative peers was incalculable. While August Wilhelm's _Berlin Lectures on Literature and Art_ (1801) and _Vienna Lectures on Dramatic Art and Literature_ (1808) remain permanent contributions to literary theory, the actual shaping of the aesthetics of Romanticism became the task of Friedrich.

The latter's amazing critical output began at the age of twenty-eight. _On the Study of Greek Poetry_, called by Schlegel's editors _Studiumaufsatz_, (_Analytical Treatise_),[4] reflects the rudimentary concepts of criticism and literary history as they were taking shape between 1795-96. Every year for the next five gave a new dimension and amplification to his theorizing about poetry and world literature in general. Raimund Belgardt argues convincingly that Schlegel never evolved from an epigon of Goethe and Schiller to an eventual Romantic break with classicism.[5] The continued growth of Schlegel's doctrine never deviates from its initial commitment to Romantic aesthetics.

Friedrich Schlegel's theoretical speculations parallel closely the Hegelian system. The parallel is not surprising given the chronology of the two thinkers and the debt their formation owed to the apocalyptic atmosphere of the fin de siècle marked by the French Revolution and by the Napoleonic Titanism of the new century. More specifically, they were both deeply affected by Fichte's cult of the ego and the syntheticism of opposites, with the reconciliation of Nature and Spirit as ultimate goal. Actually Schlegel's method, if not system,[6] had been developed prior to the publication of Hegel's major works, predating them by nearly a decade. Schlegel's principal metaphysical concerns are virtually identical with those of Hegel; they are clearly reflected in their aesthetics. Both try to elucidate the progressive evolution of Freedom and Reason toward a fully self-conscious individuation; both labor to accelerate a secular Second Coming, only in the case of Hegel the final synthesis is expected to reveal itself as the Absolute Spirit or Knowledge, and Schlegel envisions it fulfilled as "progressive universal poetry."

Prior to 1796, Friedrich focused his attention on the study of Italian poetry and mainly, on Dante. At that time, his periodization of classical Western literature into the classical Greco-Roman and "modern" or Romantic had taken already a fairly definite shape. The post-classical epoch of "Romantic" literature he breaks down further into "older" Romanticism, pace-setting and nearly perfectly self-realized during the Christian Middle Ages and the Renaissance, and "new Romanticism,[7]" developing in Schlegel's own time as a rebellion against "the strictly ordered life of the Enlightenment.[8]" This "new" Romanticism is therefore in a state of flux, as yet not perfected, but most promising as fulfillment of the highest aspirations of modern mankind.

In this first stage of his doctrine's development (1795-86) Friedrich revived Herder's concept of a "Romantic way of thinking" (Denkart), as it evolved in the Middle Ages.[9] Schlegel believed that this aesthetic experience could be brought up to date in the nearest future through an awareness-rousing criticism and revival of the creative genius of older Romanticism. This then is Schlegel's evaluation of the development of post-classical literature in the West according to Belgardt.

> At the beginning there is the flowering of Romantic poetry [of the Middle Ages and the Renaissance], next comes [a period of] degeneration in Schlegel's own time, followed by a soon-to-be-reached achievement [of poetry's] novel mission.[10]

The idea of a closely interacting cultural community of the Romance countries,[11] a medieval Romania,[12] was viewed by Schlegel as a powerful stimulus to the development of the "older Romantic poetry" out of a close association of language, cultural awareness and the novelistic genre, the latter called by Schlegel "typical" of this Romantic-Romance world view.

Unexpectedly, Schlegel turns in the very same Analytical Treatise from the drive to identify the Romantic element as a continuous, universal and vital strain in the "modern" literature of the West to an apparent reclassification of both trend and novelistic genre as classical. On closer scrutiny, this shift proves to be purely terminological.

First of all, classical, i.e., Greco-Roman poetry remains for him a model of absolute perfection, even though its actual viability is "now" in a disintegrated state. Secondly, classicism as such best answers the demand of universality, Schlegel's most fundamental postulate for Romantic art. Classical poetry was "natural," while "modern" poetry has "artificial origins and character." This artificiality is not to be taken negatively for it makes -- potentially, of course -- for "the right [literary] rules, enduring perfectibility and... total satisfaction." These features were absent in Greek poetry which was a result of "natural education," whereas in "modern" poetry intellect is the leading principle of aesthetic formation, in spite of all the Romantic Phantasterei, "fantasticism.[13]"

In a daring double negation worthy of Hegel, Schlegel insists that the "onesidedness of modern literature can be rectified" and the "highest favor of nature," read, classical literature, "can be compensated." The "flabbiness" typical of contemporary literature becomes a "favorable sympton," even though, as a reaction to deadening rationalism, it springs from "a violent, often over-wrought striving." This very violence presupposes "the highest degree of strength,[14]" which is expected to contribute to the regeneration of the literary reality of Schlegel's time.

Thus infinitely progressing self-perfection is set as goal for the "new, artificial" literature. Only through "spontaneous self-initiative (Selbsttätigkeit), through spirit, intention and freedom," can there be established harmonious order. The "imperfection of the beginning" of this modern poetry "would thus be overcome[15]" and literature will eventually enjoy what Schlegel calls later in his programmatic 116th Athenäum Fragment "a limitless growth of classicism.[16]" In this synthesis of order and fantasticism, modern "depraved" Romanticism has the potential to soon become something higher than both, combining the robust finiteness of its classical predecessor with the never-ending drive for the infinite of the frustrated Romantic.

In its second stage, the so-called "early Berlin-Jena period" (1796-98), his thought revolves around the redefinition of the novel. Schlegel reaffirms Herder's view in the key signifiance of the novelistic genre in literature and its function as a Romantic life style setter.[17]

In the light of these suppositions it should come as no surprise that Schlegel classifies Dante's Divine Comedy as a "novel" and a "Romantic one[18]" at that. He breaks down the genre into three categories, the mimic novel, which predominates in Dante's Inferno, the sentimental, exemplified by Dante's Purgatory, and the fantastic, typical of the Paradise.[19] Even though Schlegel views all poetry as Romantic,[20] Cervantes the poet-novelist is, in the final analysis, "more Romantic than Shakespeare,[21]" and Don Quixote remains "the only thoroughly Romantic novel.[22]"

Such an all-inclusive definition of Romanticism leads of course to a near destruction of the term's usefulness.[23] This notwithstanding, Schlegel continues to explore further all the themes dealt with in the Analytical Treatise. Romanticism as embodied in "the absolute novel is, by definition, a transcendently-oriented "Christian poetry," a conviction echoed by Hegel's much later published Philosophy of Fine Art (1835). The novel as Christian poetry is for Schlegel a "symbol of the absolute ideal[24]" and, finally, the "poetic ideal qua God.[25]"

Eventually, even the short novel or novella, being both "romance and novel,[26]" as well as the "sagas and fairy tales[27]" are included in the ever-expanding novelistic category. A new dialectic dimension is added to the Romantic work of art; its fundamental need for self-transcendence makes it "potentialized poetry," or a synthetic, sublated "poetry of poetry[28]" which includes literary criticism and the artist's self-criticism.[29] The resulting dialectic involvement of objective criticism with the purely subjective act of creation makes "objectivity the principal requirement of a novel.[30]"

> In all novelistic categories all that is subjective must be objectified; it is erroneous to consider the novel to be a subjective literary genre.[31]

Following through the dialectic process, "criticism itself must submit to objectification,[32]" a requirement one would expect of a classicist, but then, classicism is really one of the dialectic poles of Romanticism and its eternal paradigm.... Objective novelistic creation and criticism suggest a new key concept that Schlegel will develop some three years later: the function of irony as reflective framework arising out of the work of art itself.

The principle of novelistic as well as critical objectivity suggests a dialectic tension between the individual and the universal. The idea of the individual as a <u>Versinnlichung</u>, a perceptible representation -- or objectification -- of the universal goes back to the <u>Analytical Treatise</u>; this objective representation was to guard against the "individual" and that which is specific becoming a onesidedly "self-serving" perversion of "free art" into an imitative <u>Geschicklichkeit</u>, dexterity.[33] Now the tension between the real individual and an abstract idea is to be reconciled at a new, more highly potentialized level. As modern poetry renews its bid for the infinite, "the absolute mood," the goal of its effort so far, becomes equated with "prophecy," and "asolute poetry" as true ideals, ideas and yet individuals.[34]

Gradually, the speculations of Schlegel the avowed enemy of systematic thought acquire a very Hegelian sophistication in daring syntheses seeking ever-higher potentializations of the Romantic mentality. In an apparent swing toward classicist measure, the absolute novel's principal concern becomes Selbstbeschränkung, self-limitation sought by the finite individual who nevertheless -- and because of his finiteness -- gets to represent all of infinite Becoming. Through this act of representation he actually becomes infinite, yet retains an existential and aesthetic profile of clearly determined, finite outlines. If there is a paradox in this, it is cavalierly resolved in the synthetic concept of irony. Belgardt views Schlegel's idea of individuality inwardly infinite with finite outward delineations as

> a mediation between the necessity of the drive for the infinite and the consciousness of the achievement of a "complete coincidence.35"

If this "coincidence" is viewed as ironic, Schlegel's vertiginous reconciliations of subject and object, as well as the claim of classicism for absolute Romanticism, become somewhat more plausible. If we can accept the proposition that "everything is jest in representation," and "everything earnestness in the moment of elevation," the resulting synthesis as "true irony" can indeed be instrumental in "acquiring infinity.36"

In 1797, during his first stay in Berlin, Schlegel's struggle for the Romantic Absolute, pursued by the means of an ironic objectivity, shifts from analyses of the "absolute novel" to the determination of a poetic ideal, only to move on towards a critical encompassing of the whole of Romantic poetry in 1798. In his own speculative fashion, Schlegel parallels the contemporary genesis of Friedrich Hölderlin's mythological poetry. Despite the shifts in focus, Schlegel's ultimate purpose remains the capture and embodiment of the infinite through finite means, thus reconciling eternity with time.

In his early Analytical Treatise on classical

antiquity, Schlegel spoke of the Golden Age of poetry when "divinity walked about in earthly garb," when "the infinite had been achieved," and "the law of eternity became visible in mortal works.[37]" In 1797 Schlegel is confident that the time has come to find again a "mystical unity in multiplicity." This unity can only be "Romantic," a compendium of

> complete poetic, logical or philosophical and historical, rhetorical, ethical [individual unities]....[38]

On the strength of these insights, a fuller explanation of the progressivity of the universal Romantic phenomenon can be offered beyond simply postulating it as a <u>never-ending thrust to infinity</u>.

The "natural formation" of Greek culture had collapsed, but it has been kept from suffering a permanent relapse into primal chaos by a tension between "self-creation and self-destruction," the latter never being complete,[39] thanks once more to the dialectic principle of double negation.

> Classical poetry has annihilated itself historically... but progressive [poetry] has not; it destroys itself often enough, but it recreates itself right away.[40]

This is a faithful parallel to Hegel's concept of universal but abstract Being-in-itself as opposed by the particular and concrete Being-for-itself, the latter by definition alienated from the former's abstract essence. The two rise through mutual mediation to become a Being-in-and-for-itself; existing in eternal flux, this higher, more self-conscious existence never statically <u>is</u>, but eternally becomes what it ought to be, and, becoming this ought, no longer <u>is</u> what it <u>was</u>. Schlegel's bid for a universal progressive Romantic existence has, in his own words, a "peculiar nature, which can eternally only become, but never be perfected,[41]"

The apocalyptic visions of both Hegel and Schlegel typically stop short of the real concretization of the Absolute. Schlegel admits this openly.

> Even the most universal [and perfected] works... stop short of the goal of harmony, remaining incomplete.[42]

As indicated earlier, Schlegel solves the impasse between promise and fulfillment through the synthetic quality of irony. At this point he introduces the concept of wit[43] as the ultimate "artistic," i.e., Romantic, tool of fulfillment; the same function serve parody[44] and satire.[45] But wit is also essential to philosophy, being for it "what prophecy is to poetry.[46]" Again wit is redefined qua form as "the appearance of an absolute antithesis.[47]" Belgardt calls Schlegel's concept of wit an equivalent of philosophical syntheticism. Wit is "the law of mixture," which combines "the widely separated... and the apparently contradictory.[48]" In Schlegel's own words,

> The Romantic imperative demands the mixing of all genres. All nature and all science must become art. -- Art must become Nature and Science.[49]

This shows how much Victor Hugo's bombshell of mélange des genres, sprung on literary classicism in 1827 in the Preface to the drama Hernani, owes to Friedrich Schlegel's concept of wit.

The earlier postulate declaring the artist an objective, "scientific" critic is rephrased between 1797-98 as "poetic reflection," a synthesis between producer and product;[50] put differently, this means Sichselbstmitdarstellen,[51] a "self-representation simultaneous with the representation" of an object. Poetic reflection is Selbstbespiegelung, a "self-mirroring," endowed with "the divine aura of irony," a self-reflecting reflection "washing, as it were, in an endless row of mirrors." The Absolute, the

Infinite, the Whole "can be only intuited, and this can be achieved only by wit.[52]"

The same process toward the ultimate "witty" intuition will produce a kind of meta-poetry that Romantic poetry potentially already is, a "poetry of poetry;" because of its "relationship to the whole[53]," this higher art <u>has become</u> the whole. Belgardt interprets this cosmic syntheticism as a reconciliation of "purposiveness of art work with its lack of purpose," of "one work of art with all works of art, of one with all other arts, of all poems with one poem.[54]"

A sweeping afterthought summarizes the insights of the second period of Schlegel's doctrinal evolution. <u>The universal "truth of the Eternal" achieves, as it had in the past, first a mirroring of itself in "appearance" which is the deception of the finite</u>; secondly, <u>it can achieve absolute perfection if this deception is viewed as allegorical and symbolical</u>. As a result this potentialized deception has acquired <u>Bedeutung</u>, meaning, the only reality in <u>Dasein</u>, our "Being here,"

> because only the <u>Sinn</u>, sense,
> the spirit of Being-here,
> originates from and returns
> to that which is elevated above
> and beyond all Being-here.[55]

The brief span between 1799 and 1800, referred to by Schlegel scholars as the "late Berlin-Jena period," represents the third, "mythological" stage of his doctrine. The earlier call for a universal Romantic "ideal" is expanded to include the creation of a new "mythology," which, in Belgardt's view, is to "reflect the spiritual tendencies of the times.[56]" The art of classical Greece continues to be prototypical for Schlegel; but the earlier suggestion that "the Ancients can be surpassed in their very classicism[57]" now becomes a definite prospect of a "limitless growth of classicism" postulated by the earlier-mentioned 116th <u>Athenäum Fragment</u>.[58]

In the "Speech on Mythology," Schlegel declares as essential for all "real" poetry a transcendent "point of reference," a "center" grounded in the Divine. Here Schlegel comes to grips with the fundamental impasse of all Romantic theologizing. The Romantic bid for the synthesis of Spirit and Nature is, by definition, pantheistic. The totality of Goethe's *pan*, the whole, learned from the anthropomorphic theology of the Greeks, is reaffirmed by Schlegel in its radically this-worldly, immanent, secular nature. And yet, like every other Romanticist, Schlegel searches for a World Ground, a center *transcendent* in the Platonic and Judeo-Christian sense or, at best, for a *transcendental* orientation towards a kind of Kantian noumenon, an unapproachable, unprovable mental ground, absolutely necessary for the understanding of the phenomena. Like the speculative peregrinations of Hegel's Spirit progressing toward the Absolute, the pantheist-this-worldly essence of all Romantic metaphysics and theology remains a thorny obstacle to the transformation of mankind through an apocalyptic aesthetics *nobler* than this world, but still *of* this world.

Schlegel's bid for a modern mythology gravitates toward Platonic and Christian *transcendentism*, rather than Kantian *transcendentalism*; this fact prefigures his eventual conversion to Catholicism. His Paris studies of the relics of Western literary traditions convinced him that "man has not begun his earthly career without God.[59]" In his *Ideas* he speaks of "longing and a quiet melancholy[60]" via-à-vis transcendent creation and "in respect to its human analogue.[61]"

The "reflection of divinity in man[62]" as the ultimate poetic act has, however, clearly Dionysian overtones.

> The form of poetry must be
> religious -- sacrifice --
> feast, orgies -- the temple.[63]

This brings Schlegel closer to Nietzsche's *amor*

fati, love of man's this-worldly fate, and the "Saturnalia of the spirit," celebrated by Nietzsche in Merry Wisdom. The "mystical science of the whole,[64]" and "the inner living relationship" of all things, and "inseparable union of nature, man and God,[65]" are not new except in their unusual breadth and sweep. They are admittedly taken from Spinoza, whose system Schlegel considered the "center" and "point of reference" he needed for his new mythology and mysticism.[66]

Inevitably, this mythology tends to become a base for the sciences of the rejuvenated Romantic century. The final reconcilition of man, nature and God is pantheistic anthropology; the novel becomes "the highest representation of physics,[67]" Spinoza's view of Nature and Spirit as two complementary aspects of one infinite substance is Schlegel's theology; his aesthetics claims to have laid hold of the sought-after "center" which is "humanity, beauty, art," with the Golden Age as center of this center;[68] the earlier-stipulated acceptance of the infinite and hence a must in the fulfillment of ideal poetry is Schlegel's eschatology; otherwise, the prospect of poetry's "completion" would equal "the coming of the Messiah, or the conflagration of the Stoics.[69]"

It is Schlegel's psychology which stands at the "center" of his mythologically grounded system of sciences. "Fichte has given an example for a new mythology,[70]" but what he sees as "object" is merely "a product of creative imagination" and hence, not concrete enough for Schlegel's mythological needs. Fichte's consciousness was filled with "unconscious reflections;[71]" Schlegel intends a synthesis of the materialistically-oriented metaphysics of Spinoza with Fichte's idealism; once this is accomplished, reality will be viewed as

> a point of indifference between [the Fichtean consciousness and Spinoza's infinite substance].... the infinite has reality for consciousness.... Everything is in

one and the one is all.[72]

And yet, for all these pantheist velleities, Schlegel cannot quite shake the shadow of Platonism. The more he moves in the direction of an eventual Nietzschean superman in his idea of all ideas (which is the idea of the Divine to be developed in all men[73] giving them a direct share in Divinity), the more he is fascinated with the pre-Socratic concept of pais paizon, the boy-god at play destroying and creating worlds on a whim,[74] the more surely he does return to the Platonic symbology of the "pious fraud," necessary for the explanation of an otherwise absurd phenomenon of existence. This point was not lost on Belgardt who finds Schlegel's symbolic world view grounded on

> the unification of opposing elements, or inner mutual penetration of reality and ideality, a possibility of cognition and knowledge only through the symbol, the necessity of deceit, whose product is nevertheless the highest truth.[75]

Schlegel's earlier concepts of "poetry of poetry" and "self-reflecting reflection[76]" as potentialized aesthetical existence find now a parallel in a rejuvenation of life itself, a kind of Romantic biology. As at first an unconscious Selbstgesetz, a self-given law or, literally, an autonomy, life becomes gradually conscious of itself, potentialized to a "double life" or "life of life." From the "unlimited fullness of new invention," opposed by "general communicability," arises "living Wirksamkeit, efficacy,[77]" higher than either of its components.

The progression from the initial unconsciousness of reality toward God-in-man suggests the possibility of mangodhood for the Romantic artist and aesthetician. "Man invents (dichtet) this world poetically, only he doesn't know it right away." The artist's development of poetic creati-

vity into a conscious effort to transcend himself
and create poetically a world is another Hegelian
parallel. In his "Letter on the Novel" (1800)
Schlegel claims this initial unconsciousness also
for the Divine Spirit.

> Fantasy spares no effort to
> express itself, but the Divine
> can communicate and express it-
> self in the sphere of Nature
> only by indirection.

This indirect manifestation of the Divine (but immanent!) World Ground is once more salvaged for
consciousness by wit, "the only thing left in the
world of appearances of what was originally fantasy.[78]"

In the broadening base of Schlegelian speculations, wit is given yet a new, higher function
of the ultimate and most certain epistemological
tool in the Romantic encyclopedia of sciences.
Its "combinatory faculty" is

> capable of identifying simi-
> larities between objects other-
> wise quite independent, different
> and separate, thus binding into
> unity what is most manifold,
> disparate.[79]

Once enrolled in the service of mythology, wit becomes "a peculiar form of intuitive spirit (an-
schauender Geist)." Schlegel's wit is the unique
mode of approaching what has been mentioned earlier
as Hegel's universal, unconscious and abstract Being-
in-itself. Schlegel himself calls this target of
particularizing wit "the primary-original and in-
imitable," "the indissoluble," contradictory in
its "naive thoughtfulness (Tiefsinn)" and shot
through with "the appearance of the perverse and
the deranged, or of the simple and dumb." It is
wit that rejuvenates, because it

> thrusts us once more into the

> fair confusion of fantasy, into
> the original chaos of human nature
> for which I am hard-pressed to sug-
> gest a fairer symbol than the bright
> welter of the ancient gods.[80]

Ultimately, it is the ironic attitude of wit that enables us to come to "reasonable" terms with the absurdity of existence.

As a supposed guide to a new, "Romantically artificial" Golden Age, wit is hailed as "the highest principle of cognition" for it

> gives to [the] fullness [of Being]
> discovered by divination a scien-
> tific form through combination and
> so expands the narrow orbit of what
> is known with certainty [the speci-
> fic laws of logic, science, etc.]
> into the great wealth of the mani-
> fold [collective, unconscious
> universality of Being].[81]

In contrast to the natural growth of classical mythology, this new "witty" variant is expected to be "built out of the deepest depths of the spirit.[82]" This brilliant anticipation of the Jungian archetypes grows into a vision that vies in daring and ingenious postulation with the Hegelian apocalypse. Unlike the "old mythology" which was closely tied to the world of the senses, Schlegel's version

> will be formed from <u>nothingness</u>
> through the spirit <u>which has for
> the first time in history achieved
> self-determination and self-knowledge</u>.[83]

At the close of Schlegel's "late Berlin-Jena period," a new, terse definition of Romanticism reads:

> the truly Romantic is what re-
> presents for us a sentimental
> content in fantastic form.[84]

This sounds hardly like a prescription for Romanticism progressing dialectically toward "a limitlessly growing classicism" as postulated in the earlier-mentioned 116th Athenäum Fragment. However, viewed through the self-raising tension between the infinite complexity of spirit -- the sentimental content of the above formula (consisting, according to Belgardt, of mythological "allegories, personifications, symbols"), and the finite determinateness of fantastic form, i.e., "the historic aspect of the characters, of actions and their picturesque execution,[85]" -- what arises here is indeed a realism of wit which takes itself seriously in the realistic recognition of its ever-elusive, ever-incomplete perfection.

But the poet Novalis on whom Schlegel heaped posthumous praises in his journal Europa[86] as a potential "agent in the transition from novel to mythology," died in 1801.[87] It is also easy to see why the general public showed little enthusiasm for Schlegel's fascinating but complex and apparently irreconcilable postulates and conclusions. In 1801 Schlegel declares an end to his efforts to define the guidelines for a new poetry, religion and aesthetics; instead, he promises to dedicate his efforts henceforward exclusively "to literary history and criticism of philosophy.[88]"

His thought matured but unabated in its soaring flights, in the years after 1800 Schlegel decided to bring Romanticism to fruition through the medium of public addresses. Between 1803-04 he delivered a series of lectures on the "History of the Art of Poetry" in Paris and Cologne. Their principal thrust elaborates the old concern to bring together "the particularity of art with the incommensurate whole.[89]" He tries to develop a Bildungslehre, a "theory of education," as a "physics of fantasy," and, eventually, "an encyclopedia[90]" of sciences. Literature is to become the developer of the "higher faculties of understanding, i.e., of fantasy and feeling.[91]"

One by one, concepts that have apparently reached the maximum limit of signification are pushed beyond that limit. Schlegel calls for the "art of all arts;[92]" as the human will becomes united with the Divine, poetry will transform itself into the science "of what is alone truly real;" physics will rise, Spinozist-fashion, to the level of "a material expression of idealism, a sensory and living representation of the highest truth.[93]" Had Novalis lived to complete a series of novels along the lines of his Heinrich von Ofterdingen he would have brought about a boost to poetic fantasy unparelleled since the "dialogues of the Ancients." Here Schlegel means primarily the Platonic dialogue; only Novalis and Schelling have offered a similarly exhaustive perspective of existence.[94]

In his Vienna lectures dedicated to the History of the Old and New Literature (1812) and his essay On the Nordic Art of Poetry (1812) Schlegel gives preference to the Nordic over the Southern-European literatures, praising the former's "bold Romantic spirit, its elaboration of the Roland legend and the Charlemagne sagas," and their respective contributions to the poetry of the Crusades.[95] Schlegel contrasts the Nordic heroic songs as a "primal history of man" with the "artificially conventional" courtly epic. The heroic sagas reveal "pervasive, deep running feelings for love and nature typical of the Germanic psyche," as well as a "bent for freedom,... nobility and honor.[96]" He distinguishes Indo-Germanic "spirituality," i.e., divinization of natural phenomena from Hellenic "materalism," a tendency to explain creation by the means of "atoms and primeval chaos.[97]"

Catholicism is extolled as "a world view embracing Being and Becoming, Nature and History;" since all other religions are "included a priori in Christianity, they have become superfluous.[98]" The Christian-Romantic love-feeling dissolves the "tragic sternness of the theology of the Ancients" into a "merry game of fantasy.[99]"

Shakespeare is a "universally Nordic and truly

German poet," having produced a "heroic chronicle of the British nation.[100]" He excels in depicting the "physical depth and natural secrets of the soul," whereas Calderón's spiritual symbolism succeeds best in a "Christian transfiguration" of reality. Shakespeare's tendency to delay in his dramas the "solution of the deep enigma of life,... sometimes avoiding it completely," brings him closer to the Skepticism of the Ancients and the "wrack and ruin" dénouements of their tragedy. Calderón, on the other hand, rushes his conciliatory, "Christian" resolution from the opening scene of his comedia. A synthesis of Shakespeare's excessive gloom with the all-too-positive Christian metaphysics of Calderón could produce a Romantic dramaturgy more perfect than either.[101]

Such new, "higher" poetry promises to reconcile "the self-evident, optimistic faith" in a "higher destiny... and divine origin of man," and the equally universal feeling that man is "at quite a distance from this origin.[102]" Finally, poetry is called upon to solve indirectly, through symbolic means, the enigma of the existence of a world in the first place.

Never satisfied with finding evermore ambitious functions for poetry, Schlegel makes it both tool and mirror of the flux of Becoming and of the progression of time. Poetry should confirm "the presentiment that a transfiguration of all things is possible in its magic mirror." In this fashion, it "reaches even into the future,[103]" yet avoids the danger of a "flight from the present and reality," a danger brought about by bad imitators of Cervantes. It also opposes those who, conversely, attach themselves onesidedly "to the present" and thus "narrow down" the infinite breadth of reality.[104] Only poetry careful to avoid either extreme may aspire to "a divinely complete perfection;" only such poetry can become what it potentially is, "an analogue of the world, of God's work of art," endowed with an "eternal value.[105]"

Thus Schlegel has worked out the last, highest

synthesis imaginable for poetry as the supreme creative effort in our universe. He identifies it with the Ground of Being referred to earlier as an immanent, pantheist transcendence.[106] Poetry is to become a tool for a "sensory representation of eternity," uniting "past, present and future" in order to bring about an apocalyptic "fullness of time." Again, the stress on this-worldliness in his eschatology is crucial and explicit. Schlegel's apocalypse is no "divine glory attained in the beyond.[107]" It does not involve the "absence" or "negation" of time, but rather "time in its whole, undivided fullness." Once again, Schlegel's vision parallels Hegel's phenomenological peregrination toward the Absolute. Schlegel's call for an "eternity now" reunites time's every element,

> love past becoming renewed over and over in enduring remembrance, whereas the life of the present bears <u>already now</u> within itself also the <u>fullness</u> and hope and a rich future.[108]

A comparison with the closing lines of Hegel's <u>Phenomenology</u> shows the closeness of thought and terminology between the two Romantic archspeculators.

> This way of becoming [of Spirit achieveing Absolute Knowledge of self] presents... a succession of spiritual shapes [<u>Geistern</u>, literally, ghosts], a gallery of pictures, each of which is endowed with the entire wealth of Spirit.... Since its accomplishment consists in Spirit knowing what it is, in fully comprehending its substance, this knowledge means its concentrating itself on itself (<u>Insichgehen</u>), a state in which <u>Spirit leaves its external existence behind and gives its embodiment over to Recollection</u> (<u>Erinnerung</u>). [Thus]

> Spirit is engulfed in the night
> of its own self-consciousness;
> its vanished existence is, how-
> ever, conserved therein; and
> this superseded existence...
> born anew from the womb of
> knowledge -- is... a new world....
> [This] revelation [in Greek,
> apocalypse!] is also [Spirit's]
> <u>temporal embodiment in that this
> externalization... reliquishes
> itself, and so exists at one in
> its spacial "extension," as well
> as in its "depth" or the self.</u>[109]

Schlegel's own version of "fullness of time," as an excruciatingly present and promising gestation in the not-yet-but-already-here time dimension is, rather than Hegel's time-space reconciliation, an anticipation of the existentialist being-ahead-of-oneself, as postulated, for instance, by Heidegger. As a promise of colossal but positive changes just ahead, whose realization is, however, by no means assured, this fullness was experienced most keenly by Novalis among the German, and by Hugo, among the French poets.

This, then, was Friedrich Schlegel's version of an <u>absolute</u> cure for the "dirempt consciousness" of the <u>times</u>. He speaks of this cure as the "Romantic reality." Belgardt interprets it as encompassing both the "empirical reality and this reality's relationship to a concretely apprehensible whole.[110]" Schlegel's typically Romantic dilemma between a this-worldly transcendence and its absolute, other-worldly perfection and efficacy in the here-and-now was not solved with the continued intensification of the existential potential with which he charged and recharged the mission of poetry. He knew well that, on the one hand, poetry "still and always points back, throughout the process of investing and divesting the garments of [passing] times, to the first and the eternal," as a continuous embodiment of transcendent remembrance. On the other hand, his enthusiasm for the whole and for the relationship to it did not allow him to worship this remembrance "in the far distance of the past or the future;" he knew it had to be "seized as something present and real.[111]" The result was inevitably a secularized, and hence, in terms of the Absolute, <u>unsatisfactory Transcendent Presence</u>, a mere sum total of events, existences and objects -- Hegel's above-quoted "ghosts" -- finite and perishable for all the totality made up by their universal Being.

NOTES

[1] While August Wilhelm held regular appointments at the universities of Jena at the turn of the century and, after 1818 at Bonn, where he occupied the first chair of Sanskrit studies, Friedrich served briefly (1800-01), also at Jena, as Privatdozent, an unpaid assistant professor. However, Friedrich's erudition in Oriental languages and the pathbreaking essay On the Language and Wisdom of the Hindus (1803), earned him eventually a wide reputation. Again, August Wilhelm's position as tutor at Madame de Staël's international salon at Coppet on the Lake of Geneva (1804-17) kept him in the focus of European cultural happenings, while Friedrich's "foreign" experience was limited to the insecure existence of a student of Sanskrit and Old French poetry in Paris (1802-04). In dealing with the four principal pillars of "Romantic" literature, Dante, Shakespeare, Cervantes and Calderón, Friedrich held his own; while he argued brilliantly that the four constituted a progression of peaks in post-classical, "universal" poetry that showed a consistently "Romantic" character, August Wilhelm produced German translations of the four masters, some of which are still unsurpassed.

[2] The term Mitdarstellung der künstlichen Reflexion, "simultaneous representation of artistic reflection," calls for a fusion of the poet and critic in one person, and of intuition and understanding in one compound creative faculty. Cf. "Zur deutschen Literatur und Philosophie, Athenäumfragmente," Friedrich Schlegel, 1794-02. Seine prosaischen Jugendschriften, ed. Jakob Minor (Wien, 1882), II, Fragment 238.

[3] August Wilhelm was an epigone of Schiller in poetry and of Goethe in his poetic dramas. Worth mentioning are Friedrich's Lucinde (1799), a novel celebrating erotic license, and the drama Alarcos (1802), an experiment in synthetizing the best of

Shakespeare and Calderón with the Greek drama.

[4] *Prosaische Jugendschriften*, I, 87-178.

[5] *Romantische Poesie. Begriff und Bedeutung bei Friedrich Schlegel* (The Hague: Mouton, 1969), 64-65.

[6] Friedrich Schlegel was an outspoken critic of "tight" systems. Concerned with "universal relationships," i.e., such that avoid a subjective involvement with the merely particular, and "fullness of life as an enduring becoming," he writes in a letter to his brother: "Woe to the expert who loves his system more than beauty, woe to the theoretician whose system is so incomplete and bad that he must destroy history in order to sustain it." *Friedrich Schlegels Briefe an seinen Bruder August Wilhelm*, ed. Oskar F. Walzel (Berlin, 1890), 263. August Wilhelm Schlegel's good-natured ridicule of Fichte's and especially of Hegel's system so kindred to his own and his brother Friedrich's dialectical thinking is best summarized in a rhymed spoof entitled "Dynastic Succession in the Schools of Philosophy" included in this anthology.

[7] According to Belgardt, Schlegel spells the adjective *romantisch*, "romantic" with a small r when referring to the diachronically universal phenomenon, and especially to the "new-romantic" post-Enlightenment era, in contrast to *Romantisch* with capital R when dealing with the romantically more accomplished phenomenon of the Middle Ages and the Renaissance. In my own critical introductions to this anthology I too spell the universal phenomenon of romanticism with a small initial, but reserve the capitalized term for Romanticism proper, as the late eighteenth and early nineteenth century movement.

[8] Belgardt, *op. cit.*, 33.

[9] *Herders sämtliche Werke*, ed. Bernhardt Suphan, 33 vols. (Berlin, 1887-13), IX, 530 ff. .

[10] Belgardt, op. cit., 53. This and all of the following translations of German authors discussed in this section are mine.

[11] Jugendschriften, I, "Zur griechischen Literatur," 94.

[12] Cf. Ernst Robert Curtius, Europäische Literatur und lateinisches Mittelalter (Bern: Francke, 1948). Curtius explains Romania as the association of an ethnic, cultural and literary experience. The noun and adjective "romance" meant at first "folk language but thereafter also a literary work in that language, at first, still without limitation to a particular genre.... In the fifteenth century "romance" emerges as a term for a literary genre, the novel, Roman in German. Op. cit., 39 ff.

[13] Jugendschriften, I, op. cit., 97-98.

[14] Ibid., I, 113.

[15] Ibid., I, 144.

[16] Jugendschriften II, "Athenäumfragmente."

[17] Herders sämtliche Werke, XVIII, 109.

[18] Friedrich Schlegel, Literary Notebooks, 1797-01, ed. Hans Eichner (London: The Athlone Press, 1957), 76; 846.

[19] Op. cit., 851.

[20] Ibid., 973.

[21] Ibid., 1209.

[22] Ibid., 1096.

[23] Much of what Schlegel calls Romantic is in the light of modern scholarship a Baroque phenomenon. The contrast between the two will be

established in the forthcoming discussion of Spanish Romanticism due to the powerful and lasting imprint that the Baroque experience had left on Spanish art in general, and because of the unusually controversial reactions to Romanticism in Spain.

[24] Literary Notebooks, 1049.

[25] Op. cit., 735.

[26] Ibid., 1102.

[27] Ibid., 962.

[28] Ibid., 579.

[29] See footnote 2.

[30] Belgardt, 85.

[31] Literary Notebooks, 828.

[32] Op. cit., 642.

[33] Jugendschriften, I, 135.

[34] Kritische Friedrich-Schlegel-Ausgabe, ed. Ernst Behler, Jean-Jacques Anstett and Hans Eichner (Paderborn, München, Wien, 1958 ff.,) XVIII, 316.

[35] Belgardt, 101.

[36] Literary Notebooks, 500.

[37] Jugendschriften, I, 124.

[38] Literary Notebooks, 209.

[39] Jugendschriften, II, "Kritische Fragmente," Lycäumfragment 28; 37.

[40] Literary Notebooks, 150. My italics.

[41] *Jugendschriften*, II, "Athenäumfragmente," Fragment 297.

[42] Op. cit., Fragment 451.

[43] *Jugendschriften*, II, "Brief über den Roman," 31; *Kritische Friedrich-Schlegel-Ausgabe*, XII, 403, and *passim*.

[44] *Literary Notebooks*, 1959 and *passim*.

[45] *Literary Notebooks*, 65; *Jugendschriften*, II, "Athenäumfragmente," 238.

[46] *Literary Notebooks*, 537

[47] Op. cit., 540. Author's italics.

[48] Belgardt, 123. My italics.

[49] *Literary Notebooks*, 582.

[50] Belgardt, 124.

[51] Op. cit., 123.

[52] *Ibid.*, 123-24.

[53] *Jugendschriften*, II, "Zur deutschen Literatur und Philosophie," 427.

[54] Belgardt, 127.

[55] *Jugendschriften*, II, *ibid*.

[56] Belgardt, 133.

[57] *Literary Notebooks*, 111.

[58] *Jugendschriften*, II, "Athenäumfragmente."

[59] Belgardt, 147.

[60] *Jugendschriften*, II, Idea 104.

[61] Belgardt, loc. cit.

[62] Jugendschriften, II, "Zur deutschen Literatur und Philosophie," 361.

[63] Literary Notebooks, 2063.

[64] Jugendschriften, II, op. cit., 365.

[65] Kritische Friedrich-Schlegel-Ausgabe, XVIII, 152.

[66] Jugendschriften, II, ibid., 363.

[67] Kritische Friedrich-Schlegel-Ausgabe, ibid., 155.

[68] Ibid., 197.

[69] Literary Notebooks, 2090.

[70] Jugendschriften, II, loc. cit., 363.

[71] Kritische Friedrich-Schlegel-Ausgabe, XII, 30.

[72] Ibid., XII, 6 ff.

[73] Op. cit., XVIII, 414.

[74] Poetry and existence are "game and feast in the highest sense." Cf. Literary Notebooks, 1808.

[75] Belgardt, 155. My italics.

[76] See notes 52 and 53.

[77] Jugendschriften, II, "Zur deutschen Literatur und Philosophie," 359.

[78] Ibid., 371.

[79] Kritische Friedrich-Schlegel-Ausgabe, XII, 463.

[80] Jugendschriften, II, 362.

[81] Kritische Friedrich-Schlegel-Ausgabe, XII, 404.

[82] Jugendschriften, II, 358.

[83] Ibid., 359. My italics.

[84] Ibid., 370.

[85] Belgardt, 177.

[86] (Frankfurt am Main, 1803-05), I, i, 56.

[87] Belgardt, 181.

[88] Jugendschriften, II, "Abschluss des Lessingaufsatzes," 423.

[89] Kritische Friedrich-Schlegel-Ausgabe, XI, 4.

[90] Jugendschriften, II, ibid., 424.

[91] Kritische Friedrich-Schlegel-Ausgabe, XI. 3.

[92] Ibid., XI, 9.

[93] Europa, I, i, 47 ff.

[94] Ibid., I, 1, 56.

[95] Friedrich von Schlegels sämtliche Werke, 15 vols., 2nd ed. (Wien: Klang, 1846), VIII, 64.

[96] Ibid., VIII, 53 ff.

[97] Ibid., VIII, 69.

[98] Ernst Behler, "Friedrich Schlegels geistige Gestalt," Schriften und Fragmente, XXXVII. Cf. Belgardt, 200.

[99] Kritsche Friedrich-Schlegel-Ausgabe, VI, 285 ff.

[100] Friedrich von Schlegels sämtliche Werke, VIII, 89.

[101] Kritische Friedrich-Schlegel-Ausgabe. VI, 286-88.

[102] Op. cit., XI, 9.

[103] Op. cit., VI, 276.

[104] Ibid., VI, 274, 276.

[105] Belgardt, 206.

[106] See notes 60 and 61.

[107] Belgardt, ibid.

[108] Kritische Friedrich-Schlegel-Ausgabe, VI, 276 ff. My italics.

[109] G.W.F. Hegel, The Phenomenology of Mind, trans. J.B. Baillie (New York: Macmillan, 1955), 807-08. VIII. Absolute Knowledge. 3. The Return of Spirit so comprehended to immediate existence. My italics.

[110] Belgardt, 204-11.

[111] Friedrich von Schlegels sämtliche Werke, XV, 103-08.

CHAPTER III

PERIODIZATION OF THE ROMANTIC MOVEMENT IN

THE GERMAN-SPEAKING WORLD.

Most critics and literary historians agree on classifying Friedrich Hölderlin and Jean Paul Richter as forerunners of German Romanticism. The first was the ecstatic yet despairing prophet-poet of an imminent Second Coming; the second, a novelist of the fantastic and grotesque who had only marginal influence on the development of Romantic poetry.

The first nucleus of Romantic poets, writers and thinkers formed in Jena and Berlin. As indicated earlier, Tieck's novel The Story of Mr. William Lovell[1] was one of the earliest indicators of the emergence of Romanticism proper of 1796. The Jena-Berlin circle included two precocious geniuses destined to early death: the novelist Wackenroder (1773-98),[2] Tieck's friend and collaborator, and the poet of night, death and transfiguration Novalis.

Aside from his reputation as novelist, Tieck made a name for himself as collaborator and continuator of an epoch-making Shakespeare translation undertaken by August Wilhelm Schlegel; he also translated Cervantes' Don Quixote and was generally considered the head of the Romantic school, even after he had openly disassociated himself from the movement.

But it was the Athenäum, a journal for aesthetics and literary criticism coedited by August Wilhelm and Friedrich Schlegel, that gave the Romantic movement focus and impetus between 1798 and 1800. Great impact upon the formative period of the movement had also the Berlin lectures of the theologian Friedrich Schleiermacher (1768-34)[3] and those of the philosophers Schelling and Fichte at the university of Jena. After the death of Novalis in 1801 and the relocation at the same time of Tieck to Dresden and of Friedrich Schlegel to

Paris, the Jena center of Early Romanticism disintegrated.

The second stage in the movement's development is known under the various titles of Middle Romanticism, Younger Romanticism, High Romanticism and Heidelberg Romanticism. It flourished from about 1804 till the opening of the Congress of Vienna in 1815. Geographically it was dispersed between Heidelberg, its principal focal point, and Dresden, Vienna, Halle, Kassel, Marburg and Göttingen.[4] Among its representatives figured the trio of Joseph Görres (1776-48), Achim von Arnim (1781-31) and Clemens Brentano (1778-42). Görres started out as a student of natural sciences, partisan of the French Revolution and of cosmopolitanism; disillusioned by all three, he embraced the cause of German nationalism against Napoleon, and, like Friedrich Schlegel, he converted to Roman Catholicism.[5] Arnim and Brentano continued Herder's research in Germanic folklore and edited some 600 folksongs in The Youth's Cornucopia (1806/08). In it, the two poets paraphrased rather freely the folk originals, but in the process opened up an immense wealth of authentic themes, rhymes and rhythms that have not ceased to inspire German poets to this day. Arnim's historical novel The Guardians of the Crown (1817) and his adaptation of the Baroque poet Gryphius' drama Cardenio and Celinde under the title Halle and Jerusalem (1811) assured him a prominent place among Romantic glorifiers of the German past; Brentano's Fairy Tales of the Rhine, published posthumously in 1846-47, followed through the Cornucopia's intent to rejuvenate contemporary literature through the revival of folk art. What the Cornucopia did for lyric poetry, the Tales were meant to do for Romantic story writing. Brentano's rambling novel Godwi (1801) bears marks of Friedrich Schlegel's theorizing about the functions of irony and apparently follows some of the structural conventions of Cervantes' Quixote.

Thanks to the Brothers Grimm (Jacob, 1785-63; Wilhelm, 1786-59) Kassel, Marburg and

Göttingen became centers of the study of German philology, antiquities and cultural history;[6] but they gained international reputation with their Fairy Tales for Children (1812-15) and The German Sagas (1816-18). Berlin continued to attract other Romantics of the Middle Period. Heinrich von Kleist (1777-11) edited there The Berlin Evening News in the last year of his life; although a contemporary of the Romantic experiment, this greatest of German dramatists of his day, second only to Schiller, shared as many Romantic inclinations as he defied. He has a Romantic's taste for

> knighthood and the German Middle Ages, patriotic enthusiasm... [for] sentiment as central life force, the power of the unconscious, a yearning for death, a psychic-spiritual disharmony.

But there is in Kleist no

> dreamy, self-indulging yearning for the infinite, no self-oblivion in Christian or pantheistic mysticism, no taste for the faraway and the long-past, no reveling in fantasies, no play with the allurement of moods, no irony, no depreciation of reality.[7]

Kleist the disappointed soldier, despairing student of Kant, would-be farmer, jilted fiancé, discredited playwright[8] and, finally, suicide, deserves the title of poet of the demonic, rather than of a more broadly Romantic sentiment.

Two more significant representatives of Middle Romanticism deserve mention. One is E.T.A. Hoffmann (1776-22) who shares international fame with the brothers Grimm; this was to a great extent due to the popularity of Offenbach's opera The Tales of Hoffmann which used themes from the author's more popular narrations. Like Kleist a partisan of the magic and the tremendous that often borders on the horrid, Hoffmann was a master of all trades, but especially of the fantastic tale. Versatile to the point of dissipation, he fulfilled perfectly Friedrich Schlegel's primary requirement for Romantic art: a subjective attitude to reality that turns, due to a constant orientation toward the sum total of the phenomena, into pure, detached objectivity. Prussian jurist and bureaucrat, writer, painter, musician, he was fascinated with the phenomenon of the double symbolizing the ambiguity of good and evil in the Romantic concept of the self. His best story collections are <u>The Devil's Elixir</u> (1815-16), <u>Night Tales</u> (1817), and <u>The Serapion Brothers</u> (1819-21). Hoffmann mixes sharp and realistically detailed observation of empirical detail with accurate insights into the depth of the unconscious. The common denominator of all of his creations is the view of the artist as conjurer of diabolic forces, no doubt prompted by the pangs of his universalist genius. His works and life embody the destructiveness of the artistic urge so typical of the Romantic: to compete with the Creator in producing a universe of his own, more perfect than everyday reality.

The other poet-narrator that deserves mention in the context of Middle Romanticism is Adelbert von Chamisso (1781-38). Son of an impoverished emigré family he experienced vividly the cultural and ethnic uprooting of his generation. He declared himself lacking a "solid ground," a man "without a shadow." This feeling of alienation from all traditional values, ethnic, religious, and existential, inspired the writing of the tale for which he is deservedly famous. <u>The Wondrous Story of Peter Schlemihl</u> (1814) is an original approach to the recurring theme of the split personality. Caught in the conflict between his adoptive country and France, the land of his ancestors, Chamisso projects his existential vacillations into a hero who gives up his shadow to the devil, but stops short of selling him his soul. Once again, the author juxtaposes, without a pretense of an eventual synthesis, the world of hard empirical fact and the fairy tale, stressing vigorously the traditional duality of good and evil, so seldom clearly defined in everyday existence. Losing one's "shadow," an outward reflection of individual identification with a national collective, is one thing, but losing one's inner essence, the "inviolability of the soul,[9]" is to be realistically avoided at all cost; we have here one of the earliest indicators of how Romantic irony works for the gradual phasing out of Romanticism into realism.

This evolution becomes increasingly more obvious in the third and closing phase of Romantic sensibility in Germany. Joseph von Eichendorff, (1788-57), the poet of Waldrauschen, "forest murmurs," and master of the short novel, typifies the trend away from the fantastic, disharmonious and eccentric, so prominent in the Middle Romantic period. Sharing Eichendorff's simplicity and "warm joviality[10]" was the jurist-turned-professor of German literature and eventually, politician, Ludwig Uhland. He is best known for his paraphrases of German medieval ballads and his confortable attunement to the liberal-bourgeois Biedermeier style, uniquely typical of German mores between 1815 and 1848.

In sharp contrast to the life-affirming Romantic realism of Eichendorff and Uhland stands the haunted existence of Nikolaus Lenau (1802-50). If there was anything realistic about his person and work, it was his unqualified dedication to the tragic sense of life. His splenetic disposition, indulgence in the velleities of passion, and the disorienting pull of too many talents drove him eventually into insanity. Similarly, the religiously and ethnically uprooted existence of Heinrich Heine (1797-56) produced brilliant and bitter poetic fruit as a resentful reaction to the absence of peace and goodness in this world. Heine's corrosive and self-deriding irony strove for realism by intentionally deprecating his illusive goals, even the quest for perfection itself. While Lenau's moody dirges bemoan, echoing the melancholy plains of his native Hungary, the futility of the search for happiness, Heine's invectives lash out at the very essence of being, though actually his spleen tends often to be a pose, an irony of irony. The result can be cold indifference, cancelling itself in a dialectic of nothingness. In many ways, such realistic destruction of both Romantic irony and illusion anticipates the elegant nastiness and biting elitism of Baudelaire's pathbreaking symbolism and the life-lashing vitalism of Nietzsche's aphoristic sallies.

NOTES

[1] This novel and, to a lesser extent, the later Wanderings of Franz Sternbald (1799) helped to give to Romanticism the generally ill-deserved reputation as glorifier of amorality, taste for dissipation, rebellion against order and rationality, all in the name of self-serving fantasy. Contrariwise, Tieck's Puss in Boots (1797) is an exquisite fairy drama, where the scorn for traditional dramatic rules is justified by the ironic atmosphere of the play's setting. More on Tieck, Novalis, Arnim, Brentano, Chamisso, Eichendorff, Lenau, Heine, etc., in the textual analysis of the poems selected for this anthology.

[2] His novel The Outpourings of an Art-loving Friar (1797) is a sort of a Romantic manifesto, idealizing the spirit of chivalry and the Germanic Middle Ages in opposition to Goethe's and Schiller's Klassik, or Weimar classicism. Named after the city of Goethe's residence, Klassik came into being as a revival through native German means of the Greek control of creative genius. It is not to be confused with seventeenth century French classicisme that resulted primarily from a strict enforcement of Aristotelian formalism in dramatic plot structure, spectacle, diction, etc. The bienséances or "propriety" of the classical French drama hinged primarily on the preservation of the mostly misinterpreted unities of place and time. Neo or pseudoclassicism of the Enlightenment era is, by definition, yet another aesthetic trend. Cf. M. J. Hanak, "The Enlightenment as Secularization of Baroque Eschatology in France and England," Studi internazionali di filosofia, ed. Augusto Guzzo, Accademia delle Scienze di Torino (Autumn, 1971), 83-109.

[3] Schleiermacher proclaims in his work On Religion a "theology of feeling," where imagination is "the highest and most original part of man, and everything outside it only reflection

upon it." Cf. "Über die Religion," Sämtliche Werke (Berlin, 1843), Erste Abt., vol. I, 260.

[4] The Romantic Period in Germany, ed. Siegbert Prawer (New York: Shocken Books, 1970), Introduction, 3.

[5] In his essay German Chapbooks (1807) Görres backed up with research earlier insights of Tieck and held in Heidelberg the first lecture on the science of Germanistik, or German Studies.

[6] Jacob Grimm's German Grammar (1819-37), German Mythology (1835), The History of the German Language (1848) and Wilhelm's The German Heroic Saga (1829) were their chief contributions.

[7] Walter Clauss, Deutsche Literatur (Zürich: Schulthess, 1966), 225.

[8] As a result of Goethe's displeasure with the premiere of Kleist's Pentesilea in Weimar in 1808 which seemed to glory in the orgiastic Dionysian element, prime target of Goethe's life-long attacks.

[9] James Trainer, "The Märchen," Prawer, op. cit., 118.

[10] Clauss, op. cit., 221.

CHAPTER IV

TRANSITION FROM CLASSICISM TO ROMANTICISM. HÖLDERLIN'S MYTHIC POETRY AND DIALOGUE WITH A MUTE TRANSCENDENCE.

Friedrich Hölderlin (1770-43) continues the Hellenic strain of the Goethe-Schiller <u>Klassik</u> in a quite personal, ecstatic fashion that brings him close to the Romantic movement. His lack of sense for Romantic <u>irony</u> and <u>wit</u> as postulated by Friedrich Schlegel keeps him apart from the Romantic camp. His attempts to reconcile the alienated self with the universal world ground run likewise in an opposite direction to Schlegel's optimistic bid for progressive <u>universal poetry</u>. Hölderlin's poetic work is a tragic-ecstatic yea to finite existence. The poet insists on respiritualizing the godless universe by an act of faith in the return of the Divine that would, eventually, answer his hymnic pleas. Yet from the outset, he doesn't expect to be heard, which only redoubles his efforts until one has the impression he is "absorbed by a pantheist stream" of life, "imbued with a religious experience[1]" which grows in intensity as the silence of the universal whole continues.

Hölderlin's commitment to the reintegration of man with cosmic becoming is common to the Romatic school as a whole; specifically, it was shared by two of his fellow students Hegel and Schelling, while the three studied at the prestigious Protestant School of Theology, the <u>Stift</u> at Tübingen. Hölderlin's poetic ecstasies and Hegel's and Schelling's daring speculations owe much to their common metaphysical mentor Fichte.

Many other influences converged to mold Hölderlin's concept of the poet's mission, the principal theme that runs through his work. Herder's view of the mythmaking capacity of imagination which links poetry and religion was of great importance;[2] equally strong was the impact of eighteenth century German Pietism and the kindred mystical prophetism of Klopstock, author of the immensely influential Messiah epic. The study of theology didn't help to prepare Hölderlin for a pastoral vocation any more than it did Schelling or Hegel, but it reinforced in all three the sense of apocalyptic foreboding in a time rife for momentous changes in the wake of the French Revolution.

Böckmann shows that Hölderlin's preoccupation with the need for a new mythology is of a very peculiar kind. Hölderlin didn't attempt to create some new kind of Genesis dealing with the origin of the gods and the universe, nor did he seriously attempt a straightforward revival of the Olympian or even Christian theology. Nor did he attempt to produce a new eschatology or any other kind of systematic world view. What he wished to achieve was a simple renewal of a dialogue between man and nature, once more endowed with a Divine Presence. He realized that the faculty of language to communicate anything beyond the basic "mundane needs" withers with the disappearance of the dialogue with some kind of transcendent order. The inability to speak to God spells death for all lyrical feeling and poetry. At the same time, Hölderlin refused to engage in an internal monologue, "addressing his own I as a Thou" in order to "preserve a relation with the world," transcending a strictly innerworldly subject-object relationship. Ultimately, Hölderlin tried to develop a language with such "sweeping world-reference" (Weltbezug) "that the address would draw in the unanswering Thou of mute nature.[3]" This kind of poetry is "mythic" in the narrower sense, for it doesn't base itself on a "living," generally accepted mythology which, Friedrich Schlegel's efforts notwithstanding, failed to materalize in the Romantic era or after.

In a world left godless, first by the departure of the Olympians and, more recently during the Enlightenment, by the Judeo-Christian tradition, a renewal of intimate affective relations with nature beyond the latter's utilitarian exploitation became a generally felt need. Schelling expressed this need admirably in identifying a "precognitive," preterrational inner self,

> a secret, wondrous ability to
> withdraw from the flux of time
> into our inmost self... there
> to contemplate the eternal in
> the form of immutability.

According to Schelling this inner self-certainty predates the dichotomy of subject and object responsible for the dirempt consciousness of modern "rational" man. It alone provides access to the supersensible world.[4] Hölderlin takes Schellings's thought to its logical conclusion. The split between man and his world can be healed only when he as subject abandons the science-induced attitude of domination (Herrschaftsverhältniss) toward nature, replacing it with one of a "remembering thanksgiving.[5]"

    A taste for the panegyric ode and a hymnic bent made themselves felt even prior to 1793, the year marking the inception of Hölderlin's first period of major creativity which follows his leaving Tübingen with a Master's in theology. The poem "Greece" is one among a number of hymns dedicated to the rather abstract concepts of "mankind," "beauty," "freedom," etc. All of them bear a heavy mark of Schiller's regular rhyme and rhythm patterns. They reflect a basically sunny, "Apollonian" quest for the lost Golden Age of Western civilization. This attitude and formal traditionalism extend into the second stage of the poet's development (1796-98) which took place during his stay in Frankfurt as private tutor in the home of the banker Gontard. Soon, the didactic slant of Schiller's orderly Klassik gives way to the Dionysian ecstasies stirred up by the readings of Pindar and Sophocles. Plato's mystical rationalism shows less strongly, mostly as transcendent-erotic overtones harking back to The Banquet.

Hölderlin projected the virtues of Plato's prophetess Diotima[6] into the cultured and sensitive lady of the house Susette Gontard.

In the poem dedicated to Hercules, written still under the spell of Schiller's didacticism at the very beginning of his stay in Frankfurt, the poet invokes the demigod as a kindred suffering spirit. He exults over man's ability to approach Olympian immortality and to hold on to a portion of it which he considers his rightful patrimony, reclaimed by his own devices.

Soon, it is Susette Gontard's image as Diotima that begins to dominate Hölderlin's poetic creation. There exist altogether six versions of the Diotima poem, including the elegy "Menon's Laments for Diotima." The first version continues to employ the traditional classical patterns; the following two imitate the Alcaic strophe; the next one is written in an impeccable replica of the classical Greek elegiac distich,[7] the same as "Menon's Laments;" the last is a two-line fragment conceived in the period of progressive mental deterioration after 1802. The elegiac distich, together with the Alcaic and the Asclepiadean strophes, predominates in the second (1796-98) and the fourth period (1800-02) of his poetic evolution.[8]

"Hyperion's Song of Destiny" and "To the Fates" are poems representative of the second period. The theme of Hyperion deals with the struggle for Olympian loftiness and perfection, a symbolic re-creation of ancient Hellas. Eventually it grew into a novel entitled <u>Hyperion, or the Hermit of Greece</u> (1797-99) in which the symbolic struggle becomes a real war of independence against the Turks, waged in vain by a noble contemporary Greek youth who withdraws from the world upon the death of the embodiment of his ideals, Diotima.

The triadic pattern of "Hyperion's Song" is analyzed by Konrad Nussbächer in terms of

> the inner dialectic of thesis,
> antithesis and a reconciling,
> "sublating" synthesis; [this
> arrangement is]... the
> organizing principle of many
> [of his] poems; it is related
> to Mozart's and Beethoven's
> sonata form.... Through his
> musicality... Hölderlin estab-
> lished a genuine contact with
> the forms of Greek prosody in
> which word and tone were as yet
> not separated. In poems that
> follow the triadic structure
> of three internally related
> stanzaic groups it evolves into a
> masterfully managed tool adapt-
> ed from Pindar[9]....

"Hyperion's Song" is dedicated to the care-free, impassive immortals supposedly dwelling in the beyond; the author fully expects to be rebuffed by a transcendent cosmic silence. Hölderlin's paraphrase of the Pindaric ode, renowned for its rugged but impassioned irregularity, expresses perfectly the burning need to be heard and answered. The expectation of continued silence brings forth a new burst of praise of cosmic becoming. Neither a naive belief in dogma, nor an anthropomorphic "rational" explanation are the cause of the urge of the Hyperion-Hölderlin figure. The "blissfully bright eyes" are fixing with a "silent/ Clearness eternal" other vistas than the miserable lot of the mortals resembling water being driven "from cliff to cliff." The poem's inspiration in Goethe's "Song of the Spirits above the Waters" is evident.

"To the Fates" addresses again the questionable regiment of the cosmos. The three four-line stanzas are of the Alcaic variety; the first two progress toward a synthesis in the third. The thesis pronounced in the first is a request by the poet directed to the Fates for enough time to complete his mission on this earth; the antithesis is the poet's own answer to his plea. It deplores existential restlessness and the inability to slake the thirst for the Absolute; the only triumph left him is this-worldly and, therefore, lost in the flux of time, even though it was to be a celebration of the transcendent "holy." The resigned synthesis accepts the fact that, unlike Orpheus' music, the strings of his own harmony failed to "take him downward," into the ground of all things, to what Goethe calls in Faust the descent "to the Mothers.[10]" The overtures to Divine Transcendence -- in Heaven or in Hades -- remain unrequited. The plea itself, as an act of poiesis, creation, must be its own reward. The poem is a classically ordered expression of the Romantic yearning for the infinite and a thinly masked joy of not achieving it.

During Hölderlin's third period of creativity (1798-1800) occurs a transition from the Hellenic motivation to German-patriotic themes and, finally, the emergence of an apocalyptic, Greco-Christian syncretism. The poet had spent the two years at Homburg near his friend Isaak Sinclair who had procured him a refuge after the heartrending departure from the Gontard household. A poem dedicated to the river Main is yet another variant on the theme of an imagined Hellas, but it indicates the thrust of Hölderlin's maturing thought: the Germans must Hellenize themselves, not only by a formal imitation of their poetic forms and myths: they must synthesize their talent for "clarity of representation[11]" with the Greek heritage of openness to the Divine; only thus can the gap be closed between reason-afflicted individualism and the immediate experience of nature.

In Homburg was also conceived the project of a drama about the Sicilian philosopher Empedocles. The work didn't progress beyond several fragments, but it puts into relief Hölderlin's paramount concern with communication of the ultimate truths. He viewed Empedocles' suicide in the crater of Mount Aetna as an act of defiance on the part of a superior individual unable to convey the experience of the Divine to an unreceptive citizenry.

   It is the fourth and last period of his major poetic activity between 1800-1802 that produced the works for which Hölderlin is deservedly remembered as one of the greatest poets of the German language. This is when he wrote the grand odes, elegies and the patriotic hymns. They are spiritual products of a harrowing Odyssey that led Hölderlin in quest of tutorial positions from Stuttgart to Switzerland and, eventually, to Bordeaux in the South of France. "The Song of the German" opens a series of patriotic odes with a challenge: "Oh holy heart of nations, oh fatherland!" calling for a long-overdue self-realization of German national awareness.[12] Other odes are dedicated to Rousseau, to Heidelberg, the river Neckar and, once again, to Diotima. The Hellenic themes continue recurring in "Chiron," "Vulcan," and "Ganymed." Thematically most important and formally most accomplished is "The Poet's Calling."

   In an intentionally overlapping syntax which begins to be Hölderlin's trademark, the poem invokes Bacchus the wine god proceeding from India westward. It addresses the "daylight's angel," ostensibly the poetic-Apollonian counterpart to Dionysus-Bacchus, the poet as such, referred to also as "Master." Finally, "genius," the spirit of divine inspiration, is invoked and defended against the Philistinism of rationalists and empiricists alike, the thankless "race full of cunning," who "pretend to know/.... The daylight and the thunderer," while busily scanning and rationally explaining cosmic phenomena. The poet's calling is to serve "the Highest," whom he "suits exclusively," and to festively announce His imminent approach. But this-worldly phenomena ("wellsprings,... banks,... heights") too deserve the poet's praise and protection from scientific quantification, demythologization and spiritual death. Hölderlin defends for "us," i.e., poets touched by genius, the right to divine mania in the presence of the Absolute reentering a long since godforsaken world. It is its renewed

Presence that "siezed us by hair locks,/... Senses us silencing" and that make us "quake in our bones." The poet's response must be worthy of this bone-chilling apprenticeship: avoiding the reduction of poetry to a child's idle dilettantism, he must absorb the cultural heritage of the Orient and Hellas, and even "the thunder heard recently," i.e., the classicist contribution of Goethe and Schiller.

The last three stanzas take stock once more of the human resources capable of rendering the experience of the Absolute. "Our Father" (Zeus, Dionysus, as prefigurations of a syncretic Jehovah image) makes our survival in the world of flux and imperfection possible only by keeping us blind-folded "with [the] holy night" of perceptual and intellectual obfuscation. The world-transcendent "Olympus" remains unscaled by the violence of the rationalist-empiricist busybodies. And yet, "it still is good too wise to be," to intuit, as does the poet-prophet, the Divine Presence. Mankind, informed by fresh poetic insight, will go on "alone god facing," relying on "artlessness," as absence of dehumanizing cognition. Without "weapons" and "cunning," man will endure; should the "lack of god" become a still more terrifying certainty, it will "prove helpful" in driving the poet-human even beyond the limits of the present excruciat-ingly ecstatic experience.

A small number of rambling but powerful ele-gies that follow represents the peak of Hölderlin's dithyrambic ecstasy. All are written in elegiac couplets, again in rigorous observance of the laws of Greek prosody so skillfully adapted to the spirit of the German language that the meter seems native to it.

"Menon's Laments for Diotima" is an elegiac projection of the poet's rather Platonic affair with Madame Gontard, and the last complete Diotima variant. The poem calls for little interpretation due to its conventional syntax and imagery. The second stanza bewails the loss of man trapped by the gods in the darkness of "the death realm," symbolizing his blindness to Divine Presence. The image of Diotima, not mentioned until the third stanza, is conjured up as "something friendly inclined," standing, paradoxically, close to the poet "from afar." The second stanza enumerates the beauties of nature that had witnessed the poet's past bliss in Diotima's presence. Lovers, like poets and prophets, "have been assigned life of a different kind," far and protected from the ravages of time, which "roars out there," in the world of appearances, ruling violently the flux of becoming. The reminder of the poem deals with the pangs of the bereft lover who errs "aimlessly" through the now topical death realm of existential forlornness.

By indirection, the image of Tantalus is conjured up. Once, he used to be a guest at the table of the Olympians, but was cast out for his all-too-human presumption to test the wisdom of the immortals. For a brief moment Hölderlin allows a glimmer of hope to shine through the gloom; humans, like himself slumbering "under the flowering earth...," may expect "a season,"

>   When a miracle's thrust will them,
>   the sunken ones, force
>   To return, once again on the greening
>   ground to go wandering.

But this hope, too, is in vain, for "years went dissolving/ Since the evenings around glow with foreboding we saw." As in practically all the poems analyzed so far, only the glowing image of the "Athenian," created in the poet's mind's eye, has redemptory force for him and mankind.

>   So you're giving me proof, and tell
>   it to me that to others
>   I might tell it....

The elegy ends with an enthusiastic address to the "benign genii" who like to dwell near lovers. They are to prolong their stay on earth until such time that all humankind is raised to a measure of participatory Transcendence. As an afterthought, the possibility of seeking the absolute even in the this-worldly dimension is suggested, as long as it is revisited by the caring immortals.

The elegy "Bread and Wine" is an example of mature Greco-Christian syncretism, with Hellenic mythologism still a dominant factor. It is another lament over the perversion of Divine Nature by Reason which caused the existential disorientation of modern mankind.

Addressing his friend Heinse to whom the poem is dedicated, Hölderlin asks, "Why be poet in beggarly times?" Like the gods of Epicure -- and of the enlightened deists -- the gods of our time are alive, but beyond the pale of our utilitarian consciousness. What is worse,

> Man can only at times bear all the fullness of god.

But there seems to be some hope after all; following the flight of the Olympians there emerged "a genius, still and celestial/ Soothing...," announcing the end of "the day" of godless alienation. He and his heavenly choir had left behind "some gifts" as tokens of his presence. And yet there emerges again the crushing image of man unable to bear Divine Presence even symbolically, by the means of the sacraments,

> For too great to enjoy spirit the greater has made.

In spite of it, bread and wine as symbols of the Christian mystery of transsubstantiation, ought to bring about the respiritualization of the human condition. Bread as the "fruit of the earth" represents Hellenic this-worldliness and lust for growth, but it is also the substance of the Christian-Oriental ritual of "partaking of the body" of a dead God who is to rise again. Conversely, the immanent-transcendent complex of "wine" as the body of a dead god in the process of resurrection corresponds to the Olympian Thunderer Zeus, amalgamated with his wine-giving son Dionysus, a Helenized kin of the irate Jehovah and of his divine son Dionysus-Zagreus, torn to pieces but resurrected.

The final stanza presents a compelling vision of Christ the Redeemer and director of the cosmic regiment. He not only "balances day against nighttime," but, thanks to his "perpetually greening" life vigor, he guarantees the return of the gods, i.e., of the spirit of Hellas. Through Christ's mediation modern man can hope to see the fulfillment of ancient prophecies of a Second Coming and universal redemption.

>   Look at us, we are they, fruit of
>   Hesperia we!

Jehovah's son, "the Syrian" brings about through "us," the poet-seers, the final reconciliation of all existential opposites; even the Titans, the rebels against the race of Jovian gods, slumber more gently in their underground prisons. Cerberus, Hell's intractable guardian, relents long enough to drink and sleep.

In "The Rhine" the Germanic-patriotic and Christian elements begin to predominate. It is probably the best of the "patriotic hymns" in sweep, force and in formal as well as structural originality and intricacy. The rhythmic and stanzaic structures are entirely of Hölderlin's inventing, a mixture of Greek echoes and of wide-flung arches of subordinate clauses dictated by the subject matter's mighty movement. This encompasses the birth of the infant river, its growing pains as it unwinds out of the mountain ranges and is being forcibly directed westwards away from its desired goal in Asia. Eventually, the poem digresses to expound on the poet's own inner struggles to finally encompass the sum total of cosmic becoming.

The hymn is constructed triadically, consisting of fifteen stanzas or five triads. Each triad develops from fifteen verses in the first stanza upward to sixteen in the second and back downward to fourteen in the third stanza.[13]

There is a major break and contrast between the first section of the first two triads ending with stanza six, and triads three and four, ending with stanza twelve. The last triad (stanzas twelve through fifteen) reconciles the first two sections, in Hölderlin's own words, through an "extended metaphor" that runs through this last "synthetic" section.[14] The first section builds up the thesis: a concrete description of the unwinding of the river's inception. The second section draws conclusions from the objective description of the Rhine's course that have wide-ranging metaphysical and moral implications. There is an additional break (and contrast) in the middle of this first section, at the opening of stanza four, broadening the meaning of the river's struggle for spontaneous self-determination

> A riddle's what springs from purity.

"Need" and "training" can do much for the self-discipline of the intepreter of the Divine, "yet nothing matches/ What birth can achieve." Once again the hymn's principal thrust is toward the elucidation of the <u>enigmatic origin of the urge to achieve the Absolute in the here-and-now</u>; this urge is god-given and he who is capable of uttering it is god-touched, sprung from the ultimate purity of being which transcends this world.

Beissner identifies the introductory theme as an "alert restlessness of the individual in times of transition;[15]" it is on this same note that the composition concludes. "Suspecting nothing," the poet learns "a fate," from the "lamenting Rhine" at its headwaters. Nussbächer detects in this statement "an inner connection with the poet's own fate" and, eventually, also with that of the sons of gods (stanza three) and demigods (stanzas two and ten) who, just like men,

being children of divine light and
of Mother Earth, must endure
trouble, torment, and the
blessings of their dual nature.[16]

    The poet's soul yearns to fly East to view the Greco-Roman cradle of Western myths in Italy and on Moreas, the Peloponnesus. This flight is paralleled by the struggle of the "freeborn Rhine" to continue its original direction eastward, "to Asia," the cradle of all civilization. The Rhine is as blind in its struggle against "what is fated," and just as unsuccessful, as the blindest of all creatures, the "sons god-sired," poets of the Divine like Hölderlin who lack the common sense of average humanity as well as the instinct of beasts.

    Like the gratuitous grace of traditional Christianity, "the light beam" continues the theme of the importance of "pure origins." The poet alone can fulfill this "immortal wish" to head toward the source of the universe. The vision of the youthful Rhine stream reemerges. Resembling the infant demigod Hercules it "tears up the snakes of importunate tributaries, dragging along everything including forests and mountains that would obstruct its course.

    Forged in this harsh smithy, as "things genuine only," it eventually becomes free to meander broadly at will through the lowlands, supporting "like a father his children" the industrious cities that had sprung up along its banks. The first section that gave an objective description of geographic phenomena ends here on a down-beat note suggesting appeasement.

    The second section opens the vast panorama of human hybris in the "rebellious ones," the "drudges" who transgress the bounds set to humans by the "foolish-godly" wine god. The result is tragic for both: the gods flee into the beyond and men are left in a metaphysical void. Nussbächer traces this irreverence to become "even as the gods" to the butchers of the French Reign of Terror.[17]

On the other hand, the hard-tested demigods, the "likes of the Rhine," never forget their noble origins and the privilege of being assigned arduous tasks. Here Hölderlin introduces the principle of human participation in the Divine reminiscent of Plato's definition of Eros in The Banquet.[18] "Another one," the divinely-attuned poet, must exercise human feelings for their benefit "as sharer," the type of man the gods "have need of." In a letter written in 1795 Hölderlin writes to Hegel explaining this sharing in terms of Fichte's "Absolute Self," rather than in the light of the conclusion of Plato's Diotima tale.

> The gods cannot feel anything by themselves because their unconditional and independent self-sufficiency cannot apprehend anything outside themselves... [Fichte's Absolute Self] must be, on account of its demand for all, quite objectless, and therefore cannot possess any consciousness....[19]

The competitor, rather than sharer and mediator of the Divine, having become a rebellious drudge in his relationship with the infinite, will destroy himself and his microcosm -- all that "is dearest" -- and thus increase the universal obfuscation of modern humanity.

Unlike these murderous supermen-manqués the true prophets of a higher mankind deserve the praises of their brother-in-suffering, the poet of the Divine. Foremost among them is Rousseau whose memory is conjured up in stanza ten, opening the second half of the second section (stanzas ten through thirteen). The image of an Arcadian landscape in stanza nine concludes the first half of the second section. In stanza ten the peace of Arcadia clashes with Rousseau's tragic and restless Titanism that parallels closely Hölderlin's own fruitless search for a peaceful and satisfying existence. The extended image culminates in the vision of the Bielersee (in French, Lake Bienne) in the Bern Canton of Switzerland where Rousseau had spent in 1765 a few precious days free of tribulation. Rousseau's enthusiastic description of the virgin nature of the island of Saint-Pierre on that lake[20] inspired stanzas eleven through twelve. This second major section provides, according to Hölderlin's own interpretation, an antithesis to the first; it concludes with the anticlimactic twelfth stanza in a gently declining cadence:

> To the earth of today the day's
> declining.

The final triad achieves a synthesis of sorts between the geographic reality of the self-assertive, magnificent, semidivine existence of the Rhine and the questionable success of the poet's dialogue with the Absolute. This dialogue works often by indirection, through invocations and hints. It borders on a challenging demand for an answer suggesting that "A wedding feast" between "men and immortals" has again become a possibility.

But as so often before, the optimism quickly fades. All that mankind can count on is a remembrance of such a banquet, celebrated either in the mythical times of Hellas or, more likely, in the poet's mind. Remembrance, anamnesis, evokes once more, and this time unequivocally, Plato.[21] The "wise one" who "succeeded/ From noon past midnight enduring: the burden of "luck," i.e., of knowledge of the Absolute, refers directly to Socrates as he appears in the closing lines of The Banquet. The extended metaphor that elaborates the cognition of the Absolute through recollective flashes of intuition is summarized succinctly in the closing line of the next-to-the-last stanza praising Socrates' ability

> Lucid to stay at the banquet.

The final stanza addresses by name the poet's friend to whom the hymn is dedicated. Isaak

Sinclair, like Hölderlin, Rousseau and Socrates, is represented as a <u>vates deorum</u>, the announcer of gods, his soul open to the Divine Ground of Being, whatever the aspect under which it chooses to manifest itself. As indicated earlier, the concluding lines of the poem reveal a tormenting unrest in Hölderlin's search for God. The words roll off as if out of control; the daytime aspect of "the ruler," may hold in bondage the feverish forces of chaos; but at night, they reemerge in "primal confusion." Still and all, this nocturnal triumph of Dionysus is essential to prevent petrification and paralysis of the vital forces, something Nietzsche will warn against as the "disease" of conscious reasoning. Beissner comments:

> It is precisely the forces of decay and transition that keep alive; this is why the poet speaks in defense of <u>das Lebendige</u>, that which is alive.[22]

Hölderlin's insight into the night forces of the soul as the necessary and life-giving reverse of conscious speculation helped to develop Nietzsche's concept of the Apollonian and the Dionysian as a dynamic, mutually complementary duality of existence. Indirectly, Freud benefited from it in his vindication of the forces of the unconscious.

The last lines of the Rhine hymn show traces of gradual mental disintegration. The disorder started making itself felt in 1802, after Hölderlin returned to Germany from Bordeaux. Back to that year dates the last spurt of creative energy that was to spawn several vast hymns introducing an apocalyptic Christ figure with continued strains of Dionysian Hellenism. "Patmos[23]" is the mightiest of these compositions. Nussbächer traces the poem's "inner turmoil" to a keenly experienced presence of the "figure and message of Christ" and a continued tension between this Christ figure and the Hercules-Dionysus complex.[24] At the outset, the poet laments once more the difficulty in seizing and holding the Divine.

> Near and hard to hold onto is God.

The poem's crucial message is "Christ is still living." The whole betrays a crushing nearness of the Deus absconditus, the hidden God that was to prove too formidable an antagonist even for Nietzsche.

Among the latest poems that predate the definitive dementia in 1806 figures the strangely haunting fourteen liner "Half of Life." Regular in its irregularity, it offers elements akin to twentieth-century expressionism. The few words of the text are rich in flashes of the Da-sein, of Being-here, in the simple immediacy so dear to Sartrian and Heideggerian existentialism.

Much was lost of the sporadic poetic work produced during the long decades of almost uninterrupted benightedness while the poet was being cared for by the master carpenter Zimmer in Tübingen.25 What remains are a few short poems, mostly eight-liners, divided into two four-line stanzas that evoke in never-ending variants the four seasons. Formally, they are immaculate,

> simple, at times merry verses
> striving for exactness in the
> description of landscapes
> gleaned from no real impressions. Only seldom breaks
> forth something reminiscent of
> what used to be, the I is as
> if forgotten and drowned...26

Hölderlin's final act of loyalty to the mute Divine Presence was to follow it into a psychic beyond, transcending reason, consciousness and physical reality. Though not really a Romantic in the stern suppression of the self for the sake of awakening the Divine, he helped to set the stage for the Romantic act of self-transcendence, engendered in the daring speculations of German idealist philosophers.

NOTES

[1] "Epilogue," Hölderlin. Gedichte, ed. Konrad Nussbächer (Stuttgart: Reclam, 1963), 208. This and all of the following translations from German authors are mine.

[2] Paul Böckmann, "Sprache und Mythos in Hölderlins Dichten," Die deutsche Romantik, ed. Hans Steffen (Göttingen: Vandenhoeck and Ruprecht, 1967), 9-10.

[3] Böckmann, op. cit., 10-11.

[4] "Briefe über Dogmatismus und Kritizismus," Schellings Werke vol. I, 242, Cf. Böckmann, 13.

[5] Böckmann, 14.

[6] Literally "she who venerates the Divine," The Banquet, 202B.

[7] Also called the elegiac couplet which consists of two hexameter (six-foot) lines, the first of which mixes freely dactyls and trochees (stressed-unstressed-unstressed, and stressed-unstressed feet, respectively), except for the fifth foot which must always be dactylic. The second pentametric line omits the two short syllables of the third and sixth dactylic foot.

[8] Friedrich Beissner, editor of the Kleine Stuttgarter Ausgabe of 1961 defines the Alcaic strophe as "clear and rapid-storming," one that "never allows two accentuated syllables to immediately follow each other." The four-line strophe opens with two hendecasyllabic (eleven-syllabic) verses, both of which begin with an unstressed syllable(or half foot). "Each verse develops at a rapidly increasing tempo," as the first three trochees (stressed-unstressed syllables) are

followed by two dactyls (stressted-unstressed-unstressed syllables, twice, one after another). In my translation the pattern of tonic accents is the following

    Alóng the Gánges soúnded the
          pléasure god's
    Loud tríumph, ás from the Índus,
        all- cónquering

Starting again with an unstressed half-foot in the third line, the Alcaic strophe "stalks victoriously, as if after having climbed a peak, in a clear alternation of unstressed and stressed syllables." Actually, one could look at the prosodic pattern of the third line as a perfect iambic octosyllable, rather than as a heptasyllabic trochee with an unstressed first half-foot.

    The yoúthful Bácchus cáme
         with hóly

The fourth and last line starts with two consecutive dactyls (stressed-unstressed-unstressed syllables) twice in a row, ending with two consecutive trochees. The cadence of this pattern is experienced by Beissner "as a falling down a stairway toward the level of the next strophic beginning."

    Wíne and awákened the sléeping
         nátions.

The Asclepiadean strophe which allows purposely an immediate sequence of two stressed syllables one after another is, according to Beissner, "darkly thoughtful and spasmodic." An example of this strophic peculiarity is the opening line from the poem "Farewell" (second version)

    Só we wánted to párt? Thought it
       was góod and wíse?

No poem featuring this metric pattern was chosen

for this anthology. Cf. Hölderlin. Sämtliche Werke, Kleine Stuttgarter Ausgabe, ed. F. Beissner (Stuttgart: Kohlhammer, 1961), II, 502-503.

[9] Hölderlin, Gedichte, ed. Nussbächer, 212.

[10] Faust II, Act I, "A Somber Gallery."

[11] Nussbächer, 225.

[12] As the metric pattern of this opening line indicates, the ode is cast in the Alcaic strophe preferred by Hölderlin. A companion piece entitled "To the Germans" is in the Asclepiadean mode starting with "Never you mock the child when still the foolish one/ Perched on a hobbyhorse, deems himself great and high."

[13] "Only the middle stanzas in the second and fifth triad are, perhaps intentionally, one line shorter," i.e., have only fifteen lines. The last stanza of the poem was cut down in the final version from fourteen to twelve lines. Cf. Beissner, Kleine Stuttgarter Ausgabe, II, 438-39.

[14] Ibid., 439.

[15] Ibid., 440.

[16] Nussbächer. Gedichte, 218.

[17] Ibid., 219.

[18] See note 6.

[19] Beissner, II, 442. The italics are mine.

[20] Les confessions suivies de rêveries du promeneur solitaire, "V^e promenade" (Genève, 1782), 132. Cf. Beissner, 443.

[21] It appears, among others, in The Republic, Meno, etc.

[22] Beissner, 445.

[23] On this island in the Aegean sea dwelt John, the favorite apostle of Jesus to whom had been communicated in his old age the Apocalypse, the secret revelation of the world's destinies between Christ's death and His Second Coming.

[24] Nussbächer, 220.

[25] The poet's retreat was a balconied alcove in a tower overlooking the river Neckar.

[26] Nussbächer, 226.

CHAPTER V

EARLY ROMANTICISM. THE BERLIN-JENA GROUP.

1. Tieck, Master of the Kunstmärchen and the Tale of Horror.

If Hölderlin was a link between Goethe's Klassik and fullfledged Romanticism, Ludwig Tieck (1773-1853) represents the transition from the rococo banter of Wieland's Neo-classicism[1] to the self-assertion of the affects preached by Friedrich Schlegel.

Born in Berlin into a ropemaker's family, Tieck studied theology and philosophy at Halle and literature at Göttingen,[2] developing an early taste for Shakespeare, the Elizabethans and Calderón.

Tieck's unruly student existence in Halle (1792) brought him close to suicide and physical as well as mental collapse. The atmosphere at Göttingen proved more conducive to serious philological studies, but his taste for the weird and supernatural was permanently formed and endured well into his mature years. The friendship with W.H. Wackenroder, a sickly youth of acute artistic sensibility, exerted a stabilizing influence on Tieck until the former's premature death in 1798. Thanks to Wackenroder Tieck developed enthusiasm for Germanic art, customs and the literature of the High Middle Ages, as well as a measure of self-discipline. In 1793 the two friends undertook their celebrated journey through Franconia, soaking up the medieval flavor of the region and developing an ethnical consciousness of things traditionally German which they began to see as equal, if not superior, to the arts of classical antiquity.

Wackenroder's book of essays on painting and music of the old masters Outpourings of an Art-Loving Friar (1797) defended the primacy of intuition in the creative process over the systematic study of art theories. Four of the essays are probably from Tieck's pen. Goethe rejected the book but it found enthusiastic endorsement by the Nazarenes, a group of German artists living in Rome. While they professed to follow the aesthetic principles of the early Gothic painters, the masters actually extolled by Wackenroder and Tieck were Raphael, Dürer, Leonardo and Michelangelo, all men of the High Renaissance.

In 1796, Tieck published the earlier-mentioned controversial novel The Story of Mr. William Lovell, drawing on the experiences of his dissolute student days.[3] Werner Kohlschmidt traces the erosion of Lovell's moral fibre to his "schooling in sensuality in Paris and Rome;" from an innocent Schwärmer, "enthusiast," he declines to the level of "an ever-grosser epicure and world-despising cynic.[4]"

Gradually Tieck was able to bring under control his effusive enthusiasm which was to a great extent a reaction against rationalist utilitarianism and the morality of his lower class upbringing.

In 1797 he was contracted by Enlightenment's arch-propagandist Christoph Friedrich Nicolai to write edifying stories for the latter's publishing business. After Wackenroder's death in the following year Tieck continued to cultivate for a long time to come his passion for the art of the Germanic Middle Ages. Also in 1798 he published under the title The Wanderings of Franz Sternbald a series of narrations about the itinerant life of artists in Dürer's time. The novel has a loose structure freely mixing prose, lyrics and epistolary materials.[5] The author subtitled it "An Old German Tale," its geographic span extending from Nürnberg to the Netherlands and Rome. In 1799 appeared Phantasies About Art that propagated in essay form Tieck's continued admiration for the artistic reliques of the Germanic past.

However, as Kohlschmidt argues convincingly, the Sternbald novel signals a trend away from the unqualified "Germanism" of Wackenroder's heritage. Although Tieck did not return to the excesses of the "Lovell" period, he continued using the Dionysian sensuality of the Latin South as a foil to both pious Protestantism and the enthusiasm for Wackenroder's Germanic antiquarianism. By 1800, Tieck not only found his own Romantic dimension but pointed the way to Hochromantik, the "High" or Middle (Younger) Romanticism;[6] eventually, this trend would lead him in the course of his long life to a quasi-realism not unlike that of old Goethe.

    Between 1798-1800 Tieck lived in Jena, plunging into a motley but productive series of activities ranging from publishing to literary and art criticism, poetry, playwriting, recitation and, eventually, stagecraft. In Jena he met and befriended not only the two solitary pillars of German Klassik Goethe and Schiller, but the members of the Jena Romantic circle.

    A two-year sojourn in Italy (1804-06) proved to be a stimulus to his poetic Muse; more importantly, it solidified his erudition in medieval German literature. In 1825 he secured an appointment as manager of Dresden's Court Theater with the title of Hofrat, Court Councilor. Eventually, he was granted a pension by Friedrich Wilhelm IV of Prussia and ended his days in Berlin, the city of his birth.

    Tieck's literary creations of lasting quality embrace, aside from the novelist genre, the Kunstmärchen (literary fairy tale), and several plays. For the plots of the former Tieck drew mainly on the chapbooks of the German Middle Ages. The plots of The Story of Heymon's Children and of The Beautiful Magelone are of folk origin; the Fair-haired Eckbert is Tieck's own invention and still considered a classic of its kind. The Runic Mountain (1802)[7] shows a new trend in Tieck's art gravitating to yet another subgenre, the so-called Märchennovelle, the fairy tale novel. While in the literary fairy tale the natural and supernatural are closely interwoven, in the fairy tale novel the two worlds "are more distinct from one another.[8]" Here too shows Tieck's evolution toward a more sober treatment of everyday reality at the expense of the fantastic.

Aside from the earlier-mentioned spoof on Neo-classical taboos Puss in Boots (1797)[9] Tieck's principal dramatic output falls between 1799 and 1804. This includes a dramatic version of The Fair-haired Eckbert, Prince Zerbino, Genoveva, Melusine and Octavianus. It has been said that for all of his talent as Shakespeare translator and scholar, Tieck failed to learn from his idol the art of dramaturgy. Tieck the playwright is at his best in the free fusion of the farce, allegory and fairy-tale atmosphere, continually reshuffling these elements in defiance of all theatrical conventions, continually breaking and again restoring the illusion of reality.

In spite of the constant irruptions of his frivolous and often grotesque farcicality, Tieck is a master atmosphere-builder, unequaled except by the best of Brentano and Eichendorff. The vague, the gruesome, the placid and playful, all mingle in an uncanny expectation of the unforeseen, as frightening as it promises to be gratifying and novel, at the same time that it is memory-evoking. All critics agree that the following brief, frail lyric passage from his indisputably best fairy tale The Fair-haired Eckbert is the quintessence of lyrical suggestiveness, unfurling a full scale of sensations that defy conceptual explanation. In it, nothing and everything is said about finite man's immediate communion with nature's infinity through the medium of the forest. The passage earned Tieck the appellation of poet of Waldeinsamkeit, loosely translated as "lone forest mood."

> Lone forest mood,
> With joy you sway
> Me tomorrow, today,
> With you imbued,
> What joy brings gay

Lone forest mood.

The same as his fantastic tales, Tieck's comic stage takes its plots from chapbooks and general folklore. Like Friedrich Schlegel, he anticipated in theatrical practice Victor Hugo's postulate of mixed genres beyond even the latter's formal daring and virtuosity: the narrative-epic, the lyric, the purely dramatic and the comico-allegorical are this hybrid genre's structuring principles; the use of the Italianate terza rima and ottava rima, and a passion for the sonnet are only a few examples of the poetic tools pressed into service by his patriotic flare. In his last drama Fortunat (1815-16) the mélange of genres subsides somewhat into a more sober mixture of blank verse and prose that does justice to the epic breadth of the whole. Similarly, the ambitious historical novel Vittoria Accorombona (1840) deals quite realistically and, indeed, in a historically faithful fashion, with the fascinating human type produced by the Renaissance lust for life and artistic creativity.[10]

As an original and inspired poet Tieck occupies a firm if not foremost position among German Romanticists. Edited between 1821-23, his poetry covers the wide range from contemplation and, indeed, speculation about Romantic creativity, to the experience of metaphysical dread, of life insouciance throbbing with the naive libido of the Latin South; it attempts to give an account of the presence of the Divine in a cynically secular world, of the elusiveness of youth and poetic perfection, and of the yearning for the Absolute; it praises, time and again, the life-affirming virtue of wounded sensibility. If there is one universal theme that runs through all of Tieck's poetry it is the nagging doubt about love's self-fulfilling purpose.

"Music Speaks" is a modern version of a Baroque sonnet, reminiscent of the "metaphysical" sonnets of Gryphius, and even of Lope de Vega in the enumerative plethora of concepts, and of

Quevedo, in the puzzled awe before the enigma of becoming.11 The language of the innocence of being, human and preterhuman, that flowed freely in some mythical Golden Age before the Fall of all God's creatures has remained mute until its revival in the "human voice;" it

> Prays, moans, exults, breaks out to
> freedom soaring

and so triumphs over "night, fear, death, muteness, woe," all agents of existential finiteness and thus enemies of the Romantic yearning for the Absolute in the here-and-now.

In "Boccaccio" Tieck pays tribute to the Renaissance man's versatile elegance, caustic wit, and forceful balance between existential antinomies that would tear apart a creature of a less survival-and-pleasure-oriented epoch. "San Lorenzo and Bolsena" celebrates the shimmering contrasts of the Mediterranean landscape, associating it with the Renaissance banter of Shakespeare's Twelfth Night. The word *scherzend*, "bantering," is twice repeated, the second time in the closing line of the poem, constructed in a distinctive, hammering sequence of a dactyl and a trochee

> Moves around, bantering.

Like most of the poems of Tieck's Italian period except the sonnets, "Boccaccio" and "San Lorenzo" are couched in "free rhythms," the unrhymed, rhythmically sharply differentiated an liltingly irregular verse so dear to the Romantic rebel against the jingling regularity of the English heroic couplet and the French *alexandrin*.

"The Pantheon" praises the simplicity and sincerity of the grasp of the Absolute demonstrated by the Mediterranean religious attitude. Steeped in the immediate contact with concrete humanity, the poet's Nordic self-consciousness is absorbed by the "workaday noise and confusion" of the Latin ability to reconcile the humdrum with the Divine. In the splendid setting of the Pantheon in which the businesslike pantheism of the Romans universalized and secularized the ubiquitous Divine Presence, the finite melts with the infinite.

>   We like in familiar nearness
>   To see what heaven is, as well
>   as feel.

"The Apparition" evokes, first of all, figures from the German mythical past. They come to life as a result of the poet's perusal of ancient documents which he had been studying in Rome: as he passes the "Bridge of the Angels" the ghosts of Wittich, Hildebrand and Etzel[12] are replaced by a vision of the poet's first love. But the apparition passes quickly, disappearing once and for all behind the closing door of a little stone cottage. In spite of its insignificant form and size, this cottage locks away irretrievably all vestiges of the poet's past, barring forever its humanly concrete recreation. The same as in "San Lorenzo," the closing line rings out the irremediable finality of its message in the dactylic-trochaic sequence.

>   And never shows up at its little
>   door
>   A face of a human.

"Christmas" bears as subtitle the date and place of its writing: Rome 1805. Once again the poet's Nordic moodiness and bent for abstract speculation has its vision corrected by the evocative piping of the mountain shepherds giving piety as practiced in the Latin South the deeper, Dionysian dimension in which all opposites tend to be reconciled. The Bacchanalia from which were born the classical Greek tragedy as well as the farces of the Middle Ages live again in the primitive music of the affects, mixing sensuality with the worship of the Holy Virgin, "with this-worldly pomp/ What's holy... scoffing."

A similar atmosphere of universal tolerance, even in the ghoulish rites of death as developed by Mediterranean Catholicism, pervades the poem entitled "Penitential Sermons." The same as bargaining and religiosity mixed in the "Pantheon," so go here hand in hand the somber church relics, a fire-and-brimstone sermon, and a tacit arrangement of a tryst between two young people concerted in the very presence of all the paraphernalia of death and decay.

The sonnet "Life" muses over the inability of most humans to understand and interact with the business of existing in the fullest sense of the word, which spans life and death, finiteness and eternity. In this sonnet Tieck captured, better than in most, the "tartness of being." Once again in a manner reminiscent of the Baroque concept of life as "vanity of vanities," the poet analyzes human self-deception, the failure to even partially succeed in embodying, "fanning," as he puts it, the "heat of inspiration" into the "flames" of art as living existence. For the most part, the human condition is confined to a limbo between life and death, "joy and sadness;" the poem's ending is surprisingly up-beat; a mannerized metaphor harking back to Renaissance and Baroque rhetorism introduces the eyes of the poet's mistress as "suns;" he asks himself to what he owes their "favor," considering the mournful condition of average humanity.

The answer is implied in another sonnet that starts

> Through Shining Love Lament to Song
>   is Turning

The Romantic mode, in spite and because of its self-cancelling and tortuous ironies, is its own reward. Love, a compound of its divine and human variety, as manifestation of an immanent and transcendent Absolute, is its own reward. The second quatrain puts this in quite unequivocal

language. He who spurns the "holy tears" brought
forth by such love is foolish; the poet accepts
love's only apparent perversion that takes delight
in jesting on the wounds it inflicts; though he
doesn't know exactly for what his "heart is flaming," he suspects that

> ...love for more than love itself
> is mourning.

This is another concrete example of the syndrome
of frustration over wanting to transcend into the
beyond yet wishing to enjoy the fruits of Transcendence in finite, secular existence, shared by
the Schlegels, Hölderlin, Novalis and the rest of
the Romantic fraternity.

"The New Spring" is probably the weakest of
Tieck's poems in this selection. It says little
that is new in many words: in an unrhymed but
rhythmically regular trochaic pentameter (hendecasyllable), it offers an allegoric encounter between the poet and his mannerized alter ego, an
amalgam of guardian spirit, the genius of recurring springtime, and the self's better, nobler,
and more innocent half. The poet's everyday ego
is disappointed by the unspectacular arrival of
the long-awaited spring; his child-double teaches
him how to peek behind the drab and conventional
expectations of the hackneyed concept of "spring."
Once the preconceptions regarding spring can be
swept away,

> What surrounds you now will stay
> forever.

Of course, the truthfulness of the promise made
by the spirit of real, "interior" springtime depends on the understanding of the allegory by the
poet's mistress. Palpable, if gentle and naive
eroticism is the alpha and omega of Tieck's mastery of the fairy tale in prose or verse, in the
sung word or stage representation.

NOTES

[1] Christoph Martin Wieland (1733-13) was professor of Philosophy at Erfurt, tutor in Weimar's ducal family, editor of the influential literary journal Der teutsche Merkur, close friend of Goethe and Herder, and prime mover of the secularizing tolerance of the rococo phase of German Enlightenment. In his prose works (Agathon, 1766) and epic works (Musarion, 1768, and the long verse romance Oberon, 1780), Wieland extolled the Greek sense for balance between reason and sensuality, thus paving the way for Goethe's and Schiller's Klassik.

[2] His philological erudition stood him in good stead in the earlier-mentioned translations of Shakespeare and, with the aid of his daughter Dorothea and of August Wilhelm Schlegel himself, in the translation of Don Quixote. See "PERIODIZATION OF THE ROMANTIC MOVEMENT," note no. 1.

[3] The novel's literary model was Restif de la Bretonne's Le paysan perverti (1785-91) recounting escapades and debaucheries in French society during the reign of Louis XIV. This novel earned Restif the nickname "le Rousseau du rouisseau," "the Rousseau of the torrent," for his unbridled effusions and low-brow vulgarizations of Rousseau's teachings.

[4] Werner Kohlschmidt, "Der junge Tieck und Wackenroder," Die deutsche Romantik. Poetik, Formen und Motive, ed. Hans Steffen (Göttingen: Vandenhoeck and Ruprecht, 1967), 31-32.

[5] In this, Tieck anticipated Novalis' Heinrich von Ofterdingen (1800). It was Novalis who replaced Wackenroder in Tieck's life as a friend sharing a common aesthetic base and a kindred world view. This friendship too came to an early end with Novalis' death in 1801.

[6] "Der Junge Tieck und Wackenroder" op. cit.,

37-38.

[7] All three appeared in 1797 as a part of a collection of supposed folk tales under the title Volksmärchen von Peter Leberecht, (Popular Fairy Tales by Peter Leberecht)

[8] James Trainer, "The Märchen," The Romantic Period in Germany, ed. Siegbert Prawer (New York: Schocken Books, 1970), 105.

[9] An adaptation of a tale by the French classicist Charles Perrault (1628-1703).

[10] Walter Rehm, Das Werden des Renaissancebildes in der deutschen Dichtung; O. Weibel, Tiecks Renaissancedichtung in ihrem Verhältnis zu Heinse und C. F. Meyer; Cf. Oskar Walzel, German Romanticism, trans. Alma Elise Lussky (New York: Frederick Ungar, 1965), 176.

[11] Reference is made to Gryphius' Sunday and Holiday Sonnets (1639) conceived in the midst of the horrors of the Thirty Years' War, to Lope de Vega's sonnet CXXVI "Desmayarse, atreverse, estar furioso" ("To Be Fainting and Daring and to Be Furious") and to Quevedo's "Miré los muros de la patria mía" ("Upon My Country's Walls I Lowered My Glances").

[12] Wittich or Witege is a hero-villain in the German and English epic cycles about Dietrich of Bern (Theodorich of Verona). He is an ambiguous character; a companion of Dietrich's youth, he changes sides joining Ermanrich in defeating and driving Dietrich from his kingdom. According to Rabenschlacht, the Battle of Ravenna epos, Wittich murders several of Dietrich's youthful champions; with the help of the Huns, Dietrich in turn defeats Ermanrich. The Hunnish king Attila loses his sons to Wittich's powers, but, defeated and pursued by Dietrich, Wittich flees the battlefield and is drawn into the stormy sea by his ancestress Waghild. Hildebrand is the grizzly and most loyal

armorer of King Dietrich. In the anonymous <u>Der Nibelunge nôt</u>, <u>The Song of the Nibelungs</u> (12<u>15</u>?) both Hildebrand and his king... are vassals of King Etzel (Attila) the Hun; the two bring to bay the surviving "Nibelungs," the Burgundian king Gunther and his trustiest vassal, the "grim" Hagen.

2. The Magic Idealism of Novalis, Poet of Self-transcendence Through Death.

Friedrich von Hardenberg (1772-1801) did indeed justice to his assumed name Novalis, the forest-clearer[1] of Neo-classical clutter and dogmatism in the midst of which the first Romantic circle was taking shape at Jena and Berlin. A Saxon nobleman by birth, he shared with Hölderlin a Pietist background, tempered by the hard-nosed orderliness, traditionalism and efficiency of his civic-mined ancestry. Into the brief span of twenty-nine years he packed an incredibly busy career as professional mine administrator, poet-philosopher, scientist and amateur theologian.

Between 1791-93 he studied law at Jena, meeting frequently with Schiller who made a deep and lasting impression on him. In 1793 he completed the winter semester at the University of Leipzig where he developed the closest, if not always perfectly harmonious rapport with Friedrich Schlegel, termed by the latter "Symphilosophie.[2]" Novalis took his law degree in the following year at Wittenberg. A few months later he met Sophie von Kuhn, a precocious, sensitive, and necessarily immature pre-teenager. The erotic visions she fired in his imagination turned after her death in 1797 into an ever-deepening mystical worship of Sophie-Sophia (Wisdom), female mediator between life and afterlife.

In 1795, the year of his secret engagement to Sophie, he made the acquaintance of Fichte and Hölderlin, and began to study in earnest Fichte's philosophy. The following year, after a crash course in chemistry, he got himself appointed assistant administrator of the Saxon salt mine system.

In 1797, the year of the deaths of Sophie and of his brother Erasmus, he had a vision of Sophie at her gravesite, brought about ostensibly by conscious concentration on conjuring up her image. He also became a regular member and, eventually, focal point of August Wilhelm Schlegel's <u>salon</u> in Jena. It consisted of the latter's brilliant wife Caroline, Ludwig Tieck, the theologian Schleiermacher and, of course, August Wilhelm's brother Friedrich and his wife Dorothea, daughter of Moses Mendelssohn, philosopher of the German-Jewish Enlightenment. In the same year, crucial for his theoretical studies as well as his vocational training, Novalis continued to study Fichte and Kant, met Schelling and enrolled at the Mining Academy at Freiberg to study metalurgy, mineralogy and geology.

In 1798 Novalis published in the <u>Athenäum</u> his first major work, a collection of aphorisms under the title <u>Pollen</u>, and separately, the hortatory panegyric <u>Faith and Love</u> celebrating Frederick III's accession to the Prussian throne. He also began to work on an apprenticeship novel entitled <u>The Novices at Sais</u>,[3] and on a project of encyclopedic proportions called <u>Allegemeines Brouillon</u> (<u>General Draft</u>).

The years 1799-1800 saw the publication of the major poetic works that made him famous: the <u>Devotional Songs</u> and a speech on the philosophy of history called <u>Christendom or Europe</u>. At the time, he wrote most of the <u>Hymns to the Night</u> and secured an appointment to the directorate of Saxon salt mines. In 1800 he wrote the first part of his encyclopedic novel <u>Heinrich von Ofterdingen</u> and published the <u>Hymns</u> in the <u>Athenäum</u>. Medical treatment in Dresden failed to arrest his tuberculosis; he died in 1801, with Friedrich Schlegel at his death bed.

In Novalis German Romanticism was to have its last poet-philosopher and a unique embodiment of the Romantic ethics: A quest for <u>self-transcendence into infinity, a reconciliation of time and eternity ending all this-worldly imperfections, and a serene acceptance of death</u>.

As philosopher, Novalis went beyond Kant, as he tried to reconcile the split between the phenomenal and noumenal world. He foresaw the possibility of a "stepping outside oneself," a "kind of ecstatic self-abandonment." Neubauer argues that Novalis "radicalized the Kantian view of the mind's activity from a Fichtean idealist perspective[4]" by adopting a never-ending expansion of the Fichtean Self. Novalis' "higher self" is, however,

> neither inaccessible, as with Kant, nor accessible by cogitation only, as with Fichte, but <u>directly available through intuition</u>.[5]

Ultimately, Novalis declared even the rift between faith and reason bridgeable.[6] Faith, as a consstruct of the mind, is different in degree only, not in kind from the rest of the mind's products,[7] i.e., primarily from reason.

As for Fichte, Novalis rejected the penetration of the noumenal world by some "transcendental act of consciousness," and "intellectual intuition," through which Fichte allows the ego to "originally posit its own being.[8]" Novalis could not accept a drift toward an eventual identification of such absolute ego with "a mystic God who created the material world" in an act of neoplatonic "emanation," a substance remaining independent of this world while making it, conversely, totally dependent on itself as an absolute ego. Novalis recognized the death of the empirical ego as the attainment of the freedom of the absolute self,[9] and hence, as a genuine philosophic act,[10] achieved through a supposedly purely poetic insight of his own. The message of the aphoristic <u>Pollen</u> can be summarized in one pregnant sentence.

> The highest goal of education is to take possession of one's transcendental self, to reach the self of one's self.[11]

Their differences concerning the Fichtean ego-absolutism notwithstanding, Novalis and Friedrich Schlegel molded their philosophies of art into a kind of complementary system. In fact Schlegel took it upon himself to rework and expand some of the fragments of the Pollen collection. This mutually penetrating symbiosis with Schlegel is in evidence throughout Novalis' theorizing on the arts and sciences. A case in point is his definition of wit, which arises out of the contact of "fantasy and judgment.[12]" A later entry propagating a progressive Romanticization of the world has an unmistakably Schlegelian cast.

> The world must be romanticized.
> Thus will its original meaning
> be rediscovered. Romanticizing
> is nothing but a qualitative
> raise to a higher power.[13]

Novalis' relationship with Schelling also shows compatible efforts to struggle past Kant's and Fichte's postulates of the rationality of nature. Like Schelling he wanted

> to discover nature's consciousness, to "win nature back" from
> the banishment as mere object....
> As science progresses, nature
> will gradually reveal its
> idealistic design... so that
> the affinity between object
> and subject will become
> evident.[14]

Yet Novalis could not accept the radically deductive approach of Schelling's Philosophy of Nature (1797) which aimed at an encyclopedic organization of empirically observed facts into an apprioristic mold intended to encompass all phenomenal evidence. He especially objected to Schelling's rejection of the interaction between mind and body, which would have reduced natural science to a psychological observation of mental functions barring all observation of external facts. Finally, Novalis recognized the theological difficulties with Schelling's World Soul conceived as a pantheistic, transcendent and yet material-immanent entity, a problem experienced to some degree by every Romanticist.[15] Novalis' own solution was simply once more to draft Spinozist pantheism as a foil to traditional Christian monotheism, and to produce out of their mutual tension a potentialized "new" Christianity. In this fashion, the world would remain "divine and... God transcendent.[16]"

This new religion finds its first outline in The Novices at Sais. In it Novalis hoped to counter Goethe's and Schiller's "injunction against transgression[17]" in both meanings of the word: as transcending toward a higher awareness, and transgressing against the classically-oriented measure dictated by human limitations. Likewise, he saw

> surrender to the desires of flesh... not [as] a debasement of human dignity... but a surrender to an omnipresent divinity.[18]

In Christianity or Europe, this erotic, Dionysian view of Christianity will eventually acquire the quality of Allfähigkeit, an omnipotent capability.[19] It was to produce a pantheistic Christianity embracing all earthly things as "the bread and wine of eternal life.[20]" The same as in the case of Friedrich Schlegel, Novalis' interiorization of imperfect outwardness leads to a poetization of the sciences, to "imaginative mathematics[21]" and "algebraic poetry." More specifically, Novalis envisions a "compositional art of numbers," which would provide a "mathematically cyphered base[22]" to the decoding of nature's mysteries absconded in world-immanent phenomena. In this Novalis followed closely Leibnizian rationalism rather than Bacon's and Locke's exhaustive "enumeration of empirical particulars.[23]" Neubauer stresses the importance of semiotics in Novalis' view of poeticized science. In the General Draft he hopes to lay the groundwork for a "combinatorial analysis" of word signs that would be recognized as in and by themselves "meaningless," "self-contained" and "transparent," allowing thus the structure of their sums to produce new, hidden meanings. Like musical notes, words were to become "non-referential;" such

> empty individual letters
> [would acquire] a general
> meaning within a formulaic
> combination.[24]

With this structural, algebraic repoetization of aesthetic symbols Novalis expected to do away with the rift between man and nature. The failure to reorganize the "dispersed colors of his spirit" accounts for modern man's "sickly disposition.[25]" Language is admirably adapted to the birth of a "logical physics"[26] which could go beyond the emotional abstractions produced by Plotinian emanations.

Novalis' semiotics are every bit as challenging as Hegel's and Schlegel's metaphysical insights, and are often argued more convincingly. A fair match for Hegel's abstraction of matter and concretization of spirit, Novalis' epistemology ultimately postulates the function creative symbols for "concepts of matter." Far from being "signs for material objects," they become means of self-transcendence with which one could "boldly reach into universal chaos and forge [one's own] order from it.[27]" This "new science" is a clear variant of Schlegel's Romantic poetry[28] of the imminent future, coming about from a synthesis of imagination and constructive intellect.

> Only when imaginative materials
> and forces are made into regu-
> lative standards of natural
> materials and forces shall we
> become physicists.[29]

The reliance on the negating and, by implication, dialectically potentializing function of the process of interiorization also anticipates Hegelian idealism. In a series of notes written probably in early 1798 Novalis postulates a "magic idealism" through a gradual "reduction of our dependence on sensory stimulation," and the replacement of "external physical impulses by psychic ones.[30]" In a letter to Friedrich Schlegel Novalis confirms the negative function of Christianity, expecting it to become, qua "absolute abstraction,"

> the projecting force of a
> new world-structure and mankind... -- annihilation of
> the present -- apotheosis of
> the future -- of this actual,
> better world....[31]

Novalis was no revolutionary in the leftist-liberal sense. Although his ambiguous praise of the Prussian monarchy in Faith and Love shocked the Philistines among the thickheaded bureaucrats and nobility, all it really called for was a full potentialization of what seemed a fairly promising status quo. He expected the King of Prussia to become a universal yet concrete representative of the noblest potential of his subjects, leading and ruling through example rather than force.[32]

What may have taken aback the powers that be was the poet's insistence on monarchy's self-cancelling mission. The king's function as educational model for his subjects should lead to co-option of all citizens to kingship: "the true king will become a republic, the true republic, a king.[33]"

Actually Novalis' involvement with political theorizing was only a small segment of his apocalyptic speculations considering the prominent role played by poetic existence as means to and goal of his reformatory endeavors.

Christianity or Europe breaks down the history of the European West to six epochs linked dialectically through mutual negations in a chain of progressive cultural peaks and self-cancellations. "The resplendent days" of the early Middle Ages are cancelled "from within" by the Reformation. It, in turn, is countered and checked again by the counterreformation of the Jesuits; this cultural achievement and collective awareness brings forth, again from within itself, the rationalist Enlightenment, as a reaction against the "infinite faith" preference of the Church. The subsequent deism and "mechanism" divinized secular knowledge; only to turn

> the infinite creative music of the cosmos into the monstrous clatter of a monstrous mill... which was supposed to be a mill-in-itself without builder or miller... a self-milling mill.[34]

The philosophers and encyclopedists seeking to propagate such "mill," are "cold, lifeless, icy peaks of bookish intellect," who will inevitably produce a second "more comprehensive Reformation," the French Revolution. Revolution does in turn renew "religious enthusiasm," whipping up emotions to the maximum, threatening "to complete [religion's] complete destruction." By another "dialectic inversion,[35]" the passionate excesses of revolution become "the most favorable signs of [the] regeneration[36]" of religion.

In his ambitious encyclopedic novel <u>Heinrich von Ofterdingen</u> Novalis adds little to the metaphysical and theological speculations discussed above. Inspired negatively by Goethe's <u>Wilhelm Meister's Apprenticeship</u>,[37] Novalis intended to write an "apotheosis of poetry" by tracing the coming of age of a sensitive youth who passes gradually from the medieval setting of merchants, knights, poets and hermits into the world of "myth and fairytale.[38]"

The novel focuses on Novalis' principal

existential concern: "the transition from the real world" of the everyday human ego "into the secret one -- death -- last dream and awakening.39"

The work has a simple, undramatic plot.

> The first part, entitled "Die Erwartung" ("The Expectation"), traces the journey of young Heinrich and his mother from Eisenach in Thuringia... to... Augsburg. The visitors arrive amidst a festivity... which includes the poet Klingsohr and his daughter Mathilde. Heinrich and Mathilde instantly fall in love. Heinrich's subsequent dream foreshadows Mathilde's death,... Klingsohr acquaints him with the principles of poetry, and [the] engagement to Mathilde becomes official.

There are, to be sure, secondary plots, such as "fictional inserts,"

> obliquely integrated in the main plot through a network of mirror effects according to the technique developed by Goethe... The combinatorial techniques are applied not only to the characters and the inserted stories, but also to the different genres, styles and modes of discourse as defined by Friedrich Schlegel [for the sake of developing] his "progressive universal poetry.40"

The purpose of Ofterdingen's encyclopedic and caleidoscopic vistas is not a realistic evocation of the Middle Ages or even of a medieval mood and ambience, but the genesis of a poetically interiorized grasp of reality which itself passes first into a prophetic dream and then into the dream's gradual realization.

The author's optimism concerning the evolution of existence toward a more peaceful and harmonious state of affairs finds support in his view of geological evolution as a trend away from the monstrous and catastrophic. Miners are viewed as artists who derive aesthetic satisfaction from unearthing evidence of the earth's "fabulous primal ages." As "inverted astrologers,[41]" they contribute to the understanding of the future that promises "increasingly [more] intimate harmonies, more peaceful communities;" nature, Novalis would have us believe, "approaches man" in noble spirituality; what he may lose in violent procreative power is compensated in the social forces that "shape and ennoble.[42]"

Heinrich's meeting with an hermit helps to reinforce the drift away from the egocentric particularism of the empirical ego toward a higher, purer self. Put differently, it recommends the gradual abandonment of the human ego's worldly glories. Count Frederick of Hohenzollern teaches Heinrich the importance of a temporal and spatial self-distancing from events for the sake of their correct evaluation. The count's reminiscences of his active, violent and passionate life as crusader bring about an "ultimately poetic view of history.[43]" Having thus been enlightened as to the real value of faith in the future through the purifying memory of the past, Heinrich is ready to be edified by Klingsohr on the virtues of poetry. Only then can he seriously take up the pursuit of the "blue flower." In time, this quest will become universally accepted by German Romantics as the symbol of fulfillment-through-non-fulfillment.

The novel's second part subtitled "Fulfillment" remains a fragment. It was to elaborate the idea of cheerful resignation to this-worldly imperfection as a means of keeping alive a further quest of perfection in the beyond.

    The prophetic dream of Mathilde's death comes true in the novel's second part. Her voice prompts Heinrich to sing in her honor; the song is answered by the appearance of the "poor girl" Zyane, whose name, derived from the Greek kyanos, blue, suggests the cornflower and an appropriately humble fulfillment of Heinrich's erotic and even of his aesthetic needs. In all its aspects the novel points unmistakably to a final reconciliation and cancellation of all particular, finite forms. It blends literary genres (poems, narrative inserts, dramatized conversations, reminiscences, tales), temporal dimensions, it eliminates structures of time and place, all this to prepare the gradual release of the "blue flower" into a world, itself transfigured by the flower's immediate yet eternal presence. Typical of this fullness of time and space is the last stanza attached to the "Song of the Hermit[44]" celebrating the elimination of every imaginable life-stifling abstraction and a definitive reconciliation of all opposites.

    Novalis the lyrical poet chose at first the memory of Sophie to be his mediator with the Absolute. Gradually, this memory takes on the features of Christ and the Madonna, as two specific soul-guides, away from the senseless chaos of Becoming and into what first appears to be the night of death. The atmosphere of annihilation is gradually brightened by a new, higher-than-earthly "light of the night," and "aura of erotic pantheism[45]" developing around a millennial transfiguration of Christianity itself.

    The first of the six Hymns to the Night had been rewritten from the original unrhymed, free-rhythmic verse in a heavily cadenced poetic prose. It starts with the praise of sunlight, the life giver, which is, however, also the determining factor of finiteness, and the prime mover of endless, self-destructive, ever-changing Becoming. The poet turns away from worldly light, from the imperfect abode of the "splendorous stranger," to contemplate it from a vantage point in the beyond. From this angle he sees it "submerged in a cavernous vault," its aspect "lone and barren." Memories, wishes and dreams, fulfilled or not, all come "in gray attire," befitting their ephemeral and imperfect existence. In their stead, night begins to unfold her ineffable mysteries. Mood soars and the soul, soothed by the opium of an other-worldly quietude, advances to grasp, with "gladness frightened," the reconciled coexistence of opposites reflected in the face of the Savior as He shows "cherished youth" to the Mother-Virgin. In this apocalyptic representation of the temporal intersecting with the eternal, light, the terrestrial life giver, appears "poor and childish," and the departure of the day of life "enjoyable and blessed." God's creation of the universe, intended his "omnipotence to herald," and the recurring Incarnation loom brightly in "those infinite eyes" that resemble and encompass the star-studded heaven.

The concluding lines dissolve in a staccato of broken sentences, filled with the ineffable vision of Christ's eyes, seeing without the need of light, probing the endless universe as well as the depths of man's soul. Christ, sent by Night, is her "amorous sun," awakening the poet to an erotic union with Him, the beloved "Bride." This composite Sophie-Christ figure is a cipher of eternity, infusing the poet with real "life" and making him only now truly "human" in the midst of the eternal nuptials of Night.

In hymns one through five the metric and gradually rhymed verse begins to predominate; the sixth and final hymn entitled "Yearning for Death" is cast in a perfectly regular and rhythmic form. Neubauer argues convincingly that the gradual ascendancy of the traditional verse form over the initial poetic prose reflects a progressive -- if rather unorthodox -- Christianization of the poet's inspiration.[46]

The end of hymn four is written entirely in

rhythmically regular two-stress verses distinguished by a haunting cadence; it evokes what Nietzsche will call in his <u>Merry Wisdom</u> the "art of declining." The eroticism of the imagery is at the same time explicit and suggestive, unparalleled in its joy-in-sadness mood, except by the best mystical flights of St. John of the Cross. Sleep, the flame of erotic ecstasy, the fusion of two-in-one, self-annihilation and self-renewal are inextricably bound up in one voluptuous gasp.

    The last hymn is a naïve but magnificent summation of the poet's farewell to finiteness. Neubauer points out the usage of Pietist terminology. This results in an individualistic approach to the Divine, and yet it communicates a "communal faith." Furthermore, the "uneven pulsation of the first and the subsequent prose hymns" reflects the author's progression from transcendent but personalized eroticism to the "simple vocabulary of the sixth hymn.[47]" The culmination of the communal experience is simply and tersely expressed in the closing couplet of the second six-line stanza:

        We lost the urge abroad to roam,
        We yearn for our father's home.

    The rest of the poem is a reconciliation of past and future, of immanence and transcendence. The remembering soul moves from the mythical-Biblical past of supermen-prophets and of the still "youthful" Divine Presence in the guise of Incarnation, Passion and Resurrection to a joyful surrender of the self. In the concluding hymn, Jesus is once more hailed as "Bride;" as in the second part of the "Song of the Hermit" in which the Savior is compared to a "caring wife" of the human soul, this is a case of an intentional inversion of the traditional symbolism developed by Christian mystics who assigned to Christ the role of the "Lover" or "Bridegroom" and to the soul, that of the "Bride" or "Belovèd."

    <u>The Devotional Songs</u>[48] were an instant success

with the public as well as with Novalis' poetic peers. Friedrich Schlegel reported to Schleiermacher they were the "most divine" Novalis had ever written, "unmatched, except for the most intimate and profound early short poems of Goethe.[49]" Novalis himself wrote them as a reaction to the all-too-cerebral hymnic poetry of the Pietist tradition in an attempt to achieve "liveliness, fervor, and to appeal to universal feelings free of Church dogma.[50] In addition, he wished to overcome the affected crudeness of folk song imitations by the Pietist Zinzendorf (1700-60).[51] The seventh devotional song entitled "Hymn" blends masterfully the Dionysian ecstasy of carnal lust with the Christian communion of worshippers, priest and God in a celebration of the mystery of transsubstantiation. Spiritual-carnal communion, attunement of souls, mutual fusion of bodies, participation in the mystic rites between a humanized deity and divinized flesh, a literally exercised symbolism of "body and blood," all are harmonized in a sweeping rush toward the infinite. Knowledge in the broadest sense, from carnal to the mystic apprehension of cosmic totality, pursues the incomprehensible, willingly losing itself in the unfathomable depths of the enigma of being. The insatiability of love is praised as the highest good of the ardent, self-consuming initiate, contrasted with the "sober ones" who had never tasted the "nurture" of infinity.

The fifteenth and last song of the series embodies perfectly the final "ordered" dimension of Novalis mystical rapture. It marks the trajectory from the "free rhythms" of "Hymn" to the impeccably regular, almost monotonous cadence of alternating female and male verse endings cast in the likewise alternating rhyme pattern ab ab, and the starkly concrete vocabulary. The result is a most intimately personal experience of the beauty of the Mother of God, unutterable and incommunicable in its ecstatic immediacy.

The earlier-mentioned "Song of the Hermit" is representative of the poems and songs incorporated in <u>Heinrich von Ofterdingen's</u> first part, and those intended for the novel's unfinished sequel.[52] It typifies the culmination of a drift toward a less ecstatic and more controlled experience of the Second Coming in the guise of a communal affair. What starts out as a mildly Dionysian reminiscence of an erstwhile "crusader" for beauty in the-here-and-now, moves from subjective sensual experience ("the love cup's fullest measure") to a cheerfully conceived resurrection of the dead, surrender to a returning Christ and universal divinization of nature.

    Among the late <u>Miscellaneous Poems</u> "Eyes on Living Men I'm Training" is perhaps Novalis' very last poem. Formally, if not thematically, it is quite different from the devotional song, nocturnal lyricism and the longing for self-transcendence. The structural devices of epiphoric repetition,[53] balanced juxtaposition of the same or slightly altered words, and other means suggesting the structure of the fugue and counterpoint in music, anticipate the rhetoric repertory of Arnim and, especially, Brentano. In terms of thematic inspiration the poem shows singular disinterest in self-transcendence, stressing instead an almost classicist acceptance of the transcendent-immanent rift between humans and gods, and an apparent affirmation of the active life. Neubauer calls the poem "meditative, confessional and intellectual rather than narrative symbolic and folksonglike,[54]" disregarding its quasi-folkloric formula pattern which was to become so popular with the poets of the Middle-Romantic School. The great herald of mystical self-transcendence may have suffered in this one last instance of intuiting the essence of reality a momentary inclination toward positive this-worldliness.

NOTES

[1] Derived from "Novali," people from land reclaimed from the forest whom he claimed for ancestors. Cf. John Neubauer, *Novalis* (Boston: Twayne Publishers, 1980), 40.

[2] "Symphilosophy," a word coined after the pattern of *sympathy*, suggesting a mutual intuitive attunement between the two friends. Cf. *Novalis*, *Schriften*, ed. Paul Kluckhohn und Richard Samuel, 2nd. ed. (Stuttgart: Kohlhammer, 1960-75), IV, 491. The two friends repeatedly clashed over Novalis' admiration for Schiller, and Schlegel's admiration of Fichte's purely deductive system.

[3] Inspired by Schiller's poem "The Veiled Statue at Sais."

[4] Neubauer, *op. cit.*, 30.

[5] *Ibid.*, 42. My italics.

[6] *Schriften*, II, 387.

[7] Neubauer, 24.

[8] Johann Gottlieb Fichte, *Ausgewählte Werke*, ed. Fritz Medicus (Darmstadt: Wissenschaftliche Buchgesellschaft, 1962), I, 292.

[9] Neubauer, 24.

[10] *Schriften*, II, 374.

[11] *Ibid.*, II, 425. Actually Novalis attempted to counterbalance Fichte's Absolute Self with Spinoza's determinism of the self and the self's surrender to a one single Absolute Substance of the universe. He thus hoped to achieve a synthetic stance higher than either of the two extreme attitudes, a God-like reconciliation of egoist freedom with pantheist necessity. Cf. *Schriften*,

II, 157.

[12] "Blütenstaub," *Novalis. Die Dichtungen*, ed. Ewald Wasmuth (Heidelberg: Lambert Schneider, 1953), I, 316.

[13] *Schriften*, II, 545.

[14] Neubauer, 35.

[15] See the preceding discussion of the theories of Friedrich Schlegel. Neubauer explains Schelling's World Soul as "a spirit hovering between the polarities of nature -- an immanent rather than transcendent spiritual power." Cf. Neubauer, 26.

[16] Neubauer, 88.

[17] *Ibid.*, 66.

[18] *Ibid.*, 88

[19] *Ibid.*, 89.

[20] *Schriften*, III, 523.

[21] Neubauer, 53.

[22] *Schriften*, III, 360.

[23] Neubauer, 55.

[24] *Ibid.*, 54

[25] *Schriften*, I, 82 ff.

[26] *Op. cit.*, III, 179.

[27] *Op. cit.*, III, 179.

[28] Compare *supra*, II, "FRIEDRICH SCHLEGEL'S VISION OF PROGRESSIVE PERFECTIBILITY," note no. 85.

[29] *Schriften*, III, 448.

[30] Neubauer, 60.

[31] Schriften, IV, 273 ff.

[32] Neubauer, 82.

[33] Schriften, III, 490.

[34] Schriften, III, 515.

[35] Neubauer, 95.

[36] Schriften, III, 517.

[37] In which, as Novalis claimed quite correctly, "the romantic sinks to ruin." Cf. Schriften, IV, 646.

[38] Neubauer, 127-28.

[39] Schriften, I, 342.

[40] Neubauer, 131.

[41] Schriften, I, 252-260.

[42] Ibid., 261 ff.

[43] Neubauer, 143.

[44] Starting with "When numbers and clear spatial features/ No longer count as key to creatures"

[45] Neubauer, 108.

[46] "The prose poem form was a new departure in the history of modern poetry, though it relied on the loosened poetic form in the odes and hymns of Klopstock and the young Goethe. Appropriately, the Christian creed is finally reaffirmed in the stricter form of rhymed verse." Op. cit., 105.

[47] Op. cit., 108.

[48] Some Novalis recited at the November 1799 meeting of the Romantics in Jena. They were written between 1798-1800.

[49] Neubauer, 110.

[50] Schriften, III, 588.

[51] Protestant theologian and composer of Pietist hymns who organized in 1722 Bohemian and Moravian exiles living on his estates into the Herrnhut Community in Saxony.

[52] As edited by Benno von Wiese, Echtermeyer, Deutsche Gedichte (Düsseldorf: August Begel, 1966), 330-32, the poem consists of three sections, the first starting with "Late at night it gives me pleasure," the second with "In the distant East it's dawning," and the third, "When numbers and clear spatial features." The first section, the "Song of the Hermit" proper, is directly incorporated in the novel's first part; the other two appear in Wasmuth's edition under the subtitle "Gedichte" ("Poems") as part of the Geistliche Lieder (Devotional Songs) Cf. Novalis. Die Dichtungen, ed. Ewald Wasmuth (Heidelberg: Lambert Schneider, 1953), I, 419 and 461.

[53] An epiphor is a figure of speech repeating once or several times the ending word or words in two or more verses.

[54] Neubauer, 119.

3. Brentano's Manifesto of the Romantic Ethos: Sublimation of Meaning Into Music and Legend.

   Clemens Brentano (1778-42) is a link between the programmatic poetry of the Berlin-Jena school and the purely poetic verse of Middle Romanticism. His father was an Italian-born merchant, his mother Maximiliane de La Roche a cousin of Wieland, and, in her youth, one of Goethe's ladyfriends. The boy grew up surrounded by the intellectual ferment of Goethe's and Schiller's Weimar, and the ecstatic unrest of the Jena Romantics. Fascinated by the whimsical, impulsive and irregular, he found a kindred spirit in Tieck, imitating the latter's irreverent experimentation with traditional poetic forms. The musicality of Tieck's poetry, admittedly a spontaneous Reimspielerei, "an interplay of rhymes" often limited to a mere ear-pleasing badinage, became for Brentano a serious compositional principle. In Willoughby's succinct analysis

> text and music for Brentano were as inseparably connected as they are in Volkslied [folksong]; the former was the natural inevitable expression of the latter. Brentano's poetry becomes Volkslied; it is characterized by the same melodious background from which the various arbitrary themes emerge in endless variations and are loosely held together by the refrain.[1]

The involvement with folk lyrics remained Brentano's lifelong avocation, but its greatest triumph came from the song-gathering enterprise undertaken with Achim von Arnim, the product of which was the earlier-mentioned pathbreaking Youth's Cornucopia (1806/08).

Brentano made Arnim's acquaintance in Göttingen; theirs was a friendship of aesthetes, typical of the late eighteenth-century passion for a complementary companionship between two poetically-inspired individuals.[2] Brentano married the poetess Sophie Mereau and in 1804 moved to Heidelberg. The following two years were possibly the most productive and certainly the happiest of Brantano's life, filled with the intellectual excitement of the picturesque university town. This euphoria came to a quick end. The year of publication of the Cornucopia coincides with the death of Brentano's beloved Sophie, a blow which had deep and lasting effects on his life and poetic development.

Between 1809-18 Brentano lived mostly in Berlin, falling first under the spell of the youthful poetess Luise Hensel who became instrumental in his returning to the Catholic faith of his youth. The Romances of the Rosary (1809, published posthumously in 1852) were a direct product of this liaison; next he became spiritually attached to the stigmatized nun Anna Katharina Emmerich. He spent the years 1819-24 literally at her bedside recording her mystical experiences. The last two decades of his life alternated between religious meditation and spiritual disarray. Brentano undertook no new major projects after his conversion, restricting himself to redrafting some of his earlier tales.

Like Tieck before him, Brentano made his literary debut with a controversial novel which launched a sweeping attack against moral and literary dogmas. His Godwi (1801) is more than an apology of impulsive sensuality. It put to test several principles of Friedrich Schlegel's theory of creativity: the fertile dialectics between self-creation and self-destruction,[3] the concept of wit as "naive thoughtfulness" shot through with "the appearance of the perverse and the deranged,[4]" and the force of self-determining spirit as creator of a new mythology from nothingness.[5] Had Godwi been taken seriously as model for a new novelistic structure, it could have very well done away with the genre as a whole. Godwi's approach to reality and its poetic rendition is an excellent key to the comprehension of Brentano's poetry and his Kunstmärchen.

What there is of a plot in Godwi's desultory narration is, eventually, totally aufgehoben in the Hegelian fashion. What is actually left is a vague feeling of sublimated events, characters and ideas; in the words of Claude David, "the action is annulled; Godwi is a novel in which nothing happens.6"

David lists other, apparently well-planned breaches of the novelistic convention: the characters are outlined vaguely, as concepts, not as individuals; in their relationships they love and leave one another, barely coming in contact; the dialogues are "arbitary improvisations," mere responses "to the mood of the moment;" the universal "anarchism potentialized to blasphemy" cannot be explained simply as the author's "youthful wantonness;" it appears in the later works in a "dampened and spiritualized" guise.[7] Brentano himself defines the ethics of his self-authenticating libido in no uncertain terms

>He who is born to debauchery
>and fails to exercise it leads
>a truly vicious existence.[8]

What is done, cannot be undone; but it can be recast in "a beautiful representation of the action.9" David interprets this as

>a work of art become an aesthetic dream in which takes
>refuge the weight of being-
>there (Dasein)[10]

Faithful to the Schlegelian Selbstaufhebung, self-annihilation for the sake of fulfilling the absolute whimsicality of the self, Godwi as a self-mirroring process of a "pure," existentially uncommitted game lacks any transcendent ground that could serve as a logical or even mystical explanation of its purpose, for there is no point to its being except a momentary gratification of a perfectly gratuitous whim. David calls it "the word, pure and simple, as sound and shape," a "delighting in the word sound," a "game with assonances," often degenarating into "endless word accumulations, arbitrary digressions, puns in poor taste.[11]"

In very few people did poetry and the poet's existence become blended as closely as in Brentano.[12] This was the opinion of his friend Eichendorff who compared the "swift, unexpected changes of emotion" in the folk song to those of Brentano's moods.[13] Godwi's world is spiritualized to the point that all that is left of corporeality is the sensual element.[14] Anticipating Unamuno's paradoxical question whether Cervantes wrote Don Quixote or vice versa, Brentano asks: "Does the world create me or I the world?[15]"

Brentano is without doubt the foremost master among Romantic poets and philosophers -- not excluding even Hegel -- who succeeded, at least to his own satisfaction, in totally deobjectifying the phenomenal world. While the end product of Hegel's phenomenological process was the epiphany of absolute knowledge qua free, concrete spirit, in Brentano it is an "atmosphere, a mood[16]" that is left over from the dissolved world of objects. On the other hand, Brentano attacks vigorously contemporary system builders who would "create a world through their own act of force," but all they accomplish is to nail the "Prometheus" of human creativity "to the rock" where "the vulture of reflection gnaws on his ever-returning heart.[17]"

And yet Brentano's thematic repertory is not that of a conventional Romantic. As David points out, the Romantic concept of nature has no place in this spiritualized world, "no more than a serious treatment of the Middle Ages or an orthodox view of Christianity." Brentano's sensibility and world view stand closer to those of the "late Baroque;" quoting Friedrich Gundolf, David finds in Brentano's Romanticism

> a mixture of burgeoning
> pedantry and inmost sincerity,
> of artiness and simplicity,
> of euphony and hollowness of
> thought.[18]

In addition David points out a kinship, in terms of blood relation[19] and of the aesthetical-literary variety, between Brentano and Wieland. David speaks of the merrily melancholic spirit which pervades the atmosphere of their respective Kunstmärchen.

For the two collaborators on the extremely successful Youth's Cornucopia Arnim and Brentano, true lyric poetry combined lyrics and music into an inseparable whole in the manner of the folk song. Willoughby claims that especially Brentano's poetry becomes Volkslied in fact. As in the folk song

> the intellectual content of
> his songs is exhausted after
> the few first strophes and
> they are only intelligible as
> musical compositions.[20]

It was Brentano's imagination that created virtually ex nihilo the legend of the Lore Lay which first appeared as a lyrical insert in Godwi; joined to ballads such as "On the Rhine,[21]" it gave birth to the lyrico-epic subgenre of the Rheinmärchen, the Rhine fairy tale. But enthusiasm for the Rhine lore became widespread only after Brentano and Arnim made their pilgrimage along the banks of the river in 1802, collecting folksongs as they went along.

The Cornucopia was born from this direct exposure of the two friends to the geographic and ethnic reality of the Rhineland; Walter Scott's publication, likewise in 1802, of the <u>Minstrelsy of the Scottish Border</u> also contributed to its genesis. The collection was dedicated to Goethe who defended it against pedantic criticism of philological hair-splitters.[22] Willoughby notes an important difference between the <u>Cornucopia</u> and Herder's earlier <u>Voices of Nations in Songs</u> (1778); as opposed to Herder's cosmpolitanism, Arnim's and Brentano' emphasis lay on the traditional-national element, "in which every rank and profession is represented.[23]"

The voluminous collection was a labor of love, uncritical, arbitrary in its criteria for selection and manipulation of form and structure, showing now an archaizing, now a modernizing tendency of the editors. Willoughby finds Arnim "much more ruthless" than Brentano in restructuring the originals to suit the Romantic postulate of equating poetry with life.[24]" Oskar Walzel praises Brentano's contributions the the <u>Cornucopia</u> as well as his original poetry for "richer moods" and form purer than can be found in Arnim's poetic world; the latter succumbs to the lure of "words and phrases he has heard," repeating them <u>ad nauseam</u>. Walzel's characterization of Arnim's poetry calls to mind the Jungian category of the "naive or extraverted artist," who is "subordinate to" and as if "standing outside" his work, unconscious of his artistic intentions.[25] The melodies of others that haunt Arnim's memory are "spun out" to fill

> the rhythm of a poem which
> <u>has taken possession of him</u>
> with words, the sense of
> which has slipped his mind.[26]

Brentano's variations on a theme are likewise music-oriented-and-dominated lyrics; the best are kindred to Goethe's lyrical spontaneity, filled with tensions between sarcasm and tenderness, compassion and aloofness, irony and naiveté.[27] Undoubtedly, the impact of the <u>Cornucopia</u> cannot be underestimated in terms of moulding the German collective consciousness and inspiring not only the Younger Romantics contemporary to the Arnim-Brentano team, but virtually every new generation of German poets down to our days. Finally, it contributed greatly to the acknowledgement of the ethnic lore and spontaneous naiveté as fundamental virtues of Romantic art in general, and of all lyrical poetry in particular.

Paradoxically, Brentano's haunting musical melancholy and satirical banter that echo his yearning for the infinite are hardly "primitive and traditionalist," two essential qualities of folk poetry according to Herder. Although inspired by the "folk spirit," Brentano produced an art of highest conscious intentionality which, incidentally, "unfolded and enriched the forms and motifs" of folk poetry with "innumerable variations" and "inexhaustible volutes." Convincingly, David argues "no one's work is less folksy than Brentano's.[28]"

This tension between the spontaneous and the premediated pervades the other genres cultivated by the master of lyrical moods. To a much greater extent than Tieck, Brentano lacked the discipline in structuring the plots and the psychology of his characters requisite for the production of good drama. The lovely lyrics inserted in his comedy Ponce De Leon (1804) could not save a disorganized plot from being a total flop on the Vienna stage in 1814.[29]

The Foundation of Prague (1815) is remembered only because it sparked interest in Slavic mythology, which was to be exploited as a major thematic source by the Romantic classicist Franz Grillprazer (1791-1872). Conceived originally as an operatic libretto the play bears marks of undue theatricality. Its message is ambitious: a nostalgic evocation of the mythical matriarchate in Bohemia under the aegis of the wise princess Libussa, and its transformation into a higher, patriarchal order in the person of Libussa's husband, the first Przemislide Primislaus (Přemysl). The play intended to rekindle hopes for the Slavs as well as for the Germans of a self-determined political future, free of Napoleonic interventionism.

Brentano's ability to dilute characters, events, landscape, even feelings into atmosphere makes him the master of magical make-believe and hence, a natural teller of fairy tales.

In Rhine Tales, published posthumously in 1846-47 together with the Italian Tales, Brentano turned from simple paraphrasing of the folk tale to pure invention. As in Godwi, lyrical interpolations are frequent; as a rule, they reinforce the mood of the ambience at the expense of action. The Italian Tales (1809) were inspired by Giovanni Battista Basile's Pentamerone (1634-36), but are in fact quite original reelaborations of the Italian models. After 1835 Brentano began reworking one of tales into Gockel, Hinckel and Gackeleia (1838), "an oblique biographical confession." James Trainer contrasts Brentano's fairy tale technique with Tieck's stressing the former's primary concern for "linguistic effect" that sacrifices the visual to the auditory; the result is

> a blend of mirthful incongruity, wit and improvisation or,[in Arnim's words] frivolous coquettishness.[30]

An onomastic allegorism of people and places maintains the folk tale's faculty for characterizing human types in terms of good and evil, success and failure, love and hate, naïveté and, sometimes, of gruesome detail.

Putting into practice Novalis' theory of word-cyphers as preterconceptual signifiers capable of creating new significations and values out of new structural configurations, words are for Brentano

> units of sound which can be effective for the audible patterns they set up quite apart from [their] literal meanings....[31]

Genuine laughter, self-parody and a constant banter seem to be the only purpose of the tale. At the same time, the implicit Christian faith in the ultimate triumph of loyal service in the interest of good is more than once shaken by the author's actual existential experience. Brentano's world allows for a great deal of grotesque hybridism which lets the animal and vegetal kingdoms coalesce with the human species in an "unstartled acceptance of the impossible,[32]" which leads simultaneously to a skeptically-oriented questioning of the reality of existence. Gackeleia wanders through the world following the miraculous "Kunstfigur," "artificial figure," given to her as substitute for a doll her parents decreed she was never to have. This mechanical device run by an internal clockwork opens the world of the magic only at the cost of suffering for the parents; the curse of artificiality befalls everyone concerned.[33]

Crucial for the genesis of the unique atmosphere pervading Brentano's lyrical world view is the handling of the time progression. It is the mutual permeation of the real and the imaginary that accounts for the ambiguity of Brentano's world. Emil Staiger defines Brentano's time concept as *reissend*, "tearing and tugging" on conventional time dimensions: present, past and future; far from being overcome, the past is thus "simply forgotten.[34]"

"On the Rhine" is a seminal ballad of Brentano's Rhine mythology, drawn, virtually in its entirety, from his imagination. The moon-lit river, the wraith's fluttering shift, her own immaterial body's shivering which threatens to upset the boat, "the starlight's glimmering shine," the "many splendid cities" flying past, the voices from the nunnery, the flow of the candle light, the reddening dawn and the towers, "sundrenched, blinking in the morning sun," are the only dynamic motifs developing movement and change. On the other hand, still is the grief stricken fisherman, unable to accept the irreversible flux which includes the death of the loved-one; even the ghostly sweetheart is static in her gesture toward the mountain peaks, except when she is trying to capture the starlight on the rippling surface of the Rhine. Time flows imperceptibly, its passing merely suggested in the subtle changes taking place in the objects in space. He waits for her "till the stars are blinking/ And till the moon will shine;" the morning does not come, as a distinct and opposite phenomenon to night, but rather as a blurred fusion of both

> Belovèd maid, good morning,
> Belovèd maid, good night!

The appearance of the dead girl turns out to be in the light of daybreak a delusion after all; when he tries to wake her to the beauties of the new day, he is alone. And yet a swallow, flying from nowhere to nowhere, establishes concrete contact with the grieving fisherman whose identity begins to coalesce with that of the poet.[35] The fisherboy recedes into the background, allowing himself to float passively into the sea of an undifferentiated, collective existence which is the death of the human self. The swallow that had symbolically authenticated the link between phenomenal reality and the truth of imagination now "touches" with its presence the poet whose identity merges with that of the fisherboy drifting out of everyday reality.

> The fisher sang this ditty
> As if I sang that song!

"Lore Lay" is one of the most haunting of Brentano's songs. The legend of the Rhine maiden is another product of his early poetic Muse; it serves as a lyrical interlude and relief of the chaotic tensions of the non-novel <u>Godwi</u>.

Ironically, it was Heine's version of the Brentano myth that gave it world-wide currency, because of its unfeigned simplicity and the genuine naiveté of its musical suggestiveness.

Brentano's "original" is psychologically more demanding in its complex portrait of a <u>femme fatale</u> who is tired of being desired for the sake of her magic beauty, the only witchcraft to which she pleads guilty. The bishop is no exception; in the very execution of his office as spirtual arbiter of Lore's guilt he falls victim to the very same libido that condemns her in the eyes of men. The "witch" proves a better Christian than her judge; he uses the fire of his illicit passion as an excuse to grant the "sinner" a release from the unbearable curse of her beauty. His leniency condemns her to becoming a bride of Christ. Actually, it betrays an unconscious hope on his part of preserving her charms for himself, even if only vicariously, through the agency of a monastic institution. His rigorous adherence to canon law aimed at destroying Lore Lay's libidinous attraction works against his design. Tired of being beset upon in the name of human and divine love, Lore Lay plunges into the Rhine at the sight of a male figure in a boat that she conjures up, partially as a wish fulfillment of her perfidious lover's repentance, partially as a promise of the attainment of perfect bliss. Again, as in "On the Rhine," the poet feels himself multiplied in the triple invocation of Lore Lay, as the echo of her name rings from the <u>Dreiritterstein</u>, the Cliff of the Three Knights, named after her three escorts who failed to deliver her to the nunnery. The boatman's call, its echo, perhaps the voice of the beautiful sorceress herself and the poet's inner voice join in the triple invocation of her memory

As if all three were I.

"The Cradle Tune" is brief and self-explanatory, a gem of self-serving lyricism calculated to embody the mood of repose gradually overtaking the waking consciousness. It pretends to no meaning, message or purpose except that of lulling itself to sleep. Alliterations, the use of the narrow front high vowels i and $\bar{e}$ ("sing," "whispering," "singing," "swinging," "sweetly," "bees") add to the repetitious, incantatory relaxing of the self into sweet oblivion.

"The Song of the Spinning Woman" elaborates in an intricately repeated counterpoint yet another variant of the woman abandoned by her lover. Like "On the Rhine," it too is cast in four-line stanzas consisting of heptasyllabic verses with alternating female-male verse endings. In the earlier poem, the counterpoint of lover-beloved was built up in a parallelism of a single, powerfully contrasted inversion of moods. The "sweetheart with ringing joy" first watched "the crying boy" bathed with tears, only to be watched in turn by "the crying fisher boy." We have here a double contrast, first in the image of "joyful sweetheart" as opposed to "crying boy" and, secondly, as "the saddened boy" watches his sweetheart. The parallelism is held together by the internal juxtaposition of the two contrary ways of singing matins. Other, less complex contraries appear throughout the first Rhine song: the watery deep grows "even redder," as the boy's sweetheart grows "ever paler," etc., but none has the contrapuntal intricacy of the matins scene.

In "The Song of the Spinning Woman" the parallelism runs through the entire six stanzas. Actually, there are only two fundamental stanzas in the composition: in the first, the memory of days long past is associated with the song of the nightingale; in the second, the lone spinner woman spins away, fighting back her tears, her yarn as pure as the light of the moon and as her memory of the lover who had abandoned her. The following three stanzas are alternating variants of the first two. The only new idea added in the sixth and last stanza (variant of stanza number two) is the wish to be able to cry, so as to break the habit of bearing her grief in silence which perpetuates it.

S.S. Prawer is quite correct in noting that there is no progression in the poem, "no mounting towards a climax." The linkage is automatic "in a listlessly wistful succession of end-stopped lines." Only one mood prevails; after the first two stanzas, the "intellectual content" is exhausted. One could indeed "read the poem backwards as well as forwards, continue it to infinity."

All this is in keeping with the universal Romatic longing for the infinite and Brentano's specific need to dissolve conceptually-structured time dimensions into a continuum of non-chronological duration. To some extent this is indeed a device "cherished by the fin-de-siècle generation" of "tired late-comers and misfits" unable to cope;[36] but it is also a rather "modern" (i.e., late twentieth-century) tendency to bypass a conceptualized statement for an immediate, insistent but vague self-revelation seeking the absolute, the more esoteric its expression, the better.

The second part of "Echoes of Beethoven's Music" selected for this anthology describes the earlier-analyzed inspiration of the "naive" artist, unequal to his inspiration and driven to its musical communication disregarding his sensibility stretched to the breaking point, until the poet-musician is vibrating with music, the same as Memnon's pillar or statue, one of the seven wonders of the ancient world, said to be set off by the first rays of the rising sun. Once transposed into tone, the torment of nightly inspiration of the artist, brutalized equally by the unattainability of heaven as by the imperfection "the hell of God's earth," is transfigured into an ode of God's daytime adoration.

The third part of the poem dedicated to Beethoven's creative agony is a rhymeless dithyrambic paean to the creative self, anticipating Nietzsche's Dionysian ecstasies and surrealist imagery, though not the groundlessness of our own bent for agnostic secularism. Like Beethoven's torment-filled consciousness of creative Titanism, the musical genius whom Brentano recognizes as kindred, must do to what it is driven. Specifically, this is making "a world in his image," in direct competition with a trans-worldly Divinity, though "he," i.e., the creative Everyman, "did not intend it." And yet, the shattering realization of finite man's alienation from the One, the universal ground of Being -- a nightmare that had haunted thinkers since Pythagoras -- emerges again in the cry

> All is divided, however.
> No one can claim it all, each one
> Has a lord, only the Lord not.

The god-like nature of the singer-poet is cursed with the acutest sense of alienation: to be sure, he "renders no service," but being free to serve his own need to serve the divine, <u>he is self-serving</u>, and hence, the loneliest of mortals.

The <u>Romances of the Rosary</u> is a cyclus of poems conceived by the ageing poet after his conversion and lengthy spiritual communion with the stigmatized Anna Katharina. The work remained a fragment and was, in David's opinion, "the most ambitious of his undertakings," but also one that "could not be completed.[37]"

The Eighth Romance of the cyclus is deservedly the most popular one. It is once again couched in four line stanzas with alternating female-male perfectly consonated rhyme endings of the <u>ab ab</u> pattern. In addition, the female verse endings <u>a</u> are assonated throughout the poem as are the male endings <u>b</u>.[38]

As in all of Brentano's lyrical work, the Eighth Romance produces a uniform and meticulously exhaustive tableau of festive repose, suspending all activities of workaday usefulness. The evening falls, the colors fade, the shadows grow longer, flowers droop, meadows sink into slumber, wild game appears where the rush of a waterfall comes to rest in a pool. Roses wax silent guarding their secrets, lovers proceed to the coast to seal with silence their exuberant daytime banter. The poison of the siren's call, the same as the approaching night and the emerging earth spirit throw a shroud about the conscious mind, revealing "the blue-hued cosmic plan" of universal existence which is that of unconscious and hence, happy, repose. Even the trees seem to crowd down closer to the valley, the well springs send forth "the silent plash" of the intuitive awareness of being in whose depths conscious thoughts sadly contemplate their ever-frustrated attempts at self-comprehension. Brentano, the unruly, restless searcher for perfection-in-repose finds it in this most Brentanoesque passage: it is the sad self-cognition of rational thought in the process of becoming aware of its existential irrelevance.

NOTES

[1] L.A. Willoughby, *The Romantic Movement in Germany* (New York: Russel and Russel, 1966), 46.

[2] Such as the bond between Goethe and Schiller, Coleridge and Wordsworth, Tieck and Wackenroder and later, Tieck and Novalis. The Wackenroder-Tieck team effort set a trend toward a less than equal give-and-take between two genial artists. The same as the physically sturdier but unruly Tieck became dependent on the frailer but better disciplined Wackenroder, Brentano clung to the manly firmness of Arnim, the Prussian nobleman and eventually Brentano's brother-in-law through marriage to Bettina Brentano, a poetess in her own right.

[3] See supra, II, "Friedrich Schlegel's Vision of Progressive Perfectibility," note no. 39.

[4] *Ibid.*, note no. 80.

[5] *Ibid.*, note no. 83.

[6] Claude David, "Clemens Brentano," *Die deutsche Romantik* ed. Hans Steffen, 160.

[7] *Ibid.*, 162.

[8] Clemens Brentano, *Werke*, ed. F. Kemp (München, 1963), II, 384.

[9] *Ibid.*, 412.

[10] David, "Brentano," *op. cit.*, 163-64.

[11] *Ibid.*, 165-166.

[12] In Joseph von Eichendorff's words, "Brentano was constantly impelled by an overwhelming imagination to mix poetry into life." Cf. Friedrich von Hardenberg (Novalis), *Werke, Briefe*,

Dokumente, ed. E. Wasmuth (Heidelberg, 1953-57), II, 1059.

[13] Willoughby, The Romantic Movement in Germany, 47.

[14] David, op. cit., 168.

[15] In the preface to Godwi; Cf. David, op. cit., 169.

[16] David, op. cit., 168.

[17] Preface to Godwi, David, ibid., 169.

[18] Friedrich Gundolf, Die Romantiker (Berlin: Neue Folge, 1930), I. 328 f.

[19] As indicated above, Brentano's mother was Wieland's cousin.

[20] Willoughby, The Romantic Movement, 46.

[21] "Auf dem Rhein," also referred to by its opening line "Ein Fischer sass im Kahne." It appears as "The Fisher in His Rowboat" in our anthology.

[22] Willoughby, 49.

[23] Op. cit., 48.

[24] Ibid., 49.

[25] As opposed to the "sentimental or introverted artist" who is most of the time conscious of his intentions... against the demands of the object," i.e., the work of art. Cf. "On the Relation of Analytical Psychology to Poetry," The Collected Works of C.G. Jung, trans. R.F.C. Hull, ed. Read, Fordham, Adler, McGuire (Princeton: Princeton University Press, 1975), XV, 72-73.

[26] German Romanticism, trans. Alma Elise Lussky

(New York: Frederick Ungar, 1965), 154. My italics.

[27] *Ibid.*, 155.

[28] Claude David, *op. cit.*, 179.

[29] Roger Paulin lists as the comedy's "promising ingredients" a "French Rococo source, masks and disguises in the style of Shakespeare and Lope de Vega." Cf. "The Drama," *The Romantic Period in Germany*, ed. Siegbert Prawer, 194.

[30] "The Märchen," *The Romantic Period in Germany*, *ibid.*, 111.

[31] *Op. cit.*, 112.

[32] *Ibid.*, 113.

[33] Work of art she was, not doll,
Pretty figurine, that's all.

[34] *Die Zeit als Einbildungskraft des Dichters* (Zürich: Atlantis Verlag, 1963), 77.

[35] For an analysis of the Romantic tendency to schizophrenia and ego fragmention see Gilian Rodger, "The Lyric," *The Romantic Period in Germany*, ed. Siegbert Prawer, 162-65.

[36] Prawer contrasts Brentano's "Song of the Spinning Woman" with Gretchen's spinning song from the first part of Goethe's *Faust* which progresses, with calculated interruptions by the plastically, rather than musically evoked spinning wheel, toward a "final outburst, overflowing line-endings and stanza-endings." Goethe's song has thus a definitive cutting-off point after which absolutely nothing can be added to the classically-progressive and purposive composition. Cf. *German Lyric Poetry* (New York: Barnes and Noble, 1965), 123 ff.

[37] David, *op. cit.*, 159.

[38] The female consonated verse endings (a) of the first stanza rhyme "decreeing -- fleeing," and the male consonated verse endings (b) of the same stanza rhyme "ax-wax;" at the same time the a endings "decreeing -- fleeing" assonate with the second stanza's a endings "sealing -- reeling," while the b endings "ax-wax" assonate with the second stanza's "began-again." This "inner" consonance and outer (inter-stanzaic) assonance run through the whole poem.

4. Achim von Arnim: Reformer of Society Through the Revival of German Ethnic Consciousness.

As a poet Achim von Arnim (1781-1831) holds his place in German literature mainly as coeditor of the Cornucopia and Brentano's collaborator in the recasting process of folk materials. A Prussian nobleman of an old and proud lineage, his Muse and life style were considerably more disciplined than Brentano's. He stopped at Heidelberg in 1805 during a European tour and remained there as an active force of the Younger Romantic circle until 1808 when he moved to Berlin. A brother-in-law of Brentano, he remained his lifelong friend. In 1813 he took time out from his literary activities to equip and command a company of volunteers to participate in the Wars of Liberation against Napoleon. In 1814 he retired to his ancestral home in Wiepersdorf and dedicated the remainder of his life to writing short stories, novels, plays and poetry.

A collection of short stories (Novellen in German, in the tradition of the Italian Renaissance novella) called The Winter Garden (1809) shows traces of Arnim's long involvement with folk art. Brian Rowly calls Arnim's and Brentano's creative characters "heavily overlaid,[1]" presumably by their exposure to and imitation of folkloric elements. Like Brentano, Tieck and others of the middle-Romantic generation, Arnim indulges in digressive arabesques that do little for the essential feature of the novella which is conciseness. In structure and motivation, he shows preference for improvisations, improbable coincidences and patriotic and ethical moralizing. Often the dividing line between short story and fairy tale is blurred to the point of disappearing. Goethe who cultivated the short story genre with his usual sublime mastery warned in his Conversations of German Refugees (1795) against mixing real events such as historic occurrences with wildly roaming imagination, the product being hybrid "monsters," "at odds with sense and reason.[2]"

This is indeed what tends to happen in Arnim's historical tales and novels. Intending to renovate the German national spirit through a favorably colored retrospect of Kaiser and Reich, he dictates to the reader his own standards of credibility that customarily transcend the "reality-determining consensus" of even the most indulgent reader.[3] And yet, as virtual father of the historical novella of the Romantic period, Arnim successfully broadened the interest in the glories of the German past to include the country's popular masses.

A novel with the prolix title Countess Dolores' Poverty, Wealth, Guilt and Atonement (1819) received an accolade from Eichendorff for its religious and moral message; but the improbabilities, coincidences and laboriously stretched-out digressions make it an example of unpardonable literary self-indulgence and intentional formlessness reminiscent of Brentano's non-novel Godwi. Its message is clear: The countess' one and only indiscretion brings about a gradual disintegration of her world.

The novella Isabel the Gypsy (1812) produces in a rather more economical mode the same effect as the Dolores novel. The author follows a folk tradition about a youthful escapade of the Habsburg prince Charles (eventually Emperor Charles V), with a princess of the Gypsies; the anecdote is enriched with an apparatus of "golems" and "mandrakes."

The Mad Veteran at Fort Ratonneau (1818) shows greater promise. The plot is once again drawn from folklore; its weirdness brings it very close to the horror tales of Hoffmann without allowing the triumph of evil to endure nor remain grotesquely inexplicable; a convenient miracle cures the hero's insanity.

The best of Arnim's prose works is indisputably The Guardians of the Crown (1817). The second volume remained a fragment[4]; the book is well documented, especially in the detailed and exact descriptions of the customs of the early sixteenth century drawn from the chronicles of the day. Once again, the realist depiction of characters and the convincing local color clash with gratuitous oddities of the plot. A secret society of self-appointed guardians of the crown of the realm groom a scion of the Hohenstaufen family to replace the well-entrenched and powerful Habsburg dynasty. The machinations of the crown-guardians are laced with "mystifications and supernatural agencies," sure signs of the Romantic inability to tell a tale for its own sake.[5]" The novel hints that the glories of the Empire can be revived as long as there remains a living tradition upheld by a handful of faithful defendants of the realm. This thesis fails both as convincing literature and, especially, as inspiration to political action in Arnim's own times.

The antiquarian and ethnic enthusiasm derives from the author's exposure to the folk vein; yet his defense of the monarchic institution would concede some civic rights to all subjects. This seems to indicate that each individual can become free to the extent commensurate to his lights and station in life; the monarchic principle would thus find new vigor and authentication in a culturally awakened and spiritually renewed citizenry. Arnim was fully convinced that a national and institutional renewal could be achieved by acquainting Germany with her imperial past seen through the ingenuous eyes of folk poetry.

As playwright Arnim has to his credit an impressive number of dramas; he had the flare for the dramatic but his plays suffer from the same diffusion of effort in building dramatic plots as do his novels. He has a great ability in handling what is known in Spanish literature as <u>género chico</u>, the "small genre." He succeeds best in the hybrid combination of historical "drama" and puppet play, a dramatic equivalent of his fairy-tale-like <u>novella</u>. Like Tieck and Brentano, Arnim mismanaged Shakespeare's Renaissance (and Baroque) universality of varying moods, lyrical and narrative passages, psychological insights and reflective soliloquies. Shakespeare -- and for that matter, Calderón and Lope de Vega -- were able to blend these elements into a homogeneous and pre-eminently dramatic whole; the Romantics tended to produce a confusing medley of mutually cancelling impressions, no more than "interesting," sometimes ironically playful, sometimes gruesome vignettes.

In 1813, Arnim published a collection of such shorter plays under the title Die Schaubühne (The Dramatic Stage). They resemble somewhat the entremeses[6] of the Spanish Golden Age, but are actually spin-offs of seventeenth century English plays and Shrovetide farces;[7] some were reenactments of actual historical events with a tragic outcome, such as The Appelmann Family. As in his short prose, Arnim delights in these minor plays in a sharp juxtapositian of the broadly comic with the tragic and gruesome.

Full-scale historical and religious dramas that came from Arnim's pen are ambitious in sweep and message. Critics agree they were intended to be Lesedramen, plays to be read, not staged. Such is Halle and Jerusalem (1811). As indicated earlier, it was directly inspired by a play by Andreas Gryphius.[8] Even though the drama is brought "up to date" in terms of pure chronology (the plot unfolds in the Napoleonic era), the Baroque world view of mundane vanities is, intentionally or not, preserved. Like a Baroque hero, Cardenio's lofty, steadfast nature clashes with the mundane baseness of his surroundings. He is crushed by being unable to either overcome it or to come to terms with it.[9] The play follows through the call sounded in Countess Dolores for the renewal of traditional Christian values put into jeopardy by the French Revolution and Wertherian narcissism. Like the novel, it fails as both literature and propaganda piece. Due to its diffuse structure it also fails at its intent to render what Oskar Walzel calls "the profusion of life itself,[10]" succeeding only in individual scenes which bring to life convincing tableaux of enlightened sensibility which filled the final decades of the eighteenth century as it was phasing out into the raptures of young Goethe's Storm-and-Stress experience.

In the posthumously published drama entitled <u>Margrave Carl Philipp von Brandenburg</u> (1848) Arnim appears to have overcome most of his dramatic weaknesses. It is less diffuse, shorter and less ambitious in its historic sweep, well constructed and even though the casual linkage shows some of the incongruities typical of Arnim, the conflict between love and duty experienced by Philipp, the youngest son of the Great Elector, Friedrich Wilhelm (1640-88) of Brandenburg, is believably handled and touches the chords of universal human suffering, a talent Arnim so much admired in his great models Shakespeare and Calderón.

Arnim the lyrical poet, too, is uneven in his endowments and achievements. Gillian Rodger accuses him of "banality and dullness;[11]" Walzel, of being "ponderous and awkward.[12]" In addition, Walzel claims Arnim "does violence to the rhythm of the folk song," and seems to have made, together with Brentano, "the unintelligibility" of folk poetry preeminently the essence of the genre, espousing it, not infrequently, as a guiding principle in his own original poetic creations.[13]

But Brentano and Arnim succeeded in enriching the folk paraphrases of the Romantics by successfully adopting the Spanish "trochaic four-line stanza" rhymed, assonated and sometimes "rhymeless.[14]" As indicated in the preceding analysis of Brentano's lyric poetry, a case in point is Brentano's <u>Romances of the Rosary</u>. In the Eighth Romance octasyllabic verses rhyme intricately first as an inner, in-stanza consonance; secondly, they are externally assonated, i.e., between the stanzas throughout the poem. But in the Rhinelore poems ("On the Rhine" and "Lore Lay") Brentano prefers the heptasyllable with perfectly consonated, alternating <u>ab</u> <u>ab</u> rhyme endings.

"Too Light it is For Sleeping" is an example of Arnim's employment of the same heptasyllabic four-line stanza with alternating female-male endings. It is a simple, direct invocation of the beloved by her lover who is dazzled by her perfection to the point of losing sight of all imperfections in the beloved, in his own ecstasy and in the rest of the world which exists for him only in so far as it is filtered through her presence.

"Keep Beckoning, Trees, You that Listen" recalls vaguely a shorter poem by the Baroque poet Johann Klaj (1616-56) entitled "Landscape.[15]" The lyrical I which plays the key role in Arnim's poem is of course absent in the object-oriented effusions of Klaj; the similarity ends with the apostrophy to the landscape. The motif -- and motive -- of Arnim's subjectively-colored nature impressions is summarized in two short lines

> Feel, this instant,
> How I'm alone.

"It Feels Sultry on the Earth" is a song of water sprites celebrating the realm of perfection so dear to all Romantics, and usually relegated to the unattainable beyond, or enjoyed all-too-briefly in a rare irruption of eternity into the time dimension. Here Arnim endows the realm of the watery deep with all the virtues vainly craved on dry land. The poem fairly leaps with the motion of never-quiet water: planets gladly dip into it, all the treasures available on land come eventually to rest at the sea's bottom, as storms never cease to "send new guests."

Yet continuous, joyful motion doesn't exclude quietude. No weeping children, no love pangs, no cries of jealousy disturb the whirl of merrymaking, touched by the storms unsettling the world above only as a "glancing" effect that simply serves to cool off the underwater revellers.

A lilting, repetitious ditty that opens with

"And so You're not Forsaken," exemplifies the festive banter that is one of the mood-setting traits in the novel Countess Dolores. Cast, like Brentano's "The Song of the Spinning Woman," in four heptasyllabic stanzas, rhyming once again ab, ab and alternating female and male rhymes, it elaborates the conceit of two lovers who make up after a separation and, perhaps, an act of infidelity. The first line of each of the four stanzas ends in "forsaken" (verloren, in the German original); in fact, the first stanza repeats it again at the end of the third verse.[16] Nothing much happens here aside from the fact that one of the lovers went astray ("Within myself forsaken") in the hostile world of inner feelings and outer blandishments; quickly disabused, fooled and abandoned by the escapade, the inner voice of truth brought the straying lover back; faith indeed had been "forsaken;" but stronger than faith is love which cannot ever be forsaken permanently, because it alone is eternal.

The Brandenburg gentleman Arnim shows, for all the unruly structure of his affects that produced works of amorphous and hence, ineffective grandeur, that in moments of intimate empathy with things and feelings his poetry can be as touching as the anonymous voices of the folk psyche which he had helped to salvage for posterity.

NOTES

[1] "The Novelle," The Romantic Period in Germany, ed. Siegbert Prawer (New York: Shocken Books, 1970), 141.

[2] Johann Wolfgang Goethe, Werke, ed. Erich Trunz (Hamburg: Wegner, 1951), VI, 209.

[3] Horst-Jürgen Gerigk, Entwurf einer Theorie des literarischen Gebildes (Berlin: Walter de Gruyter, 1975), 26 ff.

[4] The second unfinished volume was published posthumously in 1854. It was intended to reinterpret the first part as "an hallucination and allegory." Cf. L.A. Willouhgby, The Romantic Movement in Germany, 109.

[5] Ibid.

[6] They were one-act "inserts," often farcical and always moralizing, sandwiched between acts of the longer and more serious comedias. They were calculated to provide comic relief and were customarily unrelated to the plot or thesis of the main play. Cervantes was one of the masters of this subgenre.

[7] Roger Paulin, "The Drama," Cf. Prawer, op. cit., 197.

[8] Supra, "Periodization of the Romantic Movement."

[9] Paulin recognizes this when he claims that the drama, "with its symbolical pilgrimage to forgiveness and grace, owes more to Calderón" than Shakespeare. Cf. "The Drama," op. cit., 198.

[10] German Romanticism, trans. Alma Elise Lussky (New York: Frederic Ungar, 1965), 272.

[11] "The Lyric," Cf. Prawer, op. cit., 150.

[12] Walzel, op. cit., 155.

[13] Ibid., 152-53.

[14] Ibid., 160.

[15] Klaj's shorter poem is an ecstatic descriptive praise of nature's vegetal beauty.

> Oh, silver bedazzling, in you are converging
> The knotty, broad shadows of linden trees,
>   surging!
> Gentle and cool unperturbed is your call,
> Acknowledged by all!
>
> What paint brush could render, through artifice clever
> Your leaves' against sunrays protective endeavor?
> None of your tree trunks with green which is graced
> The order effaced.

[16] The repetition of *allein*, "alone," at the end of the fourth verse of the second stanza and of the second verse of the third stanza is rendered as "nigh" and "I," respectively, in my translation, thus breaking the rhyme identity of the original; however, the lost verse identity was compensated by another one between the second verse of the second stanza and the second verse of the third stanza, both ending in my translation in "I," as opposed to the *hinein* (into) and *allein* (alone) of the German original.

CHAPTER VI

CULMINATION AND LEVELING OF THE ROMANTIC PATHOS.

1. Chamisso, Uhland and Eichendorff. Reconciliation of Romantic Yearning with Nature and Reality.

    The three poets who brought High Romanticism to maturation differed widely in their regional and even ethnic backgrounds. Chamisso was a son of French emigrés from the Lorraine region and an adoptive Berliner; Uhland was as firmly rooted in his Swabian regionality as Chamisso was ambiguous about his Prussian identity. Eichendorff remained throughout his life faithful to his native Silesia the memory of which continued to spark his poetic imagination. He shared with Chamisso the fondness of a childhood spent at an ancestral castle and the yearning for a return to a happier past. Unlike the skeptic French-Prussian Chamisso and the political <u>homme engagé</u> Uhland, Eichendorff was the least "alienated" of the three, at least in terms of his secure, sometimes naive intuition of a World Ground sustained by traditionalist Catholicism. Unlike their non-conformist and often narcissistically self-destructive predecessors of Tieck's and Brentano's ilk, all three had a stake in the new Germany evolving from the chaos of the Wars of Liberation during the apogee and eventual disintegration of Bonapartist hegemony in Europe. As children of the Eighties of the Enlightened Century, they were able to work out a compromise with a reality to which each contributed according to his special talents. Chamisso as a Prussian officer and natural scientist, Uhland as lawyer, deputy of the newly-formed German Diet and university professor, and Eichendorff as volunteer militiaman and magistrate. Their positive attunement to everyday existence was faithfully reflected by the orderly nature of their literary endeavors.

    Rarely before and since have lyricists and balladists of the Romantic persuasion achieved such immediate and unstrained unity of subject matter and form, of feeling and convincing utterance, of atmosphere and musical coloring. They succeeded fully in capturing the need to concretize the unfulfilled and vague yearnings of their age for universal freedom and rationality. They viewed the creative process not as an absolute escape from reality per se but rather as a recreation of the beauties of a lived or imagined past. They were capable of calmly savoring the immediate presence of natural and psychological phenomena, and of sharing them with a wide and most appreciative audience.

Adelbert Chamisso (1781-38) soon gave up his military career, in part because he was caught in a conflict of loyalties between his French past and spirit, and his present allegiance to German Prussia; partly, too, the Prussian defeat in 1806 made him face squarely the futility of an armed solution of nationalist and libertarian aspirations.

After 1807 he developed close ties with Arnim, Brentano, Wilhelm Grimm, Kleist and T.A. Hoffmann. He was acquainted with the older Romantic generation's prophet August Wilhelm Schlegel, the latter's patroness Mme de Staël, as well as with his age peer Uhland. Between 1812-15 he studied medicine and botany and took part in Otto von Kotzebue's Russian-organized naval expedition around the world (1815-18) of which he left an insightful account (1821). Eventually, he was made curator of the Berlin Botanical Gardens.

Although all of Chamisso's writings prior to 1803 were done in French, his written (if not spoken) German places him high among the masters of simple, polished style. This may be partly due to an inherited, traditionally French _finesse_, a sense for incisive analysis, especially in matters involving human psychology, and knack for abstraction and precision in poetic expression.

Professor Danton calls Chamisso "a naive poet but a poet of many moods,[1]" referring to a talent that could be further defined as a _precise suggestivity of the vaguest of moods_. This aptitude Chamisso shares with the poet of Silesian forest beauties and fellow-aristocrat Eichendorff.

The term "castle Romanticism" has been used in a derogatory sense to describe the Romantic obsession with all things medieval. It implies a more or less mannerized, "precious" evocation of the knightly Middle Ages, calculated to flatter the pre-and misconceptions of the broadest popular masses concerning the age of chivalry. It should not be applied to Chamisso's poetry nor, for that matter, to Eichendorff's, even though the typical "castle" vision figures frequently in their respective poetic worlds. Uhland's more premeditated balladry runs the risk of becoming topical and, at times, almost didactic and hence open to the application of the term.

The degree to which the three poets succeeded in evoking the past and nature, specifically through the introduction of ruins of a mighty past as symbol of man's futile endeavor to make his creations endure, depends on their respective lyrical endowments. In Uhland's ballad, the epic rules the lyrical elements; Eichendorff achieves the closest embodiment of a purely lyrical world perception, but it is Chamisso who maintains a virtually perfect balance between the narrative and the personally evocative feeling of nature as the great leveler of human ambition.[2] Of the three Chamisso tends, like his younger contemporary von Platen, to the classical balance between emotion <u>qua</u> content, and restraint in the verbal expression of emotion. Eichendorff's nature realism serves only to reinforce the radically Romantic core of his poetic soul; Uhland's drive for the preservation and restoration of ancient "Swabian" virtues makes him the more <u>engagé</u> and didactic, and thus lyrically less moving of the three.

Adelbert Chamisso gained world-wide fame with the earlier-mentioned fairy tale-<u>novella</u> <u>The Wondrous Story of Peter Schlemihl</u> (1814). For his hero's name he chose the ambiguous Hebrew word <u>shelumiel</u> which can mean either "lover of God," or an awkward, bungling fellow. As the equivalent to the Greek Theophilus, Schlemihl shares with Goethe's Faust[3] a love-hate struggle with and for the Absolute; but, as an uprooted ne'er-do-well, he fails in every undertaking, great or small. This inadaptability to life's realities is more than a distorted and vulgarized mirror image of Faust's Titanism; selling one's inner essence reflected by the insubstantial but psychologically indispensable personal shadow is an authentic act of metaphysical hybris. This "lover of God" who would secularize the transcendent goal of his love to enjoy it in this world is, in the final analysis, a monstrous bungler. More clearly than the theoretical framers of Romanticism à la Fichte, the Schlegels and Hegel, Chamisso realized the psychological derailment produced in the Romantic psyche by the dilemma between the imperative of "Apocalypse now!" and its implementation by a creative act of will.

The complex structure of "Schlemihlism" arises quite naturally from Chamisso's personal alienation from his native France and a permanent feeling of unease about his German environment; but disenchantment with life as a struggle for identity that plagued the European West in the first decades of the nineteenth century had universal appeal. It was especially the failure, first of the French Revolution and then of Bonapartism, to rectify the basic iniquities of Western society that led to despair over continually frustrated expectations of a more meaningful, rational and free existence for everyone. More specifically, it was the Napoleonic phenomenon that exacerbated the feeling of frustration with the choice facing the young, the ambitious and the sensitive. This choice really was a dilemma between the short-lived and deadly glory of the naive conqueror, and the wise, calm but ineffective life of contemplation. This particular problem continued to plague the European consciousness well into the so-called realist era; it finds its most successful representation in Stendhal's novels.[4]

The popular tone of the narrative and the down-to-earth problems that face and defeat Chamisso's original antihero lend to the novel's formal dimension an aura of realism, rarely found in his predecessors and contemporaries, with the exception of E.T.A. Hoffmann. To some extent, Uhland and especially Eichendorff show a similar sobering trend in the evaluation of, respectively, the heroic past and as nature molders of the "modern" psyche of Western man. In Hoffmann's short stories, the realistic detail in the description of natural objects and psychic processes clashes with the constant threat and actual incursion of the eerie and diabolic, producing a grotesque distortion of existence which is of course totally alien to Uhland's evocative medievalism and Eichendorff's immersion into soothing, if melancholic <u>Waldrauschen,</u> "forest murmurs."

"The Women of Weinsberg" is a good example of Chamisso's view of the dynastic struggle for control of the medieval Empire and of human nature in general. Like Uhland, Chamisso uses a modified <u>Nibelungen</u> stanza,[5] to formally punctuate the sturdy if somewhat somber steadfastness of the imperial order. The "king's equity" overrules the casuistry of an unfeeling bureaucracy; even if the women of Weinsberg bend King Conrad's[6] decree allowing free passage for their prize possessions to include their husbands, the humane broadening of the king's intent by his subjects is backed up by the unshakeable commitment that is the royal word.

>What spoken is, is spoken, good holds
>   the ruler's word,
>And never by a chancellor explained
>   away or blurred.

"You My Belovèd German Fatherland" is self-explanatory.[7] The poem "Boncourt Castle" (1827) is dedicated to Chamisso's birthplace in the Champagne province of France. It is a fine, unobtrusive evocation of the past, dead and gone forever, that transcends faddish "castle Romanticism." Without pose-striking and lamenting, the entire castle scenery is gradually brought to life in an exact, perceptual reconstruction of the castle's physical layout. The eye of the narrator proceeds like a panning camera from the castle's forest-setting down to the minutest detail of battlements, stone bridge, escutcheon, courtyard, and chapel, with the ancestral crypt, tomb inscription and stained-glass window. The poem ends on a reconciling note: time devours and changes all; the glory and elegance of the <u>ancien régime</u> have been transformed into dirt and dust, but its essence, the memory in the poet's mind, continues to live in the ruins' earthly existence, now likely transformed into a fruitful, tilled field. The essence of the physical setting of the poet's youth is transfigured and preserved in the indestructible soil of France. The poet will fulfill his destiny as a roaming minstrel (a topic image dear to Uhland and Eichendorff), "to sing from land to land" his sad but reconciled love for all that is beautiful and perishable, preserving it by a humble acceptance of the process of perennial transformation.[8] Though influenced by Friedrich Schlegel, Chamisso points the way for the later Romantics away from the grandiose demands laid on poetry as a means to a cosmic apocalypse preached by the earlier, more speculative Romantic school.

The cyclus "Love of Life and Ladies" (1830) has lost much of its appeal to the modern reader due to the somewhat contrived sound and feeling of its short vignettes patterned after the Frauenlob, the Cult of Ladies, an aspect of the minnesong of the High Middle Ages.[9] It holds a permanent position among the Lieder, "songs," a genre peculiar to German Romanticism. Many, if not most of the Romantic lyrics and ballads owe their international notoriety to composers like Schumann who set the above cyclus to music (1830). However, "You Ring Around my Finger" has merit of its own as a further example of Chamisso's unfeigned acceptance of the flux of time and change that alters all. The ring becomes simultaneously a symbol of surrender and resistance to the constant transfiguration of reality, a "confirmation" of "life's infinite value" which is dedication to and acceptance of the phenomenon of existence as such, beyond any rational or ethical explanation.

"The Cross Review" shows Chamisso's mastery of rigorous poetic form, this time of an Italianate variety, adopted from Dante. His variant of the terza rima calls for an alternating hendeca-decasyllabic verse with correspondingly alternating female-male rhymes of the aba, bcb, cdc pattern. The form is handled so smoothly and surely that it sounds indigenous to German and yet it throbs with a subdued but sonorous Dantesque grandeur, a challenge to suffering and the final, inevitable acceptance of the human lot as a Calvary shared by all, with no cross lighter than any other. It seems as if "The Cross Review" were the decisive submission of Chamisso's French spirit to a still alienating but acceptable journey through a German existence.

Ludwig Uhland (1787-62) was the foremost balladist of German Romanticism. His poetry is paradigmatic of the earlier-mentioned "castle Romanticism;" in Uhland's case the term has mostly a positive connotation.

A lawyer with a degree from his native Tübingen in Swabia Uhland spent little time practicing law. Most of his energies were dedicated to literary research pursued at home and in Paris (1810-11). A freethinking deputy of the Würtenberg Diet in 1819, and professor of German studies at Tübingen a decade later he became an uncompromising defender of political liberalism. This put an early end to his teaching career, but eventually gained him national prominence as a liberal Deputy to the National Assembly at Frankfurt in 1848. He identified with the Pan-Germanic faction of the Assembly which advocated the inclusion of Austria in a future Greater Germany. A Swabian regionalist by temperament, his liberalism had strong traditionalist overtones: he opposed bicameralism yet in spite of his Pan-Germanist stance, he considered the old Swabian virtues of staunch probity and solid, sometimes stolid, simplicity and joviality unequalled by any race, inside or outside Germany.

The Biedermeier life-and-furniture style that had arisen as a reaction to Napoleon out of the spirit of the Congress of Vienna was a popularized and vulgarized version of Uhland's tenets. After the dissolution of the Rump Parliament of Stuttgart in 1849 Uhland returned to Tübingen to become the crowning phenomenon of "Swabian Romanticism."

The first collection of his poems appeared in 1815. His rich poetic output was paralleled by works of scholarly nature.[10] In his later years (1844-45) he edited a collection of High and Low German Lieder; the much earlier Patriotic Poems (1816) attracted some attention;[11] he was even less successful with his dramas Ernest, Duke of Swabia (1817) and Louis the Bavarian (1819). His lasting fame among German Romantics he owes to his balladry and to songs written in the popular vein. Together with Chamisso he typifies the late-Romantic trend toward lyrico-epic and lyric poetry which accompanied the decline of the speculative and artistically dilettantist universalism of the Early Romantics.

"The Minstrel's Curse" is a poem which has earned a permanent place in all poetic anthologies of German literature. It features the best and certainly the most typical elements of the Romantic medievalist mania: strong, repetitious and often mannerized contrasts. The poem is structured entirely on the tension between barbaric autocracy in a stylized mythical far North, and the civilizing influence of minstrelsy, between young and old, the optimism of youth and the death anticipation of old age, between the violent caprice of the male and the civilizing influence of the female element, between raw force, blind to the meaning of existence, and life's only true and sufficient interpretation through the medium of art. A perfect blending of the visual-colorful and sonorous-musical devices gives especially this ballad (or verse narrative) an unparalleled plastic profile. The rhythmic construct of the Nibelung stanza,[12] modified to suit Romantic sensibilities so aptly used in Chamisso's "Women of Weinsberg," adds its heavy-footed yet supple flow to Uhland's poem. Only Heine could compete with the Swabian master of the German idiom in coining colorful word compounds which became permanent additions to the German vocabulary.[13]

More uncanny than the full and usually effective exploitation of the emotional load of the linguistic commonplaces of the Romantic world view is Uhland's prophetic vision of a Nordic country, cursed with historical obliteration by a systematic destruction of its own highest truths, those that transcend abstract propagandism and blinding chauvinism. We are of course referring to the Nazi experiment with "The

Myth of the Twentieth Century." Even now, almost half a century after the genocidal insanity of elitist racism had been wiped off the face of the earth, German humanists feel as a rule uncomfortable about the nationalistic ardor of the Wars of Liberation, the extolling of German virtues, and the concept of the Nordic race per se. The obvious implications of Herderian, Fichtean, even Hegelian transcendental idealism, including even -- and, most undeservedly, due to a gross misinterpretation by the Nazis -- Nietzschean <u>cultural</u> (!!) vitalism, still rest buried in a historical limbo, in an oblivion due to choice, imposed by the mythology of violence for violence's sake. The neurotic drive for questionable biological and cultural excellence, the latter explained as a genetically-produced racial phenomenon, lies buried under a pall of shame, together with many indisputably excellent qualities which had been literally cursed by Germany's own best "minstrels[14]" just before and during World War II.

In "A Castle on the Sea" Uhland demonstrates a rare lyrical ability to express plastically the Romantic mood of the sweet futility of power, glory, splendor, youth and happiness. The narrative and the reality of a dream castle on the sea dissolve completely in a drive to achieve and reconcile the existential antinomy which throbs in all romantically-viewed life phenomena. It is Hegel's and Fichte's need for the final and all-embracing reconciliation of Ego = Ego = World as Ego, "a real difference without distinction." Uhland's seemingly innocent poem parallels the complex speculative insights into the infinite dialectic process of self-reconciling opposites in the world of finite phenomena. Uhland's castle yearns to embrace "the sea below" and to become one with it; the gold and rose hues are blending; the moon bends toward the castle, even as the fogs are swallowing both. The poem is cast in the form of a dialogue between an earlier, or simply differently seeing observer, and his dialectic counterpart who recognizes only the <u>Nachtseite</u>, the night face or aspect, of the idealized castle scene. The wind and the waves are silent; no sound of merrymaking, but a dirge drifts from the fog-crowded castle, the sun-like, radiant princess has faded like the sheen of the crowns of her royal parents. Love, light and happiness exist only insofar as they are aufgehoben, i.e., cancelled, preserved and finally, raised to a higher existence, which necessarily implies the annihilation of the finite, world-immanent individual.

"The Landlady's Daughter" is another permanent fixture of German balladist repertory. The recurring and usually consecutive sequence of three dactyls[15] sometimes interrupted by a trochee, and the perfectly consonated male rhyme endings convey the feeling of eternity being accomplished in the here-and-now. The triadically graduated and thus potentialized sequence of love declarations, of which the third one fuses past, present and future, love eternal and love-in-death, serves to further enhance the impression of time intersecting with eternity.

A totally different atmosphere pervades "The Blacksmith," where the "daylight" facet of the Romantic idealization of industrious and forceful manliness predominates. The female element joyfully accepts the not-so-ideal trappings such as the noise and soot as concomitants of the high-shooting flames, fanned by the lover's manly vigor.

In "The Revenge," Uhland uses once more the Nibelung strophe[16] to hammer home the efficacy of direct and prompt justice pervading the Christian-medieval order. Even though not necessarily of a transcendently providential origin, justice is done through the efficacy of faith. So deeply ingrained is faith in absolute justice in the world of knightly virtue it affects even the criminal, for even he wishes to be a knight in shining armor. He pays for this ambition, warped by the need to restructure the knightly order to his needs, immediately, fully and without a chance for appeal. Uhland's choice of the topic reflects his unshakable faith in the traditionally Germanic -- and specifically Swabian -- openness to a Ground of existence which underlies the concepts of good and evil.

"Siegfried's Sword" runs even deeper in its implications for a normative assessment of the Germanic character seen through the prism of the Siegfried myth. Youthful, lusty, proud, self-confident, totally oblivious of any limitations, invulnerable except to deceit and envy, this is Siegfried and his hybris. It suggests insensitivity to others, lack of tact, absence of classical measure, a destructive and self-destructive Titanism, shown off, almost unconsciously and certainly naively, for the whole world to see.[17]

"Swabian Lore" shows once more Uhland the perennial admirer of Swabian restraint, directness, openness, patience, stolidity and, in case of clear and present danger, swift, ruthless and effective action. The description engages just as openly and directly in macabre detail that borders on the grotesque. Still, and somehow because of it, it gives the impression of an unembellished, factual account which shies from any kind of euphemism about war and heroism.[18]

In "Bertran de Born" Uhland turns to the Provençal past to once again bring to light the force of art, music and their civilizing virtues, endemic to the chivalrous Middle Ages and not limited to the Germanic North. He chooses, most appropriately, a variant of the Spanish heroic meter, the romance.[19] Bertran de Born's[20] hybris, his vaunt that he never needs more than half of the spirit with which he has been endowed, drives him into rebellion against his liege. The king is jealous of the minstrel's spiritual strength and control over the king's own daughter and son. The tragic flaws of both cancel each other. The king loses his son in a military action instigated by Bertran, and the latter, his castle and reputation for invincibility. Yet both are redeemed; for they are noblemen whose knightly pride is balanced out by Christian humility. The minstrel advises the victorious king that his own spirit, half or whole, was not in the fight against a liege, the death of whose son weighs on his conscience; the king recognizes the nobility of his adversary, as well as the magic force of music that preserves its integrity even in the defeat of the artist. Chastened by his own and his enemy's loss, the king pardons the minstrel, bowing to the force of art, of which Bertran is merely an instrument. Uhland, the minstrel of Swabian military prowess, bows himself to the magic of music which triumphs in the non-Germanic setting of the elegant Latin South, transcending all ethnic differences and peculiarities.

If Uhland was the prime representative of "castle Romanticism," Joseph von Eichendorff (1788-57) became the master-lyricist who brought to perfection the evocation of the "Romantic landscape," in both the outwardly descriptive and the inwardly suggestive psychological sense. The outwardly descriptive landscape experience is traced easily enough to the role the poet's native Silesia played in his aesthetic formation. Like Chamisso's castle Boncourt, lost forever through political upheavals and the revolution of time, Eichendorff's birthplace, the castle of Lubowitz near Ratibor, provided the physical stimuli to his imagination and the deep-seated intimations of the hidden nature of things which defies direct communication. References to Eichendorff's "unpremeditated" response to the folksong, and his "naive" and "pure" poetic sensibility[21] have some merit; but, unqualified, they could easily make Eichendorff's poetry look like subjectively spontaneous and self-fulfilling, unfeigned confessions, resembling Goethe's "May Song.[22]" Nothing could be farther from truth; Eichendorff's "direct" communications of experience summarized as _Waldrauschen_," "forest murmurs," are essentially revelations of an inner, psychological landscape. Hence Gillian Rodger's characterization of Eichendorff's principal poetic quality as "indirectness[23]" must be adduced in order to modify the interpretation of Eichendorff's poetry as a pure and "unpremeditated" response to strictly "natural," i.e., external phenomena.

A scion of old Silesian nobility, Eichendorff studied law and philosophy, first at Halle, then at Heidelberg where he made the acquaintance of Görres, Achim von Arnim and Brentano.

Later on, in Berlin, he met Friedrich Schlegel, but Tieck's and Brentano's active involvement in the revival of the spirt of folk poetry influenced more decisively his poetic production than abstract theorizing. Danton argues that Eichendorff succeeded where Tieck had failed, having achieved a "perfect musical synthesis" between melody and meaning thanks to an effective use of metric variations that break the monotony[24] of the folk prototype.[25]

In 1813 Eichendorff joined Lützow's Freikorps, an outfit of mounted volunteers to combat Napoleon;[26] the rest of his life was relatively uneventful. He spent the years 1831-45 in Civil Service as magistrate of the Prussian Ministry of Education and lived his life out in simplicity, in an unfeigned, deeply experienced harmony with nature, thanks to his unassailable Catholic faith in God's creation as the best of all possible worlds.

This does not necessarily mean that Eichendorff's art and thought are free of doubts, apprehensions and an occasional flash of despair. It is precisely the pervasive feeling of universal futility which constantly threatens to upset his existential aplomb without ever overwhelming it. The tension between Nature and Spirit is synthesized in Eichendorff's poetry more solidly and convincingly than in the transcendentalist systems of Fichte, Hegel or Schelling. Professor Danton denies passion to Eichendorff's poetry; if passion is effusiveness and pose-striking, a mannerized affectation that often mars the poetry of the earlier Romantics, then it is lacking in Eichendorff, and its absence is a virtue. But Danton's claim that such poetry does not "subjectively portray the soul life of his author[27]" is misleading, unless the emphasis is placed on the subjective aspect of the representation. Eichendorff succeeds to disguise subjective attitudes through an apparently detached, descriptive objectivity of recurring nature themes: the rustling forests, and murmuring brooks, the echoes of the hunt and the hunter's or postman's horn, bells tolling in the distance, the songs of wanderers. These acoustic impressions are masterfully blended with visual themes: scenes of calm, silent decay, of the constructs of man's labors being literally overgrown with rampant nature, moonlight pouring over nocturnal stirrings and often quite uncanny, life-threatening processes. Eichendorff carries out the poet's function suggested by Novalis as the "deciphering" and "freeing" of nature through the poetic word or, as Volkmann-Schluck puts it,

> a transformation of objective nature in self-encounters of the spirit exclusively through the power of the word.[28]

What else would be these "self-encounters of the spirit" but moments of acute self-awareness, the true "soul life" of the poet? At the same time, they are the not always clearly defined self-transcending goals of Fichte's, Schelling's and Hegel's theorizing about a poetic transformation of reality. It is ironic that it should be Eichendorff, the deceptively straightforward and "objective" poet of brief, apparently simple nature vignettes who succeeds through the power of suggestion where the master-theoreticians of the Romantic movement failed, mostly due to the convoluted and circuitous nature of their speculations that tend to alienate the average reader.

Eichendorff's repeated elaborations of the "forest world" complex is only a vehicle of the movements of Eichendorff's soul, his apprehensions, hopes, fears, jubilations and grief. He himself defines the phenomenon of poetry as

> merely the _indirect_, that is the _physical_ presentation of the eternal, of the universally and timelessly significant.[29]

Such views indicate a great deal of speculative premeditation and hardly a spontaneous reaction to the simple beauties of nature. It is, least of all, an unreflected and imitative rendition of nature's colors and sounds. Eichendorff's Catholicism runs at times the risk of pantheism, but Divine Spirit and Nature remain separate entites for him, the former transcendent to the latter. At the same time, the spiritual does constantly permeate the material. It is the tension between this immanently filtered Presence of the Absolute, sensed in the depths of Eichendorff's soul, that accounts for the uncanniness of its apparently innocuous but omnipresent and affectively extremely forceful manifestations. The tension between this Presence and its material medium, Nature, produces that charm and shudder that pulsate through his poetry.

In addition, this existentially authentic and vivid, sometimes excruciating sense of tension gives the answer to the poet's invocation of the Absolute, something sought in vain by the infinitely more complex questioner of the cosmos Hölderlin. It also follows step by step his objectified self-projections into actual wanderers "envied" by the poet, or his own spiritual peregrinations, or even the yearning to go aimlessly roaming, as if competing with the flux of becoming. This often produces the effect of chaotic, compulsive traveling, running, passing and being passed, and longing for a constant, feverish change of scenery. Without imitating the repetitious refrains of the simple, untutored and often clumsy poetic devices of the folk song in the manner of Tieck, Brentano and Arnim, <u>Eichendorff's will to roam is a direct but intentional and wholly conscious reflection of the flux of life</u>.

Eichendorff's chief prose works, the fairy tale-novella <u>The Marble Statue</u> (1819) and the novel <u>The Life of a Good-for-nothing</u> (1826) deal with, each in its own way, this pursuit of the gratuitous flow of reality. The first reaffirms the superiority and triumph of Christian values over Bacchic revelry and pagan sensuality. The minstrel Fortunato breaks the spell of Venus with the aid of "another lady's image," the Marian symbol of chastity and compassion. The resolution of the tension between earthly, Graeco-pagan love and its Divine avatar parallels the clash between psychological and aesthetic value judgments of Goethe's and Schiller's <u>Klassik</u>, and the religious-traditionalist element of German Romanticism.[30] Yet Eichendorff could hardly be accused of asceticism;[31] his attunement to nature throbbing with a participatory but an essentially other-worldly spirit assures a sad and gentle acceptance of the burden of man's physical dimension and of its tormenting imperfections.

This truly realistic existential commitment to finiteness is reflected in the novel about a "good-for-nothing," amiable rogue. It is an unapologetic praise of indolence, remotely related to the picaresque genre.[32]

Clauss refers to the work as "one continuous allegro of _joie de vivre_,: reminiscent of the music of Haydn.[33] A nineteenth-century version of the Spanish _pícaro_, rogue, who was traditionally a servant of many masters and himself a master of survival, Eichendorff's "good-for-nothing" is his own master most of the time. His wanderlust reflects Eichendorff's own obsession with the unceasing flux of the phenomena. Willingly and with ease, he submits to it, practicing divine laziness[34] which is indeed a surrender of the self to the stream of becoming, to the dismay of all rationalizing and moralizing Philistines. Unlike the harshly tested _pícaros_ produced by Baroque life fatigue and spiritual elation toward perfection in the beyond, Eichendorff's engaging wastrel does not expect perfection in this world, yet never ceases to be showered with fortune's favors as a reward for his acceptance of life as it is. Eichendorff's world view allows for happiness through an attunement to life's iniquities and inequalities; there is no revolutionary Jacobinism in this most realistic of Romantic novels, no leveling of social classes and distinctions, no Storm and Stress drive for a divinely free, equal and fraternal tomorrow. The book is a sheer pleasure for a reader looking for an easy, entertaining escape from reality, itself realistically transformed into an acceptable existential proposition made even more pleasurable by the inclusion of some of Eichendorff's best songs.

Eichendorff's positive life-adjustment actually proved an obstacle to his becoming a great playwright. A cheerful reliance on a providentially structured universe was not enough to compensate for the lack of sense for the "drastic," a term used by Friedrich Schlegel[35] to designate the playwright's understanding of man's drive to action, with all the paradoxical and destructive horrors implied in his need to act consciously and effectively in order to reshape his environment to correspond to his idea of justice and happiness.

The Wooers (1833) is a light, lyrical comedy and, according to Willoughby, little more than "a graceful marivaudage."[36] War to the Philistines (1824) is a dramatized fairy tale in the vein of Tieck's Puss in Boots, aimed at the pedantry of literary critics. All considered, Eichendorff lacked both the vis comica, forceful dramatic wit, as well as a dramatically tragic sense of life.

His critical works The Ethical and Religious Meaning of the New Romantic Poetry in Germany (1847), and the History of German Poetic Literature (1857), demonstrate competent, meticulous scholarship and an imaginative synthesizing of literary-historic detail.

Eichendorff stands out of course among the best German lyricists of all times. The poem "Echoes" is a good example of the short, deceptively simple gems or cameos of feeling caught in its delicate immediacy. But, at the same time, it points to a commitment to the phenomenon of life accepted on its own inexplicable terms, yet experienced as uncanny and, in terms of individuality, as self-destructive. The poet dreams himself back to his youth for a leisurely enjoyment of life's plentitude, but the "blossom flakes" of naive happiness turn quickly into "flakes of ice," as sober reality tears the veil of the dream. The poem is cast in the earlier-mentioned hepta-hexasyllabic verse alternation,[37] consisting of two stanzas of eight perfectly rhymed lines each.

The rhythmic and stanzaic structure of "Yearning" is reminiscent of Chamisso's poem dedicated to the Boncourt castle.[38] It features most of the motifs of Eichendorff's repertory: the nocturnal silence suddenly broken by the sounds of human activity, indifferent to the pulse of natural processes. The solitary poet associates the post horn's distant tone with his own metaphysical escapism. The song of two wanderers conveys the message of the Romantic landscape which finds in this poem its fullest treatment: the wilderness of abyss and rustling forests, marble statues pointing back to aesthetically more sensitive times, now swallowed by burgeoning nature; a flash of beautiful maidens at the windows of moonlit palaces, the suggestion of lute music and the gurgle of wells, singing and complaining about life's flow, are all fused together in a three times repeated refrain at the end of each stanza:

In the glorious summer night.

"The Broken Ring" is another permanent fixture in every anthology of German verse. The poet reacts in the simplest fashion to the betrayal of his beloved by <u>wishing</u> to become an itinerant minstrel, but never actually departing. The mental representations of "yearning" are the only activity actually engaged in by the poet. He would go singing from house to house, he would ride with the troopers into battle; what he would like best, at least at this point of being devoured by existential despair, is to be rid of the burden of existence, to lapse into calm inertia. Throughout Eichendorff's poetry we encounter the conditional, "wishing" mood pervading his endeavors; the constantly repeated "as if" reflects the mere <u>suggestiveness</u> of the World Ground, as it manifests itself through and is answered by the stirring of his psyche. This is a state of indolence, but of the attentive kind, a conditioning to metaphysical receptivity and to the "openness of the soul."

The seven-line poematic miniature "The Evening" expresses perfectly this listening, attentive attitude. It is an attempt to catch and to pass on to the audience "the tender grieving" of ancient times, the "mute tremors" which make the breast swell "like summer lightning." "Moon Night" represents a further development of the evening mood of gently stirring nature, suggestive of the soul's need to transcend herself, to return to the Infinite One-and-All, in the Ground of things before it was differentiated into people, objects, thoughts and events.

"The Hermit" is a typical <u>Rollengedicht</u>, a poem of assumed personality by a poet who <u>identifies</u> with any one of a number of Romantically symbolic figures:

the hunter, the minstrel, the sailor, the wanderer, a knight sleeping on the lookout, apparently expecting some as yet undetermined event or danger. Here, the hermit figure, tired of the monotony of modern existence, has withdrawn to the forest solitude. He opens his soul to the language of the World Ground, invoking the "world's comfort," the calm of the night. Like the sailor worn out by his workaday activities, he praises the calm of the night, as the sum total of the regenerative powers capable of soothing man's existential anguish until the day of his definitive departure.

"The Night Flower" draws a parallel between night, the sea, the running clouds and the human heart; the parallel can be experienced by the heart only if we virtually "bracket out" the stifling egoism of our selfhood; only then do we realize that

> Quiet, in heart's inmost spot
> Goes on surf's soft palpitation.

"Beautiful Strange One" is a poem dedicated to the "fantastic night" astir with memories of departed gods and promises of some "great future fortune" for the poet, a fortune no doubt of a psychic and aesthetic nature. "In the Forest" is yet another short masterpiece,[39] an impressionistic flash of the passage of time and of man's joys and splendors; with the sudden appearance and disappearance of a wedding procession, the core of the poet's self-consciousness, his "inmost heart," gives a startled bound at the rapid transformation of the present into the past. "Twilight" continues to examine this dread, proceeding from the revolution of the hours, the drift of the clouds, and the constant danger of individuality confronted with universal existence which threatens to overwhelm the fragile standpoint of the human ego. No elaborate Hegelian synthesis of object with a self-reflecting subject can drive home as vividly the problem of finite individuality vis-à-vis the infinite than this deceptively simple ditty by Eichendorff.

"The Forest Discourse" is another simple and extremely suggestive variation on the Lorelei theme, broached by Brentano and eventually made world-famous by Heinrich Heine and the music of Franz Liszt. The simple closing lines, constructed as a partial refrain,

>It's late already, getting cold,
>You won't escape this forest's hold!

Suggest infinitely more than the death of an unsuspecting traveller at the hands of a notorious sorceress; here again the symbolic load of the Lorelei figure makes for a kind of role poem. She is all that is perfect, enchanting and sensually fulfilling in life -- and deadly to individual existence.

"Night Song" is yet another representation of the flux of time, life, friends, love, in the late Latin and medieval tradition of ubi sunt, "whither have they gone.[40]" Within the night stirrings of the natural processes a question is asked by the "tree" addressing "the field."

>Oh, human! What is it you dread?

The dissolution of this existential dread is simple for a man of Eichendorff's unshakable faith in a caring, transcendent Providence. The poet calls on the nightingale to join him in a hymn to the Creator until "dawn" comes. The concept of "dawn" embraces both the particular dawn following that particular night and the "dawn" of the poet's (and, eventually, the world's) transfiguration through death into life eternal.

"The Merry Wanderer" is one of Eichendorff's happy airs that became virtually a folk song. A short hymn celebrating the joy of flitting through God's creation, it affirms the positive value of all that the Lord chose to create.

"Sea Calm" introduces a topic most dear to the Romantics: a view from a ship of a city sunk in the sea. The theme attracted such masters of the lyric verse as Wilhelm Müller and Heine. Eichendorff's version centers around the dreamy figure of the old sea king, perched, "as if" asleep, "over a harp."

In his semiconscious dream state, he "seems" unaware of the busy ship traffic on the surface; yet he does hail ships that chance to pass closer to his reef, greeting them "like in a dream." The gossamer quality of the suggestions that offer themselves to the interpreter is almost too tenuous to analyze with any kind of analytical precision. All one is tempted to say about "Sea Calm" is that it is what it says; man's concerns do not reach the World Ground, except rarely. On such occasions, it acknowledges their fragmented, alienated egoes, "as if" in a dream, by hints and blurred visions.

"Divining Rod" is self-explanatory. Eichendorff defines poetry as the search for a magic key which is to free Spirit from its bondage in Nature, an insight shared by Novalis[41] and paralleled by Hegel's obsession with the secular apocalypse preached in his Phenomenology of the Spirit.[42]

"On the Death of My Child" represents a transfiguration of a personal tragedy into an existential statement about life and death in general.[43]

The poem consists of four sections. The first is the familiar eight-line stanza with alternating hepta-and hexasyllables. It marvels about the phenomenon of grief.

How soon all will be still!

repeating almost verbatim the last line of "The Broken Ring.[44]" The statement, as most of Eichendorff's lucubrations on existence, carries a specific and a universal meaning. Darkness is falling, the day has expired, yet the poet's grief continues unabated, in spite of the prospect of an imminent calming of most, perhaps all life processes in nightfall and death. The poet reminds himself that in view of the brevity of human life, his own as everyone's else's grief is indeed pointless.

The second section elaborates further on the slowing down of daily activities. This only frees the poet's mind for remembering his dead child. The two stanzas that make up this section consist of four lines each, thus equaling the verse number of the first. The verse length has been increased; octosyllables alternate with heptasyllables, with the usual ab ab rhyme pattern, but, unlike the iambic pattern of the first section, trochees are used throughout the second.

The third section is the longest. Returning to the verse length and metric pattern of the first, it consists of five four-line stanzas. It contains the essence of Eichendorff's grief. Life is "as if" a dream; the world goes its way in defiance of logic and feelings, which seems to be its essential purpose. The death of a child seems to have no significance in the scheme of things. The poet seeks distraction among "new things," in the life processes of nature, in the beauty of birdsong and of tearful flowers, in the lament of silently rustling treetops. All these manifestations of the eternal flux relieve somewhat his pain for they give him the assurance of being controlled by a universal, perhaps even benign force.

The third and last section continues the verse and metric pattern of the previous one. It brings to fruition the grief of the bereft parents. The striking clock marks the passage of time; a dim lamp shines on a bed, made up as if the child were to return, while the parents seem to wait for some signal from the outside that it is really so, that the child had only temporarily lost its way. The resolution of this self-delusion is simple and sober. It is not the dead child who had lost its bearings, but its parents, for it had found its way to its eternal home long before them.

"Abroad" is one more impressionist vignette dedicated to the irremediable flux of time. When one leaves the home of one's childhood, it is presumptuous to expect it to remain the same when one returns years later. There is only one consolation, that of the "lone forest mood." It will, in its own good time, becalm and silence the existential anguish of individuality, the poet's own as well as of those who had once known him.

"On a Castle" uses the octosyllabic trochees of the Spanish _romance_ throughout its four-line stanzas.[45] It produces an atmosphere similar to the dream mood that pulsated in "Sea Calm." While the processes of nature -- a shower falling in the distance and trees rustling through the grille -- run their automated course, the old knight, literally "overgrown" with time, slumbers away the centuries, apparently on the lookout for something or somebody, for what or for whom being quite irrelevant. Peace spreads over the entire scene, the people are gone, only birds cavort through the window arches. As so often in Eichendorff, the peacefulness of the scene is suddenly, but gently marred, first, by the incursion of the human element and, finally by a burst of grief, gratuitous and unexplained. While a merry wedding party floats down the Rhine amidst music and festivities, "the fair bride" sheds tears. For whom? The slumbering knight turned to stone, for the past splendors of a decaying castle, for herself, her lot which must proceed according to the ordinance of time? Eichendorff doesn't tell us explicitly, but hints here at the radically tragic sense of all things alive. The answer is the mood he produces and this makes him one of the leading lyrical poets of all times.

NOTES

[1] George H. Danton, "Later German Romanticism," <u>The German Classics. Masterpieces of German Literature Translated Into English</u> (New York: Ams Press 1969), V, 156. It is to be assumed that the author uses "naive" in the sense of Schiller's earlier-mentioned essay <u>On Naive and Sentimental Poetry</u>, meaning an immediate, automatic, almost involuntary and unconsciously inductive act of creation.

[2] The French lyricist, composer of popular Parisian airs and political poet Pierre Jean Béranger (1780-57) exerted a strong influence on Chamisso who admired his compatriot's light, facile Muse and dedicated Bonapartism. Chamisso translated Béranger's poetry into German; the work was published in 1838, the year of Chamisso's death.

[3] Danton, <u>The German Classics</u>, op. cit., 157.

[4] Called by the author "a chase after happiness," it is the fundamental theme of works such as <u>Red and Black</u> (1830) and <u>The Charterhouse of Parma</u> (1839).

[5] The original stanza used by the anomymous author of the <u>Nibelung</u> epos (1215 A.D.?) consisted of four lines with predominately male verse endings rhyming aa bb. Each verse (<u>Langzeile</u>, "long line") is in turn divided in two hemistichs (half-verses), the <u>Anvers</u>, "rising verse," and the <u>Abvers</u>, "falling verse." Most of the four rising verses have female endings; each has exactly three <u>Hebungen</u>, accentuated syllables; the number of unaccentuated syllables is arbitrary. Most falling verses are, as actual rhyme endings, male. The first three of each stanza contain, the same as the rising verse, three accentuated syllables. The last falling verse of every stanza adds a fourth accentuated syllable to the customary three; like all the rest of the hemistichs, the number of unaccentuated syllables is again arbitrary. The author has thus produced a sophisticated pattern of <u>repetitious regularity</u> which nevertheless allows within its strictly observed bounds so much room for

rhythmic variation (mostly due to the widely varying
unaccentuated syllables) that the result has an uncommonly musical, even haunting quality, a build-up
and decline reminiscent of the Baroque fugue. The
following is my translation of the second stanza of
a total of 1142 stanzas that constitute the epic's
first part entitled <u>The Death of Siegfried</u>.

> Of the nóblest stóck a máiden was
>   ráised in Búrgundý,
> Ín no óther cóuntry a préttier
>   thére could bé.
> Shé was cálled Kríemhilde and wás
>   a prétty máid.
> So mány mén on hér account wíth their
>   líves have déarly páid.

This rigid number of <u>Hebungen</u> and arbitrary number
of <u>Senkungen</u> is of course disregarded by the much
more regular thirteen-syllabic stanza used by
Chamisso and Uhland.

> Of Hóhenstáufen rúlers the fírst,
>   king Cónrad láy
> With troóps in frónt of Wéinsberg
>   for mány á long dáy.

Without exception, the rising verses consist of seven
syllables, three of them accentuated; all of the
sinking verses consist of six syllables, again, with
three accentuated ones each; as end-rhymes, all of
these sinking verses have male endings. This "Romantic streamlining" of the <u>Nibelung</u> stanza falls
far short of the rhythmic variations on the theme of
rigid regularity which only the peculiar genius of
Middle High German tonality was able to produce.

    [6] Conrad, founder of the Hohenstaufen dynasty,
had himself elected king in 1127 as Conrad III, in
opposition to the duly elected Lothair of Saxony
whom he fought to a standstill in 1135. The eight
years war was the beginning of the lengthy conflict
between the Hohenstaufen (Ghibelline) family and
their Guelph opponents which lasted well into the
fourteenth century. Conrad's claim to the German
crown was reconfirmed in 1138.

[7] The poem shows to what extent Chamisso identified with the pleasures, values and goals of the jovial Biedermeier life style. More on Biedermeier in the discussion of Uhland who came close to being its model embodiment.

[8] The poem is cast in four-line stanzas consisting of alternating octo-and heptasyllables, with correspondingly alternating female-male endings. The beginning syllable of each verse is unaccentuated; this produces a sequence of either one dactyl and two trochees, or two trochees and one dactyl. Even within these fairly restrictive confines the variation of the rhythmic pattern reproduces an undulating emotion restrainted by a firmly delineated and yet slightly meandering channel. Eichendorff adopted this pattern in some of his brief poems ("Yearning," "Beautiful Strange One," "Sea Calm," etc.) showing, however, a preference for a less lilting iambic hepta- and hexasyllabic combination.

[9] The *minnesong* was cultivated by *minnesingers*, a German variety of the Provençal troubadours who flourished from the twelfth to the fourteenth century. They were aristocratic poets and composers dedicated to the celebration of ideal beauty and its primary embodiment, the cultured, sensitive yet usually unattainable *frouwe*, lady.

[10] He wrote studies on the Old French Epic, on the last and greatest of all minnesingers Walter von der Vogelweide who flourished between 1190 and 1230, and on the myths underlying the Norse sagas about Thor, the god of thunder.

[11] As an attack on the French occupants of Germany, Uhland's patriotic poetry failed to produce a wave of enthusiasm with which the public greeted the invectives of another professor-poet Ernst Moritz Arndt (1769-60).

[12] Here consisting of verses of thirteen syllables each, with a break, usually after the seventh syllable, and rhyming aa bb etc.

[13] Uhland's Regenbogenglanz, rendered literally as "rainbow glow" (at the end of the first stanza of the "Minstrel's Curse") is echoed in Heine's Abendsonnenschein, literally "evening sunshine," which occurs in the second stanza of Heine's "Lorelei" version. My translation of Abendsonnenschein is the somewhat unsatisfying "sunset's glowing shine."

[14] An obvious example among many is Thomas Mann's novel Doctor Faustus (1947).

[15] Distinguished with a "free Auftakt," i.e., unaccentuated first syllable at the beginning of each verse. Once again, Uhland uses the modified Nibelung stanza, in this case foreshortened from thirteen to eleven syllables.

[16] In this case shortened to ten-and nine-syllabic verses of the rhyme pattern customary for the Nibelung stanza.

[17] The Nibelung stanza is shortened, almost beyond recognition, into octosyllabic, with few exceptions purely iambic verses, reminiscent, except for the absence of the assonance in even verse endings, of the Spanish heroic romance verse.

[18] The octosyllabic verse has mostly male endings with some female rhymes thrown in for variety's sake. This is the doggerel verse or Knittelvers in the best Germanic tradition which goes back to the Middle Ages. Goethe used it masterfully in parts of his Faust.

[19] Uhland substitutes perfectly consonated male endings for the assonated rhyme in even lines, the latter being the chief trait of the classical Spanish romance. He also broke the whole into stanzas, each of which repeats the same male consonance four times, in the second, fourth, sixth and eighth line. These even verses are actually hepta-or seven-syllabic. In Spanish and Italian metrics, each sharply accentuated male rhyme ending counts as two syllables, so that even in the even verses the octosyllabic pattern is preserved. Uhland's odd verses are fully octosyllabic, with female, unrhymed endings. The whole com-

position is structured on the basis of the number eight. There are eight stanzas, each consisting of eight octosyllabic lines.

[20] Vicomte d'Hautefort, (1140?-15), Provençal troubadour, was an older contemporary of Walter von der Vogelweide, and author of serventes, minnesongs of lady-service (idealized woman-worship). Like Walter, Bertran expressed in satirical verse his displeasure with the politics of his day. He actually intervened in the feud of Henry II of England with his sons, and sided with Raimund V, count of Toulouse against king Alfonso II of Aragon.

[21] Walter Clauss, Deutsche Literatur (Zurich: Schulthess, 1966), 219.

[22] This juxtaposition is made by Gillian Rodger in his essay "The Lyric," in Siegbert Prawer's The Romantic Period in Germany (New York: Shocken Books, 1970), 166. Rodger speaks of Goethe's lyric manner in the context of the "May Song" as "frankly subjective," "spontaneous" and "immediate," triggered by an actual love affair. Prawer in his own book on German Lyric Poetry (New York: Barnes and Noble, 1965), arrives essentially at the same conclusion in contrasting Brentano's "Song of the Spinning Woman" with Gretchen's "spinning song" from Faust. George H. Danton juxtaposes "Goethe's logic of description" and "inner objectivity," to the "haze of Eichendorff's landscapes." Cf. "Later German Romanticism," The German Classics, 149.

[23] Rodger, "The Lyric," op. cit., 165.

[24] "Later German Romanticism." loc. cit.

[25] It was this monotony that Tieck and Brentano had codified, to the detriment of their art, as an aesthetic maxim of the Romantic lyric. The best among German composers followed the urge to set Eichendorff's lyrics to music, chief among them Schumann and Hugo Wolf.

[26] One of the reasons he came to be called "the last knight of Romanticism" was the fact that he

missed the battle of Waterloo by one day. The other reason was his gentle, chivalric attitude befitting an ancien régime nobleman.

[27] "Later German Romanticism," loc. cit.

[28] Karl Heinz Volkmann-Schluck, "Novalis' magischer Idealismus," Die deutsche Romantik ed. Hans Steffen (Göttingen: Vandenhoeck and Ruprecht, 1967), 48.

[29] "Geschichte der poetischen Literatur Deutschlands," Neue Gesamt-Ausgabe der Werke und Schriften in vier Bänden, ed. Gerhart Baumann und Siegfried Grosse (Stuttgart: Cotta, 1958), IV, 25-26. My italics.

[30] The sympathies of the two principal poets of German Klassik are unabashedly pro-Hellenic and secularly humanitarian.

[31] Walter Clauss, Deutsche Literatur, 219.

[32] Initiated by the anonymous Spanish classic Lazarillo de Tormes (1554), the picaresque novel enjoyed popularity, especially in Spain and France. In Germany its best known representative is Christoffel von Grimmelshausen's Simplicissimus (1669-69).

[33] Clauss, ibid.

[34] A term coined by Friedrich Schlegel. Cf. Danton, The German Classics, 150.

[35] Schlegel gives the term an Aristotelian denotation. Both drama and drastic are, according to Aristotle, derived from the Doric verb dran, to act. Cf. "Poetics," The Works of Aristotle, ed. W.D. Ross (Oxford: The Clarendon Press, 1952) XI, chapter 3. Cf. L.A. Willoughby, The Romantic Movement in Germany (New York: Russel & Russel, 1966), 67.

[36] Pierre Carlet de Chamblain de Marivaux (1688-63) was the prototypical representative of early eighteenth-century enlightened sensibility which dissolved each affair of the heart into an acceptable

compromise with reality. "The heart," being the <u>grand frippon</u>, "the great rascal" that it is, had to be given its due, but the demands of the everyday sobering life experience had to be likewise met.

[37] See note no. 8.

[38] It features perfectly rhymed octosyllables alternating with heptasyllables in a female-male rhyme sequence of the ab ab pattern, cast in three stanzas, each consisting again of eight lines.

[39] Cast in a nine-syllabic verse with alternating male-female verse endings, forming two stanzas of four verses each.

[40] One of the best known elaborations of this topic is the "Ballad of Ladies of the Bygone Days" by the French poet-vagabond François Villon (1431-65?).

[41] See the last two verses of Novalis' "Song of the Hermit:" "Then, at a secret word you'll see/ The whole perverted being flee."

[42] See note no. 45. in I. GERMAN IDEALISM OF THE ROMANTIC ERA. "The single man can elevate himself to dominance... only if he knows the directions in which the great necessity wants to move and if he learns from this knowledge to pronounce the magic words that will evoke its shape." Johannes Hoffmeister, <u>Dokumente zu Hegels Entwicklung</u> (Stuttgart: 1936), 324. Cf. Eric Voegelin, "On Hegel, a Study in Sorcery," <u>Studium Generale</u>, 24, (1971), 341.

[43] Other poets who suffered the loss of a child were unable to find an equally conciliatory transformation of grief into art. Victor Hugo's "A Villequier" (1844-46) and "Demain, dès l'aube" (1847) is a case in point.

[44] Which reads, "Then quick all would be still."

[45] Eichendorff does not follow the strict pattern of the Spanish model. All of the odd lines have consonated verse endings, except in the third stanza

there is no rhyme at all; as in the Spanish romance, the even verses are merely assonated. In my rendition, the last stanza's second and fourth lines show also a consonated rhyme instead of a mere assonance.

2. Wilhelm Müller, Rückert and Von Platen. Stirrings of Realist and Classical Elements in the Romantic Mood.

Wilhelm Müller (1794-27) developed his poetic Muse as an epigon of the masters of imitative folk lyrics, Arnim, Brentano and Eichendorff. He studied history and philology in Berlin, fought in the Wars of Liberation (1813-14) and eventually found employment as librarian and Gymnasium teacher of classics in Dessau (1819).

A trip to Italy in 1817 produced a two-volume work entitled Rome, Romans and Roman Women (1820). A year later appeared a cyclus of poems under the unlikely title Poems from the Literary Remains of a Travelling French-Horn Player. His Songs of the Greeks, published also in 1821, show him to be an enthusiastic partisan of Greek independence. He mastered the Rollenlied, "role song" or Rollengedicht, cultivated by Eichendorff and other Berlin and Late Swabian Romanticists. He honed out his art of imitating the simple strains of folk poetry by translating Modern Greek and Italian folk songs.

His light, singable Lieder are dedicated mostly to the pleasures of travel and conviviality. Schubert set to music two of Müller's song cycles, The Pretty Miller Woman and Winter Journey. But only rarely did Müller's talent achieve the simple intimacy of the folk original. The photographic clarity of his sketches and the grinding regularity of his rhyme often border on the banal; the onomatopeic "realism" of his sound imitations is often contrived and even insincere.[1]

In "Vineta" we see at its best Müller's gift for atmosphere evocation. The even rhythmic flow of regular trochaic decasyllables and the rote-like repetition of consonated verses with alternating female-male endings is in perfect unison with the subject matter. The memory of the mythical city of Vineta[2] rises from the bottom of the sea, the same as long-forgotten memories rise to the surface of consciousness.[3] First, we have the muffled ring of its bells, then come the flashes of its gold-topped towers which remain standing even in the city's "sunken" state. Even as the sounds and flashes capture the "sailor's" heart, forcing him to return to the highly dangerous area of their emergence, so do the memories of past happiness and love invite the poet's conscious ego to immerse itself into the depth of the unconscious,

    Back into the ancient wonder town.

    Friedrich Rückert (1788-66) was known to some as the patriarch of Biedermeier family poetry. Actually his linguistic talents and scholarship, combined with a ready lyric inspiration, made him the indisputable master of experimentation with poetic form. He studied law at Würzburg until 1809 but switched to philology and aesthetics at Heidelberg. He taught briefly (1811-12) classical philology at Jena and later at Würzburg. Ill health kept him from an active involvement in the struggle against Napoleon. In 1816 he was for a brief time editor of the poetic section of a newspaper in Stuttgart. A year later he went to Italy and spent time with German artists living in Rome. In Vienna he came under the influence of the Orientalist Joseph von Hammer-Purgstall who led him to the study of the Persian language and literature. In 1826 he became professor of Oriental languages and literatures at the University of Erlangen and, following the invitation of King Wilhelm IV, he taught in Berlin (1841-48), before retiring to his estate at Neusess near Coburg in Upper Franconia.

    During the Wars of Liberation he circulated his first cycle of poems entitled <u>Sonnets in Armor</u> under a pseudonym. Expanded to include <u>Warlike Mock-and Honor Songs</u>, the <u>Sonnets</u> were republished in 1814 under the title <u>German Poems</u>. A second collection of poems called <u>Wreath of Time</u> followed, at last in Rückert's own name, in 1817.

    Between 1815-18 he also tried his hand at political comedy satirizing Napoleon. Like these imitations of Aristophanes, the historic dramas he wrote in the Forties met with little success.

Rückert's fame as poet rests on his original compositions as well as on translations and paraphrases of Oriental poetry. His brilliant linguistic talents led him to daring adaptations of Persian and Arabic poetic forms. In this he carried on labors initiated by Friedrich Schlegel and by Goethe's West-East Divan paraphrases.

In 1821 Rückert translated the Persian mystical poet Dzhelal ed-Din Rumi[4] which led to the introduction of the ghazel verse form[5] into German literature. Eastern Roses (1822) are paraphrases of Hafiz,[6] another poet of medieval Persia. The Transfigurations of Abu Seid of Serug (1826-37) imitates the Arabic makame.[7] Rückert achieved virtual independence from his Oriental models in The Wisdom of the Brahman (1836-39). A collection of fables, proverbs and narrations entirely of his invention, it offers a compendium of Oriental knowledge of man, God and the world.[8] In addition, Rückert undertook adaptations of Indian tales, of Hebrew prophets and of Chinese and ancient Arabic songs.

His original poetic work in German is vast.[9] Love's Spring (1823) was dedicated to his bride; Kindertotenlieder[10] (published posthumously in 1872) reflect the somewhat complacent and often smugly sentimental mood typical of the Biedermeier period; at any rate, these Lieder earned Rückert greater popularity than his patriotic songs, mostly due to a greater simplicity and directness he acquired as time went on. Though now dated, they excel in what may be Rückert's greatest and lasting poetic virtue: an ability to find poetic charm and value in the drabbest things and occurrences. They show acute psychology and a keen sense for the pulse of nature and of the cosmic forces.

Rückert's facile lyrical form made him a genial translator and popularizer of the Orient's most exotic poetic gems. Unfortunately, the substance of his poetry tends to be often swamped by lexical virtuosity and overly fanciful structural experimentation which ranged from the imitation of the simple folk ballad to the sonnet, the ottava rima and the poetic tale.

"Barbarossa" (1813) is one of those gems of the folk-imitating genre which has earned a permanent place in the Romantic repertory of ballads. Unlike Eichendorff's "On A Castle," Rückert's image of a slumbering king doesn't go much beyond a simple mood evocation in the framework of popular lore about the apocalyptic restorer of the Holy Roman Empire. According to legend, Emperor Frederick I Barbarossa[11] sleeps with a band of his knights in the Kyffhäuser mountain in Thuringia, ready to intervene when the time is ripe for the revival of Ghibelline magnificence. The alternating hepta- and hexasyllabic iambi[12] lend the poem the bantering lilt and folksy familiarity typical of legends about popular heroes. The emperor's promised awakening at the moment that "ravens" cease to circle his underground abode seems to indicate that the time for the renewal of imperial grandeur will come only when Germany's "raven" neighbors will have ceased oppressing her.

"As Shade in Daytime Arriving" is one of the Songs of Children Dead that owe their fame to Gustav Mahler's music. It is a short "mood" poem, such as we encountered in Eichendorff, cast in the same alternating octo- and heptasyllables, with usually perfectly consonated female-male endings. Its incantatory repetitiousness is functional; it serves, the same as the rocking rhymes, to bring about the atmosphere of a perfectly balanced acceptance of personal finiteness beyond that of Eichendorff's, as expressed in the latter's "On the Death of my Child." Rückert succeeds to achieve what is logically impossible: he expresses through his deep understanding of the emotion of grief the simultaneity of presence and absence of a beloved creature and the consequent quiet acceptance of death. An equally quiet grief continues to pulsate through this acceptance and reconciliation. The repeated juxtaposition of two almost but not quite identical verses[13] is crucial to the atmosphere intended by the poet. The two near-repetitious verses rhyme with two new, perfectly identical ones,[14] yet clash with them conceptually. This helps to weave the intricate fabric of Rückert's structurally, rhythmically and audially intertwining and tension-building versification.

"Midnight" is another "mood" poem, arising from the same suggestive tension between contrast and identity, and musicality and meaning. It captures the same ineffable but extremely keen existential frustration of the individual condemned to eventual extinction and faced with a mute and unresponsive universe. The juxtaposition of a rhymed couplet of merely four syllables with a heptasyllabic couplet, almost twice the length of the tetrasyllables, does reproduce "physically" the confrontation between the individual and his universe.[15] First, the stars fail to single out the poet with their favor; then, the infinite depth of the universe appears filled with disconsolate darkness; next, the poet's heart discovers no other harmony in the universe except the one between his heart's woe-ridden pulsations and the universal suffering that permeates the universe. In the next-to-the-last stanza the poet challenges the sum total of mankind's woes that echo through the universe, and finds no solution to them. The resolution of the existential dilemma between the finite and the infinite comes in the last stanza. The poet suspends the efforts of logic, reason and the demands of the ego-oriented human justice to acquire an intuitive certainty about an inscrutable but active Divine Presence pulsating at the bottom of individual existence. The decisive act of irrational faith is, in the final analysis, the only way out of the threat of a metaphysical void that mars the happiness of modern man. Rückert the singer of <u>faith in a transcendent, though immanently omnipresent Higher Being</u> remains squarely in the Romantic camp, in spite of his chillingly realistic evocations of the ever-present pain of having to cease to be which constitutes the human condition.

August, Graf von Platen (1796-35) resembles Rückert in aesthetic cosmopolitanism, the taste for experimentation with exotic poetic forms, and a sense for absolute formal perfection. Otherwise, the two had little in common. Born of North German nobility, he was destined for a military career. A graduate of the Munich Cadet School at fourteen, he joined the infantry regiment of the King of Bavaria in 1814 with the grade of lieutenant. Shortly after the inception of the campaign of 1815 against Napoleon he asked for a leave of absence from the military; he was never to return to his hated profession. In 1818 he engaged in studies of philosophy, philology and natural sciences at Würzburg and Erlangen. Schelling exercised a strong influence on the thought of the unstable young man. Thanks to a modest pension from King Louis I of Bavaria, he was able to travel and live abroad. Returning only occasionally to Germany, he spent the remainder of his life mostly in Italy; he died in Syracuse and was buried on the family estate of his friend and patron Mario Landolina.

Von Platen's literary work was a continuous struggle against the formal lawlessness of his Romantic peers. His worship of formal perfection was uncompromising, so much so that his concern with classically accomplished expression threatened to weaken the depth of his thought and the spontaneity of his imagination. He succeeded in interiorizing the hated discipline of soldiering into an aesthetic will to order and clarity which approached spiritual asceticism. Hence his preference for the demanding strictures of the classical forms of the sonnet, the ode and of the ghazel, made fashionable by Rückert and Goethe. Unfortunately, his creative imagination was no match for the ornateness of his innovations; consequently, rather than achieving a classical balance between strict, splendid, and objective form firmly outlined, and a content rich in emotion, his art often degenerates into self-serving and even hollow neoclassical formalism. Still, his emotional world in a steady turmoil, his struggle for the purity of form and a transcendence of the physical, was genuine. At his best, the marble-like hardness and polish of his verse comes alive with the fire of authentic inspiration.

This fire lives in the best among his Ghazels (1821), New Ghazels (1823) and Sonnets from Venice (1825). They brought applause from many prominent artists and critics, including Goethe. Although not a talented playwright, his dramatic production, much of it influenced by the Spanish drama, shows a clarity of plot superior to that of his models and,

especially, of his fellow-Romanticists. The comedy
The Romantic Oedipus (1828) attacked the trendiness
of contemporary German letters; it also earned him
the undying enmity of Heinrich Heine whose retalia-
tions embittered the last years of Platen's life.[16]
His last drama, The League of Cambrai (1833) was
written in Naples, as was the epic fairy tale The
Abassids (1830; 34). Between 1831-32 Platen wrote
the rousing Songs of the Poles, inspired by the Polish insurrection (1830-31). They sparkle with admiration for the struggle of the freedom-loving Polish patriots against tsarist troops; unfortunately,
German censorship delayed their publication until
after the poet's death.

Ballads and romances figure among the most enduring of Platen's sculptured poetry. "The Pilgrim
Before San Yuste" succeeds in producing the mood of
Baroque existential futility. The heavy sonorous
decasyllabic iambi in rhymed couplets reproduce the
physical and psychological setting of the declining
days of Emperor Charles V (King Carlos I to the Span-
iards), over whose empire the sun did not set.[17] An
uninterrupted flow of images representing the renun-
ciation of worldly honors is contrasted with those
of newly acquired trappings of monastic self-discip-
lining. Platen caught Charles' essentially Burgundian medieval-Catholic world view: chivalry, devo-
tion to God and the holy mission of the emperor, and
to the ideal of world dominance under one monarch, one
religion, one viewpoint.[18] A failure to achieve
these goals leaves the spiritually defeated secular
chief of Christendom only one course of action: total withdrawal from secular existence as penance for
having failed in keeping Christendom united and victorious.

"The Grave in the Busento" is another epic narrative or short romance celebrating Alaric, King of
the Visigoths, who died shortly after conquering
Rome in 410 A.D.[19] The ponderous couplets of "The
Pilgrim" return, only here they run in sixteen-syl-
labic trochees with a fairly regularly occurring
break after the eighth syllable. The gloom that pervades the burial proceedings is not that of ascetic
self-denial, the main motif of the preceding poem.

A verse running sixteen syllables long is hardly customary in the poetry of the European West. What it accomplishes is the impression of an ethnic mass in a state of shock. It shows a live emotion shared by thousands of warriors, civilized only to the point of being nominally Christian, and overwhelmed by the deed for which history had selected them. Resentful of the decadent, wily Romans, uncomfortable in a conquered land, superstitious but endowed with the rude honesty and sense of honor of primitive cultures, the death of their still youthful leader leaves them perplexed and disoriented. In Platen's version it is the warriors themselves[20] who do the job of twice diverting the course of the Busento to provide Alaric with a grave immune to desacration. It is the sullen, purposeful and silent dispatch with which they carry out their labors that pulsates in the gloomy, rushing couplets. They ring with the rude splendor, force and naive self-reliance of a Germanic nation who had lost their king before either could fully assess the consequences of the fall of Rome.

"The Pain One Single Person Feels" is a modified Ghazel.[21] Philosophically, it is an elaboration of the Islamic concept of kismet, fate, that reflects von Platen's questionable fatalism in the face of an impassive, uninvolved cosmic reality. Unlike the islamic surrender of individual will to the will of Allah, the German poet's attitude to the human self is skeptical of any Divine intervention, rather than that of resigned fatalism. The individual is "naught" indeed, as are individual pains, wounds, life itself and its particular goal, and lucubrations about personal happiness. The message is a variant of carpe diem, the "gather ye rosebuds" theme of Baroque apocalyptism. The momentary pleasures and insights offered by individual self-consciousness are to be enjoyed, as if the self were exempt from the universal transience of all existing things, precisely because, on closer scrutiny, life's essence is "spelled as naught." In this modification of Oriental fatalism the haunted poet, a kin to the incomparably more unbalanced Frenchman Gérard de Nerval, finds the expression of his classically impassive though languid and, ultimately, hopeless world view.

NOTES

[1] A notable exception to this hackneyed prettiness is "At the Well Before the Gate," which, like Heine's version of the Lorelei legend, became <u>Volskgut</u>, part and parcel of a folk tradition which keeps -- or makes -- the song anonymous and thus <u>public patrimony</u>.

[2] A trading post and city of the Slavic Wends and the Vikings, located on the island of Wollin, in German Pommerania (now Polish territory). It was known in the Middle Ages as Julin (Jumne, Jumneta, Vineta, Jomsburg, etc.). It flourished in the ninth and tenth centuries. Its destruction in 1098 gave birth to the legend it perished in an earthquake or a tidal wave. It was commonly believed its ruins could be seen under water off the coast of Usedom, another island near the Oder estuary. Excavations undertaken since 1934 place Vineta under the present-day city of Wollin.

[3] The influence of Rückert and Eichendorff is evident. In terms of mood evocation this applies especially to Eichendorff's poem "Beautiful Strange One." Topically, it is "Sea Calm" and "On a Castle" that appear to be precedents of this successful attempt to capture the uncanny, sad, yet strangely joyful and attractive experience of the flux of time.

[4] Dzhelal (1207-73) was the founder of the Order of Whirling Dervishes which earned him the subriquet <u>Rumi</u>. He has to his credit a <u>Divan</u>, a Persian word for "assembly" or "council," and a <u>Mesnevi</u>, a collection of 40,000 distichs of moral, allegoric and mystical verse.

[5] The word means "web" in Arabic and had been exported to Persian, Turkish and Indian poetry. It consists of three stanzas, each containing fifteen verse couplets; each verse features four stressed syllables. The first couplet is rhymed and the same rhyme returns in all even verses, while the odd lines remain unrhymed (aa ba ca da). Schlegel cultivated

the ghazel before Rückert with indifferent poetic success.

[6] Hafiz (1327-90) flourished at Shiraz. He taught at a mosque and wrote inspired love ghazels, many dedicated to the love of boys, to the virtues of wine, the beauties of nature and to his native city. The Divan was translated in 1812 by Hammer-Purgstall; the translation inspired Goethe's Divan version.

[7] The makame is a hybrid genre of rhymed prose with interpolated verses. It is an Arabic variant of the Persian divan, both terms being figurative derivations from the word "council" or, more accurately, "allocution," a customary address delivered at ceremonial court assemblies of Oriental potentates.

[8] In this collection Rückert demonstrates his mastery of French alexandrin, an iambic hexameter (consisting of thirteen syllables in the case of feminine rhyme endings) with a caesura (break) after the sixth syllable. Named after the Old French Epos about Alexander the Great, it became the masterfully polished tool of French classicisme in the XVIIth century. Known in England as the heroic couplet, it was cultivated among others by Alexander Pope. Germany's Andreas Gryphius (1616-64) imitated it successfully in German letters. Thanks to the formal mastery of Corneille and Racine, it remained the only acceptable verse form for French tragedy until the Romantic revolution.

[9] His Collected Poetic Works, published in 1867-69, consist of twelve volumes.

[10] Put to music by Gustav Mahler in 1902. The customary English translation is Songs on the Death of Children or Songs of the Children Dead.

[11] Frederick I, surnamed Barbarossa, Italian for Redbeard, Holy Roman Emperor 1155-90, was indeed one of the last knights-errant of the declining age of chivalry. A Ghibelline on his father's side and a Guelph on his mother's, he became enmeshed in wars with his maternal relatives, the papacy, the Norman Kingdom of the Two Sicilies and the Lombard cities

of Northern Italy. He succeeded in implanting the idea of an ecumenic empire in the German mind. He drowned while underway to the Holy Land at the inception of the Third Crusade in the river Cydnus (Calycadnus) in Cilicia in Asia Minor.

[12] The odd heptasyllabic male rhymes end sometimes in an assonance, sometimes they are consonated. The first and the third verse of the first four-line stanza do not rhyme at all. The even hexasyllabic lines feature a usually perfect consonance. In my version, the male endings of line two and four of the last stanza are assonated, while line one and three are consonated; the exact opposite occurs in the German original. The intricate regular irregularity of the rhytmic and rhyme structure produces the impression of spontaneous, unpolished and a most intimately experienced expression of the folk soul.

[13] "You are a light at night" (second line of the first stanza) stands in the mildest of contrasts with "You are my light at night" (the fourth and last line of the second stanza).

[14] "My heart denied you died," (last verse of the first stanza) is repeated identically in the last verse of the third stanza. At the same time, this twice repeated verse rhymes with the second line of the poem "You are a light at night" mentioned above. The second line of the second stanza which ends in "... our bond is tight" carries on the progress of thought without much of a contrast: Likewise, "A trace of you shines bright" (second line of the third stanza) stands in conceptual juxtaposition which is hardly contrastive to the image of "a light at night," the latter occurring twice, in the first and second stanzas. All of the above-mentioned verses end in virtually perfect consonances; this creates an all-pervasive contrast of sorts between audial identity and conceptual difference, if not contrast.

[15] The last two lines of each of the five six-line stanzas are once more tetrasyllabic couplets that give the impression of repulsion, of a falling back on one's finiteness. The refrain that constitutes each of the six end-lines ("In the midnight

sky") is identical and rhymes with the likewise identical six opening lines of each stanza (At midnight I). This virtually encloses the contemplative ego in the prison of its speculations, except, of course, for the last two short lines that constitute the resolution of the metaphysical dread. There at last the ego surrenders to the infinite wisdom of a transcendent Creator of both finiteness and infinity.

16 Heine had originally encouraged the novelist-playwright Karl Leberecht Immermann's mocking censure of Platen's <u>Ghazels</u>. Immermann (1796-40) had satirized Platen in <u>The Cavalier Stumbling About the Maze-Garden of Metrics</u> (1829). Platen retaliated with his <u>Oedipus</u> drama in which Immermann is alluded to as Nimmermann, or "Neverman."

17 Due to the fact that, aside from ruling the lands of the German Empire, Northwestern Italy, Flanders (Belgium), the Netherlands, Burgundy and Spain, he was titular ruler of Mexico and the rest of the Spanish holdings in Central and Latin America. Thus at no time was there a part of his empire which did not bask in sunshine. Charles was crowned King of Spain in 1516 and Holy Roman Emperor in 1519. After a lifelong struggle against the claims of the Valois kings of France to Milan, against Luther, the Protestant and, eventually, the Catholic princes of Germany, and Turkish inroads in North Africa, he abdicated in 1556, bitter and disillusioned. His younger brother Ferdinand, already king of Bohemia, received the imperial crown; his son Philip received the crown of Holland (1555) and the crown of Spain (1556) with the title Philip II.

18 Charles' idea of a world empire is summarized in a sonnet by the Spanish poet Fernando de Acuña, entitled "To the King Our Lord." The last line of the second quatrain expresses tersely the imperial formula: "One Monarch, one Empire, one Sword."

19 Born in Dacia (modern Rumania) about 370 A.D., Alaric proved to be a courageous, able and wise king of the Visigothic nation. At twenty-two he commanded the Gothic auxiliaries under Emperor Theodosius I. After the latter's death, he ravaged Greece until

stopped by the Vandal-Roman general Stilicho in 397. He was bought off with the commission of <u>magister militum</u>, commander-in-chief of Roman and allied forces in Illyricum (now Western Yugoslavia). He invaded Italy in 401 but was repeatedly defeated by Stilicho. When Stilicho was executed in 408, nothing stood between Alaric's ambition and the weak, inexperienced Honorius, Emperor of the West. Alaric plundered Rome in 410 but, on the whole, his Goths exercised restraint in the conquest. Alaric died soon after at Cosentia (Cosenza). His intent had not been to smash the Roman world but to restructure it so as to accommodate the needs of the newly-emerging Germanic element in Eastern and Southeastern Europe. The fall of the Eternal City to a "barbarian" destroyed Roman prestige and the myth of the city's invincibility. Henceforward, the focus of power and the decision-making that affected the destiny of the civilized world shifted from Roman military and civil institutions to the papacy.

[20] As a matter of historic record, the slaves that carried out the burial procedure were put to death upon completion of their task so as to assure the secrecy of Alaric's burial site.

[21] Instead of repeating the initial couplet aa in even rhymes (aa, ba, ca, etc.), this variant of the <u>ghazel</u> develops a refrain (b) recurring in the second and fourth verse, and in every fourth verse thereafter which creates the following pattern: ab cb defb ghib etc., all the way through its twenty-eight verses, ending in stvb. The meter is a regular octosyllabic iamb that alternates four times the stressed-unstressed pattern without any variations. The perfect rhymes have masculine endings which are identical ("naught"), but reach back into the verse, covering two more syllables which produces a rare combination of a female and male ending fused together ("quelled as naught," "felt as naught," "dealt as naught," etc.), consonated throughout the poem in verses 2, 4, 8, 12, 16, 20, 24 and 28.

CHAPTER VII

THE CYCLICAL PATTERN OF CULTURAL EVOLUTION AND

THE THREE PHASES OF LITERARY GENESIS. THE PRINCIPLE

OF REGENERATIVE RESILIENCY IN WESTERN CULTURE.

Three distinct phases can be identified as a recurring constant in each cycle of literary genesis. The first is the narrative, or epic mode, reflecting the breadth and immediacy of the heroic deed. The second phase responds to some ebbing in bio-cultural vitality; the artist feels compelled to probe the tragic depth of individual conscience. Literary development in full decline is the third phase which varies in length with the rate of disintegration of the "spirit of the times," as it gradually succumbs to radical skepticism.

In the two ascending phases of the cycle, the belief in a transcendent destiny of man and his culture is strong, though rarely unanimous. The third descending phase invariably tries to adjust this belief to the pressing needs of sheer existential survival. The phases of narrative breadth, of tragic speculation in depth, and finally, of skeptical insecurity have been alternating regularly thanks to the remarkable regenerative resilience of Western culture. This resiliency has been identified by Henri Bergson in _The Two Sources of Morals and Religion_ as the "fiction-making function" of man's imagination, a life sustaining force "feeding on residual instinct, which surrounds intellect like an aura." Since instinct cannot intervene directly on the behalf of life-preservation, this ability to invent fabricates fictions, myths, spirits and gods as a defense mechanism against the devitalizing conceptualizations of intellect. Myths and gods have their origin in "an indeterminate consciousness of their _effective_ presence, like the _numen_ of the Romans.[1]"

It is this effective presence of transcendence through fiction that proved to be, at least until the end of the first half of the twentieth century, a bulwark against what Bergson called "the falsification of reality undertaken by reason." It was also the driving power behind the will to survival of the spiritual heritage of Western civilization.

The initial stage of poetic genesis is, more specifically, that of the <u>epic deed</u>. It reflects the emergence of an ethnic consciousness which embodies the most fundamental values of a given society. There arises a naive exuberance over the act, a sheer delight of man imposing himself on his environment. With the candor of childlike immediacy, it tells of the truly <u>agonic</u> tension between a representative individual and an environment which resists the imposition of the values of a given collective consciousness.

The simple acceptance of man's <u>thrownness</u> into a hostile world as a heroic task begins to wear out when the ethnic consciousness grows introspective and, consequently, less sure of itself. The <u>epic agon</u> becomes gradually displaced by <u>pathos</u>, arising from the dilemma between right and wrong; in the second phase, epic heroism cedes to pathetic reflection and uncertainty which occupy man's mind after it had reached a certain stage of sophistication. The third phase of a given cultural cycle in full decline brings together the <u>epic ethos</u> and the <u>tragic pathos</u> in a final showdown of values undergoing a critical reexamination by a culture that is losing its bearings. At this stage, a true artist makes his own reevaluation of a disoriented culture. As a rule he does so independently from the moralist, the social critic, and the politician. Inevitably, an aesthetic objectivization of a value crisis will tend toward exaggeration and a mannerized <u>pointe</u> .

More likely than not, the artist's intent to rally his fellow citizens for the preservation of their common ethnic patrimony achieves the opposite effect and actually speeds up the process of cultural disintergration. The reaction of the public compounds this trend. The artist's audience is scandalized over the aesthetic exaggeration of an already crucial situation. It tends to overreact to the "message," which only intensifies the spiral of irrationality and despair consuming the spiritual patrimony of a given period. As a result, traditional solutions of man's existential torments that had worked in the past are totally discredited. In the hope of salvaging something of the cultural essence to which he owes his formation, the artist in turn submits to what he feels is a public demand for "realism" and "common sense." This means the acceptance of a purely tangible reality as antidote against the ideological content of a world view that had grown meaningless with time and use.

Aesthetically, as well as ethically, this is a "grotesque" solution. Traditional ideals, degraded to illusions by the loss of the intuitive truth that used to authenticate them, are forced to mix with pedestrian demands of survival in a workaday reality. Intending to preserve some of the cherished values whose formulation had cost past generations so much pathos -- interpreted strictly as suffering -- these realistic "solutions" hope to regenerate the ethnic consciousness of a disoriented society through the elimination of the "superstitious" ground of ethnic myths.

Such an "enlightened," autonomous spatiotemporal "reality" claiming to be the savior of the conscience of its age cannot support itself for long. Traditional conventions cut off from their metaphysical roots combine with ethic relativism and bring about a cultural twilight well ahead of the final collapse of a culture sick with itself. Only after the cultural organism disintegrates, its debris begin to serve as a matrix which will breed another cultural epoch and set off the same cycle of ethos, pathos, and existential compromise between transcendent order and immanent chaos. This historical pattern applies to all art in general; it is nowhere as keenly and painfully evident as in poetry.

From the dawn of Western culture through the first half of the twentieth century, the resilience of the will-to-live of European culture has always proved a match for the danger that any one particular period of decline might indeed be the last one, due to the saturation of Western cultural viability with too much "past." So far, the cultural context of a specific whole had always managed to somehow phase out of the cul-de-sac of aesthetic and existential despair to find a fresh beginning. The renewed matrix had always bred a "readjusted" concept of some life-guarateeing ground, capable of spawning yet another round in the agnoizing game of self-admiration, self-doubt and self-critique. From the recesses of his consciousness Western man once more gains confidence in the <u>ethos of the act</u>. Tales of naive heroism find an unsophisticate audience; soon, listeners become spectators demanding that the <u>pathos of decision</u> be dramatized. As their characters grow flabby and their senses jaded, they start looking forward to being insulted by a ruthless critic, most likely an artist, sensitive to the need for shock treatment in order to preserve the common cultural heritage. At this point, the existential compromise between the flagging transcendent tradition and the "realistic" assessment of regeneration-through-secularization becomes inevitable. The embalmed tradition of "higher values" which have lost their teeth enters into another impasse with cynical existential realism.

   A diachronic examination of literary history shows that the cycle of <u>epic ethos</u>, <u>tragic pathos</u> and <u>cynical pragmatism</u> maintains a fixed order of succession, but does not necessarily find embodiment in the media of epos, tragedy and tragicomedy. There nevertheless seem to be some genres better suited than others to the creative needs of each specific phase of the ascending and descending cycle. The accent on ethos finds a natural expression in the epos or in the epic novel, whereas the pathetic sensibility will seek outlet in tragedy or in reflective lyric poetry. The "pragmatic compromise" with the "new reality" finds its natural expression on the comic stage and in the satire. The distinction between prose and poetry is even less relevant than the correspondence between period sensibility and genre. The definitions of criteria distinguishing the two modes vary vastly and tend to disappear according to period prejudice.

The compromise with immanent reality cannot satisfy for long man's aspirations for perfection. In the struggle for dignity of the individual faced with a radically immanentized cosmos, <u>the artist tries to adjust his finite consciousness to the notion of infinity</u>. The existential compromise between man's aspirations to infinite perfection and the need to merely survive as a purely secular phenomenon cannot produce order in either life or art. <u>A higher image of man is incompatible with the radical immanentization of the cosmic vision</u>. In a culture drained of its ethic-pathetic content, the grotesque mode proves to be a constant and necessary expression of a last-ditch struggle for the preservation of a cultural heritage, redefined as existential survival. The price of this survival is the surrender of the ideological essence of a disoriented culture ready to commit suicide. Some explicitly grotesque epochs in Western intellectual history produce artistic trends resulting in fantastic combinations of physically incompatible elements. Such productions are typical of the Baroque, Romantic, Symbolist, the <u>fin-de-siècle</u> decadent-asethetic movement, and surrealism.

NOTES

[1] *Les deux sources de la morale et de la religion*, Cf. Ernst Robert Curtius, *Europäische Literatur und lateinisches Mittelalter* (Bern: Francke, 1961), 18-19. My italics.

CHAPTER VIII

EXISTENTIAL COMPROMISE OF DECLINING ROMANTICISM

WITH REALITY IN THE AGE OF EMPIRICAL SCIENCE.

HEINE AND LENAU.
1. Heine the Exasperating Proteus of Elitist Revolutionism.

a. The Lyrical Sufferer. Adolescent Worship of the Ghost Nymph.
The Book of Songs.

Heinrich Heine (1797?-56) is a transitional phenomenon, the last and perhaps the greatest German Romantic, and certainly Romanticism's severest critic. His restless universalism spanned many areas of aesthetic and intellectual endeavor. He left his native Rhineland for Hamburg where he developed a strong dislike for business, for his uncle Salomon and the latter's two daughters who gave him his first taste of female fickleness and frigidity. His studies at Bonn and Göttingen made him an indifferent lawyer but expert in German philology, history and philosophy. The Book of Songs (1827) made him famous; but his unbridled sallies on paper and by word of mouth created a number of enemies who resented his delight in paradox, controversy, and scathing criticism of what he loved best, German culture. Travel Sketches, a travelogue with interspersed poetry (1826-31) further enhanced his international reputation. In 1831 he left for Paris where he hoped to find a politically more liberal and aesthetically more stimulating climate than that of Prussian Germany. The essay On the History of Religion and Philosophy in Germany (1834) established him as arbiter of German cultural phenomena. A scathing assessment of German militarism, stilted imagination and servility appeared under the title Germany, A Winter's Tale as appendix to New Poems in 1844.

Simultaneously an unparalleled master of the

imitative folk genre introduced by the earlier Romantics Clemens Brentano and Achim von Arnim, as well as of studied intellectual invective, he combined the features of a sexually frustrated fantasist, a real-life Don Juan, crypto-Christian, enemy of rabbinical casuistry, lover of Old-Testamental Judaism, precursor of the Zionist renewal of Jewish identity, assailant of Judeo-Christian Nazarenism,[1] vicious satirist with a morbid need for self-deprecation, amoral Hellene, would-be Socialist yet admirer of the Bourgeois King Louis Philippe and friend of the Rothschilds, Teutonoman as often as Germanophobe. Since 1848 Heine remained bedridden until his death, racked by a progressive paralysis of the spine. <u>Atta Troll</u> (1849) is a satire on left-wing political liberalism and Romantic spleen, but also, as suggested by the author, possibly the "last free forest song" of "all things Romantic." The <u>Romancero</u> (1851) failed to achieve the pure lyrical immediacy of Heine's earlier verse but nevertheless contains some passages of sublime beauty. <u>Poems 1853 and 1854</u> and <u>From the Mattress Grave</u> are strongly influenced by the fascination with the decay of the poet's self which, intellectually and aesthetically, remained painfully lucid to the bitter end.

Owing to his lifelong dialecticism, it was difficult for Heine to stay faithful to a cause or friendship, to trend, nationality or ideology. He was certainly the most controversial and thought-provoking phenomenon outside Goethe, but Heine could and would not emulate Goethe's impassive triumphs over life's paradoxes. Heine represents the ambiguous phase of dying Romanticism which clings desperately to the emphasis on human affects, individuality and rebellion against the decrees of impartial reason as well as against the silence of an inaccessible Absolute. He was an accelerator of the decay of a set of ethical and aesthetic values in the name of their preservation.

In 1819 the by no means heartless uncle sent Heinrich to get a degree in law, paying part of the expenses. First in Bonn, then in Göttingen (1820-22), Heine played the role of a cynical challenger of happiness denied him by adverse fate. And yet, in spite of the gushing confessions, the complaints about the "blow to the heart," given him, successively, by his two Hamburg cousins, he exercised uncommon reticence in respect of the identity of these two flesh-and-blood creatures who served as models for his image of the generic woman: a wraithlike, potentially passionate and yet lethally impassive creature. The pose of a Don Juan-victim of his conquests' incomprehension and indifference soon took the actual shape of the loose liaisons he was to know throughout his mature years.

From the years of his first stay in Hamburg date Heine's poetic firstfruits. The first section of the Book of Songs that was to appear some ten years later is entitled "Youthful Sorrows -- Dream Images 1817-21." It came out in 1822 and received critical acclaim from A.W. Schlegel. It is actually one continuous nightmare about the poet's unfaithful bride and his own ghostly double in the process of possessing her. The visions literally pour out of the dream region of the unconscious as variations on a black-mass marriage of the poet's diabolic alter ego which achieves what the conscious self was denied: the possession and requited love, albeit in a demonic world.

Poem number two presents the lethal synthesis of Eros and Thanatos, embodied in the impassive nymph. Endowed with ambiguous pleasure-pain qualities, she appears, progressively as washerwoman of the poet's shroud, carpenter of his coffin and, finally, as his grave digger.

> She snapped: "Be still, a cold grave I
> Have dug in which you are to lie,"
> And as she spoke, the pretty maid,
> A gaping pit she open laid.
>
> And in the pit as I did look
> My limbs with icy terror shook;
> And as the chilly tomb night broke
> All round me -- from my dream I woke.

It is most significative for the consistent unfolding and reelaboration of Heine's motifs that his earliest verses offer the vision of the self mirrored in its own grave; the same theme pervades what is commonly considered Heine's last poem.[2]

The incertitudes of an unmated male, faced with an equally ridiculous, stunted alter ego and the fickleness that is woman, experiences the qualms of libido as the work of the devil. The fourth poem of "Youthful Sorrows" demonstrates this quite explicitly:

> Thus spoke the dream god, slyly showing me
> A flood of visions from a mirror pouring,
> Before an altar stood a little man,
> My sweet by him, both said "I do!" --
>   "Amen!"
> Came from a thousand fiends with laughter
>   roaring.

Poem five of the series shows figuratively explicit fears of emotional and hence, a sexual mutilation; the nightmare ends with a dance macabre of bride and double, with the poet watching helplessly the double's intimacies with the bride. The spectral dance is a leitmotif that dominates the "Youthful Sorrows" cycle. The bride's perfidy turns into the need to deprive the poet of his eternity, and a Manichaean struggle for his soul[3], resolved by the triumph of the forces of evil (poem six). The seventh poem deals with the actual wedding, introducing another stock figure of Heine's spectral repertory: the broomstick-mammy. The eighth and longest poem of the series is a culmination of the nocturnal spectral orgies, a veritable Schauerballade in the tradition of tremendist[4] pre-Romanticism introduced by Bürger's "Lenore;[5]" it is a ghoulish get-together of men who had perished for and through love.[6]

The sophomoric quality of this poetry aside, Heine displays here a singularly sharp insight into the dangers of the emergence of certain archetypical structures of the collective unconscious into individual consciousness. This is so of course only if we accept Jung's concept of the collective psyche[7] as product of a historically cummulative and universally human experience. Elsewhere, Jung called the emergence of what was commonly believed to be forces of evil, "the uprising of unconscious destructive forces of the collective psyche," the blame being put on "enlightened rationalism" and, in our era, on "the rationalism of modern life." By "depreciating everything irrational," we have "precipitated the function of the irrational into the unconscious.[8]"

Thus the tightrope act between absolute self-individuation and self-destruction becomes in Heine a much more serious game than at first suspected. Jung's words support his contention.

> Insofar as through our unconscious we have a share in the historical collective psyche, we live naturally and unconsciously in a <u>world of werewolves, demons, magicians, etc., for these are things which all previous ages have invested with tremendous affectivity.</u>[9]

The ninth poem is the best of the "Dream Images," indicating what simple, haunting beauty Heine can produce. Topically and formally, "the marble pallid maid" introduced here offers nothing new, but the economy and inner resonance of the whole make up for the gratuitous horrors of the pieces that precede it.

Poem number ten reads like a poetic, if simplified rendition of Jung's prose. It complains about the unwillingness of the "pale corpses," stirred up from the unconscious, to return to "where earlier they had erred."

The appeal to these "shadowy fiends" to release the poet from their world reflects authentic horror at the process of releasing the unconscious forces of creativity, the price for which is damnation. Here Heine's fears parallel those of E.T.A. Hoffmann's; the latter was convinced that the act of artistic creation was a bid for the Absolute. As an act of self-transcending magic it makes of the artist a competitor with divine creativity. Seen from the Jungian angle,

> one man arrogates collective virtue
> to himself as his personal merit,
> another takes <u>collective vice as
> his personal guilt</u>.[10]

In the same poem ring echoes of Novalis' quest for the "blue flower."

> The struggle never leaving
> For the flower without peer,
> What would be the point in living
> Unless I held her so dear?

    The function of the recurring nightmare of the prude, perfidious, hypocritical and lethal woman figure signifies obviously more than Heine's first taste of unrequited love given him by his Hamburg cousins. Gerhard Storz insists that "the originator of this stubborn grief" is not to be traced to any specific female figure in Heine's life;[11] in fact, it never acquires the features of a concrete individual. Storz suggests that this <u>femme fatale</u> of Heine's more or less fictitious nightmares might be a "mutation of an experience of a different loss" which the young man's "essential particularity" finds "impossible to conceive or express;" she could even be the product of Heine's courting his reader[12] with a topical and trendy theme of the <u>beau ténébreux</u>.

    Be this as it may, the frigid <u>femme fatale</u> as the unapproachable and unattainable beauty of the Absolute which resides in the Realm of the Dead and will dissolve the individuality of the seeker who dares touch her, is clearly suggested in the above-cited (fourth) stanza of the concluding poem of "Dream Images." An allegorical reading of Heine's marble-pallid revenant as <u>artistic perfection</u>, lethal to her wooer, also corresponds to a definitely neurotic but by no means uncommon <u>personalization</u> of the awareness of evil, conjured up from the collective unconscious and endowed with spectral life by the morbidly sensitive, frustrated aesthete who challenges no less than the volatility of beauty and pleasure in defiance of the prevailing cosmic order. The reference to "the flower without peer" in the above-quoted lines reveals one aspect of Heine's frustrations as the chase after the Absolute which must needs elude him.

The last poem of "Dream Images" ends with the apparent triumph of evil; actually, it confirms in a general way the holy self-sacrifice of the poet outlined in Hölderlin's "The Poet's Calling," only in a folksier, metaphysically less resonant tone. Like Hölderlin, Heine demands an assurance of compassion and sympathy uttered by his transcendent goal; the same as Hölderlin's challege to the Absolute, the question and quest remain unanswered.

>   Now that I came, you to follow,
>   Tell me you love me, my sweet!

is more than a cry of the existentially alienated and sexually frustrated male; it is a bid for perfect beauty in an imperfect world, whose imperfection *qua* individual existence Heine genuinely believes to have sacrificed for the attainment of the highest goal.

The second section of "Youthful Sorrows" bears the simple subtitle "Lieder," "Songs." The inspiration of its nine pieces continues to be a woman figure fatal to the poet's happiness; only this time her fickelness predominates over impassive coldness. The first poem deals simply with the insomnia of a lover whose beloved fails to keep their date; the sixth unfolds in a half-serious, half mocking banter. The seventh compares the cunning and deceit of woman to the "glinting surface" of the Rhine concealing "death and night" below; the last poem is an epilogue dedicated to the apparently deceased impulsive verve of their inspiration.

The third section of "Youthful Sorrows" subtitled "Romances[13]" shows how far Heine's genius has progressed in formal control and simplicity beyond the gratuitous gruesomeness of his early Muse. Still, the thematic repertory remains faithful to the preoccupation with gravesite lucubrations, indicating a mild case of implicit necrophilia. This tendency is, however, tempered by a fairly tasteful and always frivolously bantering inclination to more or less gentle self-ridicule.[14]

Romance number two entitled "The Mountain Voice" echoes the poet's still somewhat mannerized tedium vitae resulting from love despondency; but the refrain that intimates imminent death rather than erotic gratification has the impact of a lived experience. "Poor Peter" (number four) is an ironic projection of the self into a portrait of a ne'er-do-well in the affairs of the heart and in plain survival.

"The Song of the Prisoner" as the fifth poem of the series presents a peculiar association of the poetic self with a witch grandmother. The German word Muhme, a generic term for an elderly female relative, plays a significant role in Heine's concept of family and ancestry. The mother figure played obviously a dominant role in his life,[15] yet it would be absurd to portray Frau Heine mère as a witch, given her penchant for Voltairian rationalism. But the mother-crone figure added a dimension to Heine's generic image of woman, experienced in its lethal night-nymph and the virginal-Marian aspect.[16] The "feathery grandmother" of the "Song of the Prisoner" is a companion piece to the "broomstick-mammy" of the seventh poem of the "Dream Images." It goes without saying that another dimension of the crone-relative figure derives directly from Germanic lore which had left such a strong imprint on Heine.

"The Grenadiers[17]" (Romance VI) is a lyrico-epic gem of ballad-like simplicity and direct emotive communication which by itself would assure Heine eternal recognition as one of the greatest poets of the German language. It is more than the spirit of the vieille garde, Napoleon's Old Guard come to life, more than a vivid insight into the romance of Bonapartism which Heine had lived as a boy; it is a vindication of that strange paradox of the slogans of liberation, revolutionary republicanism wedded to the glory of the grandiosely imaginative usurper Bonaparte.

"Don Ramiro" (Romance IX) displays a flare worthy of Espronceda's Student of Salamanca, especially in the dizzying music and dance sequences that accompany Clara's contact with Ramiro's ghost. The long poem shows what the maturing poet can do with materials that only a few years earlier produced adolescent paraphrases of popular legends.[18] Especially masterful is Heine's poetic rendition of the suspension of the time frame in the mind of doña Clara, when the eternity of the revenant invades chronological time.

"Belshazzar" (Romance X) continues the high level of concentrated simplicity and the incredibly powerful modulation and contrasting of atmosphere. The alternation of quiet and uproar, boisterous blasphemy and chilling terror[19] is enhanced by the stark simplicity of word, imagery and meter.[20] It is unquestionably the masterpiece of the romance genre in the German language.

"The Minnesingers" (Number eleven) declares the "minnesinger," i.e., the artist in general, a misfit among simple, healthy folk who enjoy the struggle for survival; his sensibility is an unhealing wound. The following romance (number twelve entitled the "Window Watch" is a companion piece to number four ("Poor Peter"), giving the motif of spectral love a naughty, life-affirming twist, but the lethal impact of eros is not laid to rest. It will recur off and on throughout the poetic and affective growth of Heine's art.

The "Ditty of Remorse" (Romance XV) shows how insistent this association of sex with guilt can be. It demonstrates perfectly Heine's tornness between the mother-crone and nymph concept of woman. He is the squire riding through the green forest of life's opportunities and pleasures, where "merrily rustling leaves" produce the ambience of carefree abandon, quickly corroded by the pangs of conscience.

b. Heine's Lyrical Maturity and Some Leveling of the Affective Turmoil. "Lyrical Intermezzo," Dramas, "Homecoming" and the North-Sea Cycles.

Heine published his second book under the title Tragedies and A Lyrical Intermezzo in 1823. His impressions from an excursion undertaken on foot in 1824 through the Harz Mountains appeared under the title Journey Through the Harz (between 1826-31) as the first volume of the four-volume Travel Sketches. The Harz journey led to a visit with Goethe at Weimar whom he failed to impress, one way or the other. The travel kaleidoscope also reveals a progressive aversion to the stodgy Teutonism of the conservative Old-German faction of the patriotic front.[21]

The "Prologue" to the "Lyrical Intermezzo" introduces Heine as the "Knight of the Sad Countenance." It shows one of many relapses into the misfit self-image supposedly shed in "Youthful Sorrows." But in spite of the generally gentle gloom that pervades the "Intermezzo," the atmosphere has shifted from spectral to magic. "During the Splendid Month of May" (I), "The Lotus Flower" (X) and "Up North a Fir Tree Lonely" (XXXIII) are brief lyrical gems comparable in sublimity to the "Grenadiers," "Belshazzar" and "Don Ramiro" among the romances. To the same category in evocative power and simple sublimity belongs "From Ancient Tales It's Waving," a magnificent portrait of the transcendent world of Romantic perfection, present and real in imagination, but existentially unattainable. Number eleven is a sample of Heine's youthful Marian cult; "The World is so Fair and the Sky is so Blue" (XXXI) offers an exemplary case of the Stimmungsbruch, a "break" or better, "derailment of mood" that transcends mere Romantic irony, by suddenly destroying a mood or ambience which had been carefully constructed throughout the poem. At the same time, the poem is a throwback to the stylized necrophilia of the earliest "Dream Images." Poem number thirty-two continues the motif of final and enduring emotional gratification in the grave.

Poems XLVII and LI reveal the scars left by disappointments in love, friendship and by envious critics. Heine the dashing cavalier and lover as he wishes to see himself in his mind's eye (poem LVIII) prepares the setting for a mood derailment, somewhat milder than the earlier image of two lovers locked in a chilly embrace in the grave:

> What's this, preposterous horseman,
> What means your preposterous dream?[22]

"A Star is Yonder Falling" (LIX) enhances further the stark sublimity and directness introduced by the first poem of the cyclus; the explicitness of the preceding evocations of the frail beauty of Romantic aspirations and its inevitable extinction is here less openly stated through the symbols of a falling star and a fading swan song. Poem sixty-one consists of one four-line stanza in which a sympathetic rapport between "wise" nature and the "foolish" lovelorn poet is established, without suggesting nature could cure this condition. The last poem of the series (LXV) is an epilogue or rather necrologue of the "evil, ancient ditties," presumably fruits of the poet's affective torments, phobias and "ghosts" of his restless psyche. "Do you know the ancient ditty" is a refrain-like statement that echoes throughout Heine's work,[23] usually introducing a pronouncement of some unpleasant and unchangeable truth about the human condition. The epilogue is full of playful spoofs of time-hallowed relics treasured by West-German cities, chosen according to what these relics represent in terms of the monstrously huge and spiritually powerful.[24] The course toward scathing satirization of all things German which will occur sporadically throughout Heine's mature work and culminates in <u>Germany, a Winter's Tale</u>, is charted by the innocent pleasantries of this epilogue.

A brief sample of the poetry interspersed in the <u>Journey Through the Harz</u> must suffice here. It shows the crone-relative-witch complex asserting itself with unabated vigor. The magic of the old and wise, of the ages of faith, not reason, can bring about the concretization of the Romantic dream.

The year 1825 would have been a milestone in anyone else's life but Heine's. He finished his doctorate in jurisprudence and had himself baptized; neither event impressed him overly nor did it change appreciably his life except that in later years he deplored his baptism as a spiritual violation which he allowed to happen in order to be able to obtain full admission into the Christian world. The notoriety he continued gaining as poet of nocturnal terrors and cruel wit began to catch up with him; eventually, it was to bar him forever from public office in the German Lands.

Actually what produced a stormy public indignation was not so much his poetry as the two lyrical dramas published together with the "Lyrical Intermezzo" in 1823. Both Ratcliff and Almanzor glorify individual self-assertion in the face of insurmountable odds that are sure to crush the challenger. German law-and-order circles were scandalized by the idealization of a Scottish highwayman, the hero of the first drama; the hero's noble self-sacrifice for the sake of protecting the national identity failed to appeal to German patriotism. Almanzor, the hero of the second play, and the plight of the embattled Moorish minority in Spain, met with the same misconprehension. Both plays emphasized the distinctive Scottish and Moorish garb as symbols of courage to cling to religious and racial identity in a sea of hostile forces. The Jews felt the barb of Heine's reproach for having given up their own traditional attire in the face of Christian resentment; the Germans resented the parallel between their racial attitudes and English and Spanish repressions of their respective minorities. What seemed to bother no one was the lack of a truly dramatic substance in Heine's eminently lyrical art.[25] The plays are nevertheless a significant milestone in Heine's gradual gravitation to a vital, proud, even militant and mystical Judaism as opposed to its reformist, European-Christian dilution of the Jewish faith. And yet he simultaneously cultivated the pose of a Goethean Hellene, only of a more engagé variety, without the latter's Skepticism about a revolutionary reform of the human condition.

Heine's real triumph came when the Hamburg publisher Campe published the Book of Songs in 1827.[26] Like everything in his life the benefits of its success were ambivalent. Campe's helping hand came as a godsend at a time that Heine's chances for any kind of professional employment in Germany had all dried up; the perpetual rights Heine sold Campe for the paltry sum of fifty louis d'or seemed just; at the time the publisher didn't expect to turn any profit from it. The immediate and universal popularity of Heine's verse brought about consecutive reeditions for years on end and could have brought Heine a lifetime financial security. Compounding the ambiguity of Heine's success was the fact that soon after 1827 his writings were confiscated in the more reactionary states of the German Confederation.

Aside from possessing a lyrical genius of the first order Heine shares with Goethe the common fate of being misunderstood by huge segments of nineteenth-century German readership. Goethe's detached Olympianism bothered many -- Heine, among others. Goethe's aloof cosmopolitanism and the refusal to back what he considered a vicious fragmentation of the uniting force of Bonapartism was odious to most; the Left especially resented his rejection of an egalitarian Utopia, calling him, quite underservedly, "the court lackey." Heine, aside from his counter-productive waspishness, felt kinship for the revolutionaries and social Utopians, but was attracted by the self-sacrificing stance of their unsuccessful struggles for a more equitable world. Thus his revolutionism was ethically and aesthetically motivated, his propensity to the tragic pose feeling a kinship with the radicals of Young Germany. In the light of the actual state of affairs, the stance indicated compassion with failure, rather than ideological dedication to pragmatic success. In the final analysis, Heine failed to succeed in "recreating" his time according to the Goethean model of a Titanic self-objectification. Instead, Heine pursued a further inflation of the self almost to the point of self-explosion, or, at least, self-exhaustion; yet he shared, though only implicitly, the Sage's of Weimar simple, inborn elitism in the struggle for a concrete, this-worldly Absolute.

The "Homecoming" cyclus continues on the marvelous level achieved in the "Intermezzo." Song II is Heine's version of the Lorelei legend which earned him worldwide acclaim and became absolutely integrated in Germany's folklore to the point that its authorship tends to cause genuine surprise. Some of this universal fame is undoubtedly due to Liszt's music, written in 1840, but the composer's own inspiration came from the haunting simplicity of the universally intuited archetypes that impose themselves with irresistible force on the conscious mind. In "Lorelei," Heine indeed achieved the impossible; he communicates in words the conceptually uncommunicable: the sunset glowing over a gently flowing river; the lot of the male led into existential capsizing by nature's oldest, most "natural" urge; the craving for an unattainable ideal with the full knowledge that not only it cannot be reached, but it will surely destroy the ideal-gazer. The third poem-song depicts the simplest, most vividly perceived details, catalogued from the top of an old bastion. The impressionistically recorded image of a boy-soldier going through the drill routine allows the poet's real intention to well up with a sudden mood derailment: all along the poet seemed to be, and may have indeed been, savoring the idyll; but the association of a rifle with its purpose, to shoot living things, unveils the poet's real intent, an only slightly feigned death wish.

Poem number five shows the purest subtlety in suggesting some evil, a wrong-doing, a break in a mood that seemed to indicate a quiet night in a deceased forester's house, in contrast to the storm raging outside. Yet as Storz points out, this tiny simple ballad has little to do with the customary folk "tradition or convention." Here we have Heine's own balladry responding to the tensions of his age. "The distress, desperation and weariness" produced in the forester's son who is about to commit some violent act in order to shatter the boring status quo of his existence reflects "a social actuality[27]" about to be exploded. The image of the grandmother, petrified in her chair, is a now familiar archetype. Perhaps the crone symbol signifies here a mummified,

"blind" past which cannot and will not comment on
the doings of the new generation, ignoring the generation gap and indeed the break with the deceased
father's value system.

Number XIV returns to the Romantic obession
with the sunset on the sea, when the language of the
heart finds itself freed to say more than a torrent
of words. And yet, as always, even though the momentary object of the poet's affection empathizes with
his feelings -- and because of that -- she cannot
but, eventually, act the female.

> I'm by that fateful woman doomed
> Whose poisonous tears I tasted.

Poem sixteen is another jewel of stark, simple, genuine emotion. It does refer directly to Heine's love
fiascoes in Hamburg. The atmosphere of the foggy,
sad city is made palpably concrete, right down to
the last sun ray that for the last time illuminates
for the poet the place of past torments. Number
twenty continues the sentimental retracing of past
woes. The poet's double reemerges, but purely through
the magic of imagination; the poet challenges him,
as if conjuring him by calling him by his proper
name of "double," his "comrade pallid," demanding to
know why he apes his behavior of

> So many nights, so long ago.

Poems XXI and XXII are toned-down throwbacks to the
graveyard eroticism of the "Dream Images." The first
ends on an upbeat; the poet's life vigor challenges
the force of attraction exercised by "all the dead
combined." But the second one, though not explicitly, allows the skeleton-Thanatos element to triumph,
thanks to the Eros-aspect of its dual nature, over
the forces of daylight reality.

But actuality, personal, political, poetic, announces itself with an urgency that will not be stifled. The poet begins to take stock of his abilities
and accomplishments. He now sees himself as a
"wretched Atlas" who asked for and got more than he

could handle (poem XXIV). "Aut Caesar, aut nihil![28]" was a motto that Heine never betrayed. Poem twenty-five reverses the thrust of the previous complaint about woman's "poisonous tears;" with the awareness of the irreversible flux of time that corrodes all things, Heine would like to breathe out with his expiring breath the unperishable love his heart has harbored, for women in general, a woman, for beauty and truth. Poem thirty-eight comes very close to the lament over a lack of communication that was to haunt a generation later the Spaniard Gustavo Adolfo Bécquer, on whom Heine was to exert some influence.[29]

A speculation about the dangers of a radical enlightenment of reality through cold reason which brings about an inner-worldly leveling of all emotions, ranging from the religious to the aesthetic and erotic, is voiced in poem XXXIX. Poem XLII initiates a series of self-criticizing sallies concerning the repetitious treatment of his most cherished obsession. Some unkind things are said about the "same old ditty," brooding on "love eggs" and the "peep and flap infernal" of "chicks," a fitting progeny of such poetic endeavors. In poem XLIV Heine accuses himself seriously of having been a "comedian" of the Romantic style to the point he had endangered his aesthetic as well as physical existence. In poem XLV Heine lashes out against the myths of the Hindu national epics, whose zoomorphic imagery Heine apparently finds odious, pretending to take it literally.[30] "You Are Just Like a Flower" (number XLVII) belongs to the group of gems initiated in the "Lyrical Intermezzo" by "During the Splendid Month of May." It is an exulting praise of beauty, spontaneous and absolute. Number seventy-nine is another attack on literary enemies, this time of the sobbing-sweet pseudo-Romantic persuasion. "Death -- That's Nighttime's Frigid chill" (number LXXXVII) contains no break in mood; it is a sober assessment of human existence whose poles are life and death. Youth, beauty and love are dreams; in their dream dimension they are indeed eternal, for they move in non-time. Unfortunately, they remain dreams, for most people -- and in moments of worst existential vacillation even for the poet -- disconnected from the physical reality of space and time. The following poem (number eighty-eight) closes the series of poems structured usually in four-line stanzas, the two-stanza length being the norm. It is a sort of epilogue to the spirit and style of "Homecoming;" the poems that follow are cast in different structure and rhyme patterns. They are much longer and bear no numbers. "Twilight of Gods" expands in rambling blank verse on the allegory of a spectral rape of the poet's guardian angel.[31] The poem is a categorical rejection of the human condition; life, happiness, the yearly springtime renewal of young and old all go on because of human stupidity.

"Doña Clara" and "Almanzor" belong to an entirely different poetic genre. Both are written in lilting, assonated Spanish trochees; in both Heine mercilessly ridicules the pride, easy virtue and racial elitism of Catholic Castile. In "Almanzor" Heine renews his attack on the sacrament of baptism hinted at in the earlier drama bearing the same title. His special venom is reserved for the hypocrisy of those who pay lip service to Christian humility. Heine-Almanzor dreams about taking advantage of the double standard concept of virtue practiced by the Christian establishment in order to accelerate the process of inner corrosion which he hopes will topple all institutionalized dogmatism.

The earlier-mentioned Travel Sketches, published between 1826 and 1831, broadened Heine's reputation as wit, raconteur, observer of nature, social commentator and self-deriding cynic. The first volume introduced a verse sequence entitled "Homecoming" which became an integral part of the Book of Songs a year later. The last two books depict travel impressions resulting from trips to England and Italy in 1827 and 1828.[32]

The Travel Sketches also introduced the first cyclus of poems dedicated to the North Sea (North Sea, I), an apotheosis of the regenerative marine element. Both cycles are written in the "free rhythms,[33]" reminiscent of Goethe's Storm and Stress period, but also of the earlier work of Klopstock and of Ludwig Tieck. Although they address the long-gone and yet somehow lingering divinities of Olympian Greece, they avoid the metaphysical urgency and despair of Hölderlin's bid for communication with the Divine. The sea poems of both North Sea I and II (the latter followed in 1827, the year of the Book of Songs), claim to be Heine's triumph over his youthful erotic disappointments and macabre visions, as well as over the sing-song of the folk stanza and the atmosphere of imitative folk mythology. Gerhard Storz finds their predominant features to be "clarity and freshness;[34]" Max Brod calls them "conventional in the extreme" and "lacking in sincerity.[35]" Historically speaking, they are an episode in the development of Heine's poetic form; the reemergence of the hexa-hepta-and octsyllabic, rhymed (or assonated) four-line stanza of folk provenance, domestic or "Spanish-trochaic," follows immediately upon the sea poems. This imitative folk structure, stanzaic as well as rhythmic, remains a lifelong vehicle of Heine's poetic expression.

The North Sea cycles mark clearly Heine's assumption of the Hellenic pose, which remained a rather faithful expression of his gently-hedonistic attitude to beauty, truth and death for the balance of his life, at least until the loss of his physical faculties to a gradual paralysis.[36]

"Sunset" is the third poem of the First Cyclus dedicated to the North Sea. It elaborates on the pristine oneness of "Luna, the goddess and Sol the god," a cosmic existence before any individualizing fragmentation, standing truly beyond the concepts of joy and suffering, here symbolized as a primordial indistinction of sun and moon, i.e., night and day. But now,

>Alas, at night,
>In heaven wonders Luna,
>The wretched mother
>With her orphaned, starry children,
>And she glows in silent suffering,
>And affectionate maidens and tender poets
>Tears and songs bring her as offering.

Heine's eternal quest for a synthesis of beauty and

truth producing "a paradise now" acquires in his marine poetry an especially sharp insistence. The poem's second part introduces the motif of degeneration rather than demise of the "immortal deities" of the heathen era. Sickened by the "evil tongues" of Judeo-Christian dogma, these deities

> Amble, tormented
> Dismal, on unending pathways.
> Unable to perish,
> As they drag along
> Their radiant suffering.

Like in Goethe's "Limits of the Human,[37]" in poem VII sea waves murmur into Heine's ear:

> Misguided companion
> Your arm is short and heaven is broad,
> And the stars are nailed up fast up yonder.
>
> ----
>
> In vain all the yearning, in vain all the
> sighing,
> The best thing would be you fell asleep.

This existential despair is, at this point of Heine's life, more or less a pose. It is soon to become a sober fact.

The fragility of personal existence in the face of primal forces is bewailed in "Storm" (poem number VIII). It starts with a Goethean invocation of <u>Aphrodite anadyomene</u>,[38]

> Oh, sea!
> Mother of beauty of the foam-arisen-one!

Immediately, his anguish before the ancestral authority and servitude to the goddess of love gains ascendancy:

> Grandame of love, have pity, spare me!

"Calm at Sea" elaborates further on the insignificance of individual survival. Momentarily, Heine returns to the Spanish trochaic stanza.

> Calm at sea! From the sea waves
> There a smart, small fish emerges
> Warms its little head in sunshine,
> With its merry tail it splashes.
>
> Yet the sea gull from air's regions
> On the little fish comes swooping,
> And, its quick catch held securely,
> It soars high into the azure.

"The Marine Specter" figures among the poems that earned Heine international reputation. The descriptive passages add colorful historical detail to the Vineta legend which had captured the imagination of Wilhelm Müller and others. Heine's view of the undersea city is endowed with masterfully outlined trappings of sixteenth century Low Countries, worthy of a Flemish master of that period. In the city and the period Heine claims to have found again the ideal of beauty -- and of woman -- that has been escaping him.

> You, always-belovèd-one,
> You, long ago-forfeit-one,
> You, finally-recovered-one--

At the point when he is ready to join his ideal in the sea depths, he feels himself pulled back by the "captain" of his common sense who has Faustian and Mephistophelian traits.

> The captain had grabbed me by the foot,
> Me pulled from the gunwale,
> And called, angrily laughing,
> Doctor, what in the devil?

Like at the end of "Dream Images," "Purification" (number eleven) attempts to drive the visions of elemental forces coupled with the poet's phobias and desires back into their shadow realm. With its suggestive imagery of "the ancient glistening serpent skin"

> Hypocrisy,

>   Which round my soul so long has been
>   twisting,
>   The soul distempered,
>   The God-denying-one, the angel-denying
>   one
>   Ahoy! Ahoy! Here comes the wind!

we find ourselves squarely in the atmosphere of Nietzsche's <u>Zarathustra</u> and the <u>condottiere</u> mentality of Genoa in <u>Merry Wisdom</u>.

The sixth poem of the Second Cyclus "The Gods of Greece" uses the title of Schiller's famous poem to refute the latter's balanced Hellenism. It glorifies the Dionysian, irrational aspects of the Greek pantheon, once again anticipating Nietzsche's dithyrambic vitalism. Heine is striking a blow for the "Young Lions" so savagely "rationalized" by Socrates in Plato's <u>Gorgias</u>.

>   The young ones repress the old ones,
>   As you yourself did your hoary father,
>   Jupiter Parricida![39]

Then comes the break in mood: "I have never loved you, you deities." Heine the "Hellene" now claims an "aversion" to the Greeks; but, reversing himself quickly once more, his sympathy returns to the "abandonded deities," when faced with

>   The new ones, dominant, dismal deities,
>   Malicious, dressed in humility's sheep-
>   skin --

Heine the superman-manqué proclaims in galloping dactyls his triumphant love for the underdog.

>   And in feuds among the deities I will be
>   One of the faction of those who were
>   humbled.

The following poem (number seven) ends in unequivocal epistemological nihilism.

>   The waves go on rumbling their rumble

> eternal,
> The wind blows on, the clouds go on
> flying,
> The stars are blinking, indifferent
> and cold,
> And a fool waits for an answer.

c. Heine the Paris Emigré. Maturing Political Thought. <u>New Poems, Germany, A Winter's Tale, Atta Troll</u>.

In 1827, the banner year of a mixed ascendancy of Heine's reputation and fortunes, he was invited by Cotta, the prestigious publisher of Goethe's and Schiller's works, to become editor of the <u>New Political Annals</u>. Published in Munich, the journal enjoyed a wide and informed readership. Heine's tenure as editor was brief; his heart was apparently not in the business of editing the thoughts of others, though he did invite and publish contributions "not deliriously demagogic, but gravely exhortatory.[40]"

On the conclusion of an Italian journey in 1829 Heine returned to Hamburg to spend there the last two years of his "German" existence.[41] Hoping that the July Revolution of 1830 that brought to the throne Louis Philippe would provide him with a politically and aesthetically freer and more stimulating climate, he left for Paris in 1831 as correspondent for Augsburg's <u>Allgemeine Zeitung</u>. At the time he didn't intent to make France his permanent residence. Once in Paris he threw himself enthusiastically into the mainstream of social and political activities. He became an active supporter of the Saint-Simonian socialist Utopia, but remained faithful to his ever-ambiguous fashion of embracing a cause, movement or ideology. Although he had no quarrel with Saint-Simon's <u>New Christianity</u>, an amalgam of socialism and the teachings of Jesus, before long he was involved in an argument with Buchez, leader of Saint-Simonism's moderate faction which was too "Roman-Catholic" for Heine's taste.[42]

Somewhat more harmonious were Heine's relations with the composers Meyerbeer, Chopin, Liszt and Berliotz, and with the foremost <u>litterati</u> of the period: Hugo, Béranger, George Sand, <u>Balzac</u>, Gérard de Nerval,[43] Musset, Alfred de Vigny, Alexandre Dumas <u>père</u>, etc. Preceded by his notoriety, Heine was received in Paris with open arms and a warm heart.

Till his dying day, Heine was destined to vacillate between the light of French reason and the darker regions of Germanic intuitionism, between the French tendency to direct action and the German propensity to meditation.[44] This tension between the clearly delienated, concrete particularism and the vague universalism of the quest for the infinite kept him likewise captive in the Romantic experiment with a never-ceasing struggle for self-transcendence and absolute individuation in an imperfect world. Yet this world was rapidly moving toward a categorical rejection of what was now considered unproductive games of the self with the infinite choices of self-realization. His vacillating allegiance, now to French "sunshine," now to Teutonic "fog," eventually provoked unjust attacks against most of his French compeers; Victor Hugo especially drew Heine's wrath.

Between 1835-40 Heine published a collection of his earlier newspaper articles under the title <u>The Salon</u>. They are musings on current politics, on the human condition in general, on all things German. They reflect Heine's complex, uncompromising and always exasperating search for truth and justice, for some synthesis of the fundamental problem of existence torn between the commands of reason and the demands of irrational forces. Max Brod emphasizes Heine's care to avoid all simplification[45] of the complex issues of national and individual being. And again, even in the years immediately following his euphoristic praises of French life and libertarian constitutionalism, Heine avers:

> I love what is German from the bottom
> of my heart more than anything else in
> the world... in my bosom are the archives
> of German emotion, just as in my... books
> are the archives of German song.[46]

No such accents sound in the mock-epic <u>Germany</u>. <u>A Winter's Tale</u>, a sequel appended to the <u>New Poems</u> of 1844. Ostracized or not as traitor to liberalism, Heine resumes in the <u>Winter's Tale</u> his attacks on German stodginess, stilted imagination, militarism and subservience, once again anticipating Nietzsche's identification of German <u>Geist</u> with the <u>Geist der</u>

Schwere, spirit of heaviness. Nothing escapes Heine's corrosive assessment: the Customs Union,[47] introduced in scholastic-metaphysical terminology of outward, material unity as opposed to the inward, truly ideal unity which Heine sarcastically suggests should come from censorship; the "dome of old Cologne," so fervently sung in "The Rhine, the Splendid River,[48] is now "the Bastille of the Spirit," a standing reminder of inquisitorial book-and-people burnings. Head VII of the Winter's Tale makes the Germans uncontested rulers of "the regions of aerial dreams.[49]" The Teutoburg Forest, scene of the defeat of Varus' three legions by Hermann (in Latin, Arminius), chief of the Cheruscan tribe in the year 9 A.D.,[50] is for Heine the "classical morass," and "dirt" in which the German nation found its ethnic identity. Somewhat incongruously, Heine slips in the portrait of his "poor cousin" Jesus whom he chastises for trying to reform mankind, a crime to which to a large extent Heine too would have to plead guilty (Head XIII). But the tension between the spirituality of Jesus and the no-nonsense attitude of the High Council parallels Heine's own rationalizing Francophilia that is skin-deep when compared with his lifelong love-hate affair with Germandom. A similar tension between Heine's "objective" assessment of the Middle Ages and the Romanticizing Teutonomania of "knights in spats" (Head XVII) shows Heine's perennial problem of finding himself constantly in the camp of his enemies, and assailed by those who should have been his friends. Head XXIII is one version of the recurring theme of the this-worldly frailty of things good and beautiful. It reemerges in Atta Troll as a quotation from a Schiller poem, and in the last lines of Heine's very last poem.

    The New Poems is a compilation of earlier-published verse[51] grouped under several subtitles. Poems that make up the series "New Spring" ring with echoes of the "Lyrical Intermezzo" and "Homecoming." Heine returns to the folk song, two-stanza structure, rhyme and tone, employing virtually the same devices that made up the bulk of the Book of Songs and was supposed to have been "lived down" in the buoyant Hellenism of the North-Sea cycles. Yet according to Storz the New Poems are conceived in a new atmosphere, ringing with "the keynote of Heine's later polemic with Romanticism." The "poetic apparatus" is symptomatic of a "different purpose and effect," becoming a parody of "the old manner." The author shows an unprecedented self-assurance in the manipulation of "ironic-comical devices;" what is toned down is the old Byronic dilemma between "feeling and reflection.[52]" Actually, the old narcissism, plaintive self-doubt and self-vindication are replaced by a more cynical but also more realistic assessment of human woes on a broader scope than that of a jilted lover suffering slow spiritual extinction. And yet, the Romanticized involvement with Eros remains the central theme with the same old disastrous corrolaries.

"Through My Mind Soft Accords Wind" (poem number six of "New Spring" is one more of those lyrical flashes of mood which say everything about the spring-like regeneration of the psyche touched by the thrill of loving and being loved in return.[53] "The Slender Water Lily" (poem XV)[54] is a deceptively simple image of a flower aspiring to transcend its earth-bound condition, and experiencing "shame" over its inability to go beyond touching the "reflection" of eternity. Poem twenty conceals an equally sophisticated metaphysical proposition: is sensory -- and sensuous -- beauty endowed with a cognitive consciousness of its own being, or is beauty an unconscious, "soulless," almost automatic phenomenon? The same question is restated in "Depravation," poem number eight of the "Occasional Poems" series of New Poems.

> I also doubt if she has feelings,
> The nightingale, of what she sings;
> They go too far, her sighs and trilling,
> A matter of routine, methinks.

Poem XXIX intones once more the refrain of the "old ditty" bewailing the fate of all that is pure, absolute and hence, beautiful; goodness and beauty cannot possibly survive in this world. A related and intricately complex problem with no solution is suggested in poem XXXV. Modern humanity has become so conceptualized and "enlightened" that it will mistake the fire of love for simply "poetry," i.e., something "made up," or art in its artificial, unreal sense.

> Our world lacks faith in fire
> It will think it's poetry.

The same disastrous results of rationalistic conceptualization deplores poem number forty. When the affects are overlaid with "wit" -- in the best Schlegelian sense -- the synthesis is not "progressive universal poetry," not a potentialized, "higher" existence but a virtual drowning of the self in emotion overlaid with a veneer of reason:

> My heart is so wise and witty
> And it bleeds to death in my breast.

The next series of New Poems bears the title "Miscellaneous." It contains poetized reminiscences about ladies of Heine's acquaintance during the first years of his Paris exile. In poem VII of the sub-series dedicated to Seraphine Heine goes beyond and actually counter to Spinozist pantheism[55] in demanding a this-worldly synthesis of the Old and New Testaments resulting in an apocalyptic "Third New Testament" which would do away with all dualities and opposites and, especially, with the phenomenon of pain. As the difference between good and evil is obliterated, God's omnipresence will shine in every aspect of existence. The same demand for an aesthetically (and politically) implemented paradisiac existence rings in the introductory lines to Atta Troll (Head I) assailing "that ancient lullaby," the belief in punishment and reward in the beyond, good only for lulling to sleep "the people, the big yokel." Here Heine is quite explicit in the ultimate goal of his earthly endeavors:

> Already on this earth, dear friends,
> God's realm we will establish.

Poem X of the "Seraphine" series shows Heine the cynical tease, mocking Romantic Weltschmerz. He laughs at those who experience a pining empathy with nature's cyclical processes and its burdensome impassivity. The style and vocabulary of this miscellany show a drift to the vernacular,[56] a phenomenon steadily gaining ascendancy in the balance of Heine's work. Storz points out that even the meter flows more evenly;[57] the dactyls that used to break the basically iambic metric pattern, producing a constant ruffling of the affects, grow now rarer.

Number five of the poems dedicated to Clarisse acquires the pathos if not the grandeur of Heine's French contemporary and fellow-Romantic Lamartine in his treatment of the ubi sunt, "whither have they gone" motif.

> Where are the flames that were extin-
> guished?
> Where is the wind that blew away?[58]

In "Catherine" (poem number seven) Heine confesses to metaphysical jealousy of Christ, deploring the Redeemer's moral standards, set too high for mere humans.

> Oh, he means well, this I know --
> No one is so pure and noble --

In the sixth poem addressed to Emma the author's existential despair achieves remarkable incisiveness and economy.

> But, alas, what end distressing
> Follows down love's noble path,
> Loveless woes along come pressing,
> When life's over there comes death.

Storz calls the form and tenor of this poem those of a chanson,[59] a music hall or cabaret-style song, heralding the Paris of Toulouse-Lautrec, sin capital of the world and center of free cultural -- and erotic -- experimentation.

"Tannhäuser" is a lengthy satire in three parts parodying in a rather wooden and crude fashion the medieval legend about a Christian knight who gradually overcomes his servitude to Venus and turns his sensuality into service of Divine Love. It is just another sally against "knighthood in spats" voiced in the Winter's Tale.[60] As Heine lashes out against Catholic dogmatism in faith and morals, insisting that, through exposure to this dogmatism, the deities of "heathen" Greece have become "satanized" into antagonists of the Christian God.[61]

> The pope uplifted his hands and wailed,
> These wailing words had spoken:
> "Tannhäuser, oh you wretched man,
> The magic, it can't be broken!
>
> ---------------------------------
>
> The devil who is Venus called
> No other is as clever,
> To rescue you from her pretty fangs
> Would be a vain endeavor.
>
> Now for the lust of flesh you must
> Pay with your soul eternal,
> You are cast out, you are condemned
> To lasting pain infernal.

The third major group of poems in the cyclus New Poems aptly entitled "Abroad" contains a lament over a crisis of ethnic identification. After all the invective and ridicule hurled at his native land, Heine now discloses an incurable yearning for it. "Once I Did Have a Lovely Fatherland" (poem III of the series) provides a new insight into Heine's hate-love dialectics: <u>never is his declaration of loyalty to cause, race, religion, thought or act more contradictory than when it claims to be a univocal and positive statement of praise or condemnation</u>. Given Heine's restless search for paradoxes and his need to reconcile them, had the Germany of his day been a Liberal's dream come true, Heine would not have been able to give himself to her without reservations of such severity that, eventually, he would have come to hate her.

The overt dialectic tension between French insouciance bent on more or less rationalized action and German brooding moodiness is of course nowhere clearer than in "Night Thoughts," the twenty-fourth of the "Occasional Poems.[62] But the insistent ridicule of Germany's "solid stance" and enduring "health" suggests a bit of envious admiration. By the same token, the exultation

>There comes my woman, like fair morrow
>She laughs away the German sorrow.

is not entirely self-assuring. The scorn for the wooden orderliness of the German mind that animated the <u>Winter's Tale</u> returns in the poem "An Assurance" (number twenty of "Occasional Poems). Again, if nothing else, Heine's overstating his case makes his derision sound hollow.

In the fourth series of <u>New Poems</u> entitled "Romances" Heine returns in isolated instances to the stylized necrophilia of his youth. The case in point is "Conjuration" (romance number IV). A friar's black magic conjurs up the spirit of a deceased beautiful woman, but the consummation-in-the grave which for young Heine represented the only possible attainment of an Absolute, remains in suspense. In the final analysis, Eros <u>through</u> Thanatos fails; this prefigures Heine's attitude to the bid for perfection in this world expressed in a citation from Schiller which Heine will give in <u>Atta Troll</u>:

>What as song should live forever,
>It must perish in this life (Head XXVII).

"Conjuration" focuses on the whole problematic nature of magic, read, artistic creativity of a demiurge producing a higher-than-earthly reality. And yet, even the sacrifice of self-identity (i.e., madness, such as in the case of Hölderlin, Hoffmann and Nietzsche) which the Romantic seems to seek for the sake of self-transcendence toward an other-worldly Absolute, proves unable to bring about this ultimate Romantic endeavor, simply because it pretends to enjoy other-worldly perfection in this world.

Romance twenty-three belongs to a sub-series called "The Underworld." It has an Eichendorff cast and theme, but the epistemological thrust is pure Heine. The poet projects himself into King Harald Harfagar held in bondage by a beautiful sea nymph. The latter is of course a transfiguration of the spectral bride, but her function remains the same: to demonstrate the ambiguous nature of Eros and its lethal grasp on the male against which not even the decay of old age can protect him. It also demonstrates the mind-numbing spell of absolute beauty, in this instance, residing in a watery beyond. The possession of the Absolute can be achieved only at the expense of one's individuality; because of this, the resulting gratification can be had only in a dream state. The existential exhaustion caused by the acquisition of the Absolute is expressed cogently in one four line stanza.

> At times he thinks he hears in the wind
> His Normans' voices calling,
> His arms shoot up in a friendly salute
> But soon they sadly are falling.

Among the poems of the fifth series of <u>New Poems</u> entitled "To Ollea[63]" figures one dedicated to Helen of Troy, but as she appears in the Goethean garb of <u>Faust</u> II, a revenant brought to life by Mephistophelian arts. Once again we see the communion between the finite force of man and the infinite force of the libido-arousing female struggling over the male and, apparently, thwarted in their ultimate communion.

The searing "voluptuous heat" of the ideal conjured up by the artist-magician's temerity cannot be stilled by any finite individual. Here at last we have the key to young Heine's apparently gratuitously ghoulish aesthetics. It is the dead who partake in the Absolute; they dwell in non-time, which is eternity. Like the gods of Hölderlin (and in Plato's <u>Banquet</u>), they require Eros as communicator of what eternal beings lack, which is life in terms of breath, i.e., individualized sensations.[64]

> Implant your mouth upon my mouth,
> Divine is human breathing,
> I'll drink your soul out, for the dead
> With unstilled flames are seething.

Naturally Heine's view of Eros' position <u>metaxy</u>, inbetween the perishable man and eternal gods, is much less classically optimistic than man's participation in the Divine as seen by Plato and Aristotle. The latter's <u>athanatizein</u>, immortalization, derives from

Plato's participatory metaphysics and is thus limited in the extent to which man can "touch" eternity.[65] Heine's and the Romantics' this-worldly immortalization was an absolute possession of it, <u>aut Caesar, aut nihil</u>; the <u>nihil</u> invariably won out. The already mentioned poems "An Assurance" and "Night Thoughts" (poems XX and XXIV of the sixth and last series of <u>New Poems</u>) offer little beyond what has been said <u>earlier</u>. In its tenor and convictions of the moment, "The Silesian Weavers" is kindred to the "Occasional Poems.[66]" It was written in 1844 when Heine saw himself driven by the force of economic and social circumstances in Germany once again closer to the radical Left. Unlike most of his pronouncements about Germany, the "triple curse" Heine's weavers weave into the shroud of the old order is more than a momentary outburst of sympathy. It is a heartfelt, consistent identification with the underdog and indeed a prophecy of a violent overthrow of the iniquitous establishment which came true, though only at the end of World War I.

<u>Atta Troll</u> (1847)[67] is another mock-epic, a potpourri indeed of sallies, insights and echoes of the author's earliest obsessions and, of course, of laments for the pining away of the Romantic Muse, a condition for whose morbidity Heine was greatly responsible. The plot is secondary to Heine's intention of writing a spoof of the radical Left as well as an epilogue to Romanticism. <u>Atta Troll</u> is a tamed bear who runs away from his dancing master during a performance in the Basque region of the Pyrenees. He is ungainly, naive, honest and, eventually, unsuccessful in his bid for absolute freedom, just like the left-radical German revolutionaries. But for all these unendearing qualities, he remains Heine's hero even though, paradoxically, the poet sets out on a bear hunt to kill him. The paradox is of course <u>aufgehoben</u>, cancelled, by Heine's dialectic of assailing what he loves best. Besides, his potshots at the German would-be Jacobins were meant to kill their reputation.

Heine's imagination roams far and wide; the Pyrenean setting brings to mind the heroic struggle and death of Roland and his paladins in 778 A.D. at

Roncevaux (Rencesvals), as well as memories of Novalis' "blue flower."

> Ronceval, you noble dale,
> Whenever your name is mentioned
> Full of blue-hued flower fragrance
> It will set my heart aquiver. (Head IV)

Atta Troll returns to his "romantically" wild and savage cave, showing an equally romantic tenderness for his brood and a yearning for their mother who must remain in human captivity and will, eventually, quite easily get over the loss of her mate. This gives the author a chance to indict human elitism which makes men assume they have inherited the regiment of the earth. Finally, with the same dart Heine strikes at aristocratic privilege that survived the Revolution and Napoleon, and reimposed its sway on all the Atta Trolls in Europe. All this leads to an ambiguous attack against the self-evident truth of human rights. The attack is of course ironic, but the juxtaposition of human <u>rights</u> as opposed to the <u>laws</u> of nature shows the ambiguity of Heine's allegiance to unqualified republicanism. In the name of human rights men defend their right to usurp nature.[68]

> And they think they are entitled
> To commit this heinous misdeed
> Specially against bears directed
> And dare "human rights" to call it.
>
> Human rights, the rights of humans,
> Who on you has them conferred?
> Nature never did such thing,
> Nature cannot be unnatural (Head V).

We hear quite distinctly Heine's own elitism rumble underneath this attack on any elite that had lost the moral right to claim leadership.

Atta Troll inveighs next against ossified institutions that had arisen out of the theories of natural right and the law of custom.

> What by law of nature always
> And hence, too, by the law of custom
> Guaranteed had been for eons,
> With bold cheek is hereby cancelled
> (Head VI).

What follows reveals Heine's scorn for unqualified egalitarianism.

> We're all strictly equal! Let each
> Donkey seek the highest office,
> In his stead, the lion will be
> To the mill with grain sacks trotting
> (Head VI).

And so it goes, the targets of Heine's derision broadening the vulgarization of the act of dancing which, once upon a time, was performed as a prayer ritual by King David to honor Jehovah. There is a vicious attack, meant once again only half ironically, against the atheism of the neo-Hegelians Feuerbach and Bruno Bauer.[69] Heine's praise of pantheism, however, is free of irony, since it reflects his own theological convictions. With the same breath, Heine caricatures the transcendent nature of Judeo-Christian, and by association, Platonic theology, allegorized as a "colossal polar bear" in whose other-worldly majesty "the lowly Troll" hopes to some day participate (Head VIII).

A vindication of this-worldly sensory existence (Am a beast, ungainly, boorish,/ Am the waddling beast uncouth/... Not ashamed am of my background Head IX) is followed by a paraphrase of Proudhon's attack on private property (Head X). This sally is overtly ironic, given the contempt in which Heine held Proudhon's teachings.[70] Next comes a mock-imitation of Hannibal's oath in which Troll makes his son swear eternal enmity to humankind[71] (Ibid.).

The civilizational retardation of "Visigothic" Spain and "Ostrogothic" Germany comes also under attack. The sight of the Pont d'Espagne, the Bridge of Spain, throws into relief the contrast between these two countries and France.

> That's the name the bridge was given
> Which from France to Spain there reaches,
> To the land of West-Barbarians,
> Who're retarded one millenium.
>
> One millenium they're retarded
> In regards to global manners,
> While my country's East-Barbarians
> Are retarded but one century (Head XI).

The motifs of the revenant and wise crone-relative reemerges, this time in Uraka,[72] the mother of the poet's guide and fellow bear hunter Laskaro[73] who is apparently a zombie, kept alive by his mother's magic ministrations.

It is through her stratagem that Laskaro fells Atta Troll whose fur eventually winds up in the poet's Paris apartment, but not before we are treated to a nocturnal ride of witches, specters and historic personages thrown together helter-skelter from different periods and cultures. Charles X of France (recently deceased) rides side by side with the great hunter and great-grandson of Noah Nimrod and King Arthur. Of particular interest to Heine's never-resting libido are some provocatively clad huntresses. Their dual nature of heathen deities and Christian fiends is a familiar, oft repeated theme. As for the Eternal Feminine, Heine is not too favorably impressed by its nature.

> If a devil or an angel
> I can't tell. One can't exactly
> Tell where ends the angel and where
> Starts the devil in a woman (Head XIX).

The reason why it is Herodias who among all those legendary huntresses catches the poet's eye is simple: her hate-love relationship with John the Baptist. After having him ordered beheaded, she dies of grief at the sight of the prophet's severed head.

> She kept crying and went mad,
> By love's madness she did perish
> (What? Love's madness? That's redundant!
> In itself love is but madness!) Head XIX).

The suggestive looks Herodias sends the poet in his feverish dream are a throwback to the grave site eroticism of his youthful Muse. They are a further proof that the "Dream Images" were more than adolescent reflections of a legend-cluttered mind and a bent for the macabre. Aside from Heine's ambivalent view of the Eros-Thanatos complex, the shade of Herodias reflects his ever more assertive Jewishness.

> You I love more than the others,
> More than that Hellenic goddess,
> Than that Nordic nymph more even,
> You I love, you long-dead Jewess!
> (Head X X)

Next comes under attack the Romantic School of Swabia which flourished between 1830 and 1850 whose chief representative was Uhland. Sarcastically, Heine is ready to concede to the Swabians "character," but never passion or genius (Head XXII).

Throughout the epic reverberates the sempiternal concern with bringing eternity from the beyond down to earth. In <u>Atta Troll</u> Heine literally shoots down the ideal of <u>imminent</u> apocalyptic perfection to claim it as his trophy, purified of the rabble-rousing excesses of Romantic Leftists. Head XXVII reads in part:

> Oh, how often have I, barefoot,
> Stood right upon this <u>earthly</u>
> <u>Ruddy husk</u> of my great hero,
> On the fur of Atta Troll! (My italics).

The idea of spontaneous love, innocence and Rousseauian attunement to unspoiled nature is here literally brought to bay and trampled. In the following stanza Heine gives the earlier-mentioned quotation from Schiller:

> What as song should live forever,
> It must perish in this life!

Obviously, since these are exactly Heine's feelings, the use of Schiller's thought has no ironic intent.

The concluding lines of the epic (Head XXVII) bewail the demise of the cherished Romantic feelings of Heine's youth, the "blue nights filled with moonlight," the ringing of the "long lost forest chapel" as well as the dialectically self-cancelling irony, the "teasing interruptions/ Of the too familiar coxcomb." But the image of the bears' "drone bass," transfigured into "ghostly whispers," is another sally against Romantic excesses, foremost among them the shrill contrasts that Heine so loved to construe, leaving them unreconciled. Atta Troll, the last "free forest song" of all "things Romantic," anticipates the Romantic experience bowing out "with a whimper."

As we have been trying to show throughout this long and complex exegesis of the Heine phenomenon in which man, work, and dreams are so inextricably interwoven, his love-hate affair with Romanticism found no workable synthesis of the existential paradoxes. All of Heine's efforts to bring about a compromise with newly emerging concepts of beauty, feeling, and truth backfired, on him and on what he loved best about the ambience that had shaped him and which he in turn helped to shape. The last stanza of Atta Troll expresses this succinctly.

> Different seasons, different birds,
> Different birds and different singing!
> Perhaps I could like them too,
> If the ears I have were different!

The Paralipomena to Atta Troll (Head XXIII) contains no new insights, except an intensification of the poet's self-criticism. He pleads guilty to singing about himself more than about his "bears," as he takes one last hard look at the Romantic grimace which makes him what he is and must needs unmake him in the end.[74]

d. Heine the Hesitant Rediscoverer of Transcendence. Tension Between Nazarenism and Hellenism Unresolved.

By 1848, spinal paralysis put an end to Heine's ability to get around; eventually, he could not even see well enough or move his fingers to write.[75] Yet his output during his last years (1849-56) is absolutely amazing in quantity and even quality. Understandably, his poetic visions lack the immediacy, optimistic vigor and exuberance of the Book of Songs and New Poems. And yet the three-volume Romancero and the latest poems dating from 1853 and 1854 stand out as repositories of an interiorized combativeness. In them, at last, he achieved a synthesis of sorts between acceptance and condemnation of the human condition in spite of the condemnation of all beautiful and good things to early demise in this world.

In his last years the pose of life and love weariness had become an awesome reality. The palpable presence of decay had sobered up his Byronic spleen and withered his Hellenic sensualism. The realization that the struggle for the Romantic apocalypse will die with him showed the way to transcend, in a modest and, as usual, ambiguous way, what he continued to consider the essence of reality, the here-and-now. Actually, this was not too radical a departure from the this-worldliness of his more vigorous days, only a shift of emphasis toward a transcendent ground as conceived in Scriptural Judaism, with the hope of transfiguring his broken self to some enduring dimension, but without the ritualistic trappings of Jewish Orthodoxy.

The works of the Fifties attest to this drive toward spirituality by the means of a peculiarly Heinesque apotheosis through suffering and death. In the Romancero his Muse once again ranges broadly from the harsh persiflage of pseudo-Romantic posturing and Jewish apostasy which pervert the stark radiance of Apollonian sublimity in "The Apollonian God" ("First Book -- Stories"), to the kinder satire of the antics of Polish patriots in the Paris exile ("Two Knights," ibid.).[76] The short epic "Witzliputzli" shows already in the title an intent to burlesque a reality containing very few comic elements. Heine's irreverent corruption of Huitzilopochtli, the bloodthirsty war god of the Aztecs, to a name that sounds extremely funny in German shows a strong need to laugh at what is rather terrible. The poem inveighs against the decayed life vigor of Europe and of her institutions, explaining the poet's own spooky appearance as a result of lifelong dealings with moribund matters, foremost among them his early love for Teutonic lore. The gloomy nature of this obsession is symbolized by the Kyffhäuser, legendary abode of Frederick Barbarossa, the Venusberg where Tannhäuser had been held captive by the satanic wiles of Venus, the heathen goddess of love, and by the traditional black-red-yellow colors of the German Empire, "colors of the monkey rear...." Heine gets at last to tell his story; it deals with the <u>noche triste</u>, the "sad night" of June 30, 1520 when Cortés and his men had to fight their way out of Tenochtitlán (Mexico City) leaving back much of their loot and some of their companions who then became the main actors of the play called by Heine <u>Human Sacrifice</u>. While those who managed to escape look on helplessly, the captives are gruesomely sacrificed to Huitzilopochtli and devoured, for the Aztec barbarians have as yet not learned the art of representing symbolically man's participation in the Divine. In the Christian ritual, red wine substituted blood,

> And the corpse that had preceded
> Into a quite thin and harmless
> Mealy wafer was transfigured. --

But Huitzilopochtli knows his days and those of his worshippers are numbered. The crone-relative symbol reappears to comfort her well-fed but not-too-happy "nephew." Before Heine packs off the Aztec god to Europe, there to join the Greco-Roman pantheon in the process of satanization and hence, in lucrative employment, he cannot resist taking a swipe at the Marian cult, the Mother-Virgin aspect of woman, once so dear to him in his youth.

> And there is an ancient proverb:

> Will of women godly will is,
> And the will is doubly godly
> When the woman is God's mother.

An entirely different spirit pervades the "Hebrew Melodies" of the <u>Romancero's</u> third book. Actually, the melodies are only partially Hebrew; most of them are dedicated to Spanish Jewry.[77] "Princess Sabbath" reflects the dying poet's yearning for the Jewish lore to which he had been only inadequately exposed as a child. His memories of the Sabbath service stir in his soul a feeling of a safe, enduring existential ground, something denied him throughout his adult life. The resentment against centuries of antisemitism which had given the Jews of Europe the identity of a dog, explodes here with intensive, impatient vigor. The World Ground in the process of communicating with the faithful gives them, at least for a few hours, back their human dignity. At last, unequivocally and with final validity, Heine finds the way to the reconciliation of time and eternity, of the finite and the infinite, of the human and the Divine.

> Through the house mysterious
> Whispers run and silent stirrings,
> As the house's unseen master
> Awesomely in silence breathes.

In "Jehuda ben Halevy[78]" Heine achieves yet another synthesis, that between the Hebrew culture of twelfth century Toledo and the minstrelsy of Provençal troubadours. At the end of the poem's first part Heine defines another positive, unshakeable existential foothold, gained as a declaration of independence from good and evil by the God-inspired poet:

> He to God alone must answer,
> Not to people -- for in art
> As in life -- may men inflict
> Death on us, but judgment, never. --

The second part of the poem rearranges the motif of the Jew's dog-like existence in the vision of Heine the generic sufferer whose wounds are licked by time, as Job's were by a dog. The old, irreconciliable Romantic ambivalence between time and eternity, life and death returns with a vengeance:

> Thank you dog, for your saliva --
> But its coolness only soothes --
> Death alone can make me whole,
> But, alas, I am immortal!

Once more Heine witnesses his spleen "simmering down" and flying off; apparently, the admission of immortality of a definitely inner-worldly, generically-racial kind, does tend to allay somewhat the existential anguish that used to torment Heine most of his life. It also helps to put to rest some of his Romantic élan and irony, transfiguring it to an almost classically idealist world view. Identifying with Halevy the poet, Heine sees the "God-filled soul" as the immortal, perennial goal toward which all aesthetic and existential striving must be oriented. Next comes the noble parallel between the troubadour Jaufré Rudel[79] whose old-age infatuation with Mélisande, Marchioness of crusader-held Tripoli brought him to North Africa to die at the feet of a woman he had never seen before, and the Hebrew poet Halevy, Rudel's equal in loyalty to his God-given art.

> Thus died also ben Halevy,
> At the feet of his belovèd,
> On her knees his head while resting,
> Knees of his Jerusalem.

There was to be also happiness for Heine the lover in his last years which he found in the hard-tested but enduring love of a simple, untutored, vain but spontaneous Parisian shop girl. Unable to speak German and taught late in life how to write French by Heine, "Mathilde[80]" loved him for his essential self, bruised by life, sick and dying, not for his fame and adulation by a fickle readership. In spite of some stormy domestic feuding, their love withstood the test of his gradual physical deterioration; Mathilde's patience and selflessness, assisted by the naive optimism of the eternal child, made his last years somewhat more bearable.

To the same book of the Romancero belongs another long poem called "Disputation." Patterned after a real occurrence[81] it reiterates Heine's scorn for proselytizing Nazarenism which occludes the soul's openness to the Divine, degrading the religious experience into a jousting bout unworthy of the two great religions that Judaism and Christianity potentially are. Casuistry, the need to totally discredit and destroy the opponent (Heine's own often-practiced vice), invocation of dogmas as if through magic incantations clash intermirably and without achieving any kind of a decisive victory. Like the wrongly stated premise that there is only one true religion, the poem trails off into nothingness, without an end or solution. The poem is an elaboration of a much shorter and pithier "disputation" written in Heine's earlier days. "To Edom[82]" was published in a Supplement to Heine's collected works; it shows not only a finely honed resentment of the millenary persecution of his race but, what is more important, the fear that the poet -- and, by implication, his coreligionaries -- are indeed achieving a normalization of sorts in the Christian world, a most undesirable synthesis imaginable:

> I myself have started raving
> And became almost like you.

Typical of some of the poems not published in the years of their writing that make up the Supplement is "The New Alexander," which appeared in 1846. It is a rather nasty spoof of Goethe's poem "The King at Thule[83]" and the grace of classical sobriety in life enjoyment and resignation to human finiteness which inspired Goethe's version. Goethe's king remains loyal to the memory of his spouse beyond the grave, yet keeps on practicing the art of living to the last appointed hour; he departs from life with no regrets, returning to the elemental forces of nature (the sea) the symbolic bond between him and the queen he is about to join. Heine's king, on the other hand, is a drunk, guzzling expensive champagne. By turning the order of things topsy turvy, he has convinced himself that this is the only way to world conquest. Alexander ran out of energy because he couldn't hold his "wine," read, the fire of emotions and creativity. The new Alexander-Heine has convinced himself he can handle the destructive element in creativity, simply because he has a greater capacity for it. Besides, apparently the only way to "conquer," i.e., be able to put up with this world built on paradoxes, is "by stumbling from jar to jar." The magic of art and the art of magic have become the art of staying drunk.

Poems 1853 and 1854 contain some of Heine's finest. In "Castle Affront" the ageing poet relives the "youthful sorrows" of his Hamburg years. His imagination, alive with the bear allegory of Atta Troll, sees uncle Salomon now in the guise of the old "growl bear Boreas,[84]" now as the cluttering "weathervane," tyrannically regulating the conversation and opinions of the castle's "subjects." More importantly, Heine gives us yet another clue to his youthful obsession with the diabolical and spectral forces welling up from the unconscious. The stanza

> It grinned at me, that spectral green
> With scorn my presence seemed defying,
> And from the yew trees there came next
> At me a groaning, rattling, sighing...

shifts the locus of what Jung calls variously "a primordial experience of the non-ego," and an "unknown, inhuman feeling[85]" from the collective unconscious to the deindividuating elemental force of nature which, together with the old "growl bear," threatens the needs of Heine's inmost self.

A sub-cyclus entitled "To Lazarus" (number VIII of Poems 1853 and 1853) explores the leper-like existence that have become Heine's last years. Time and again, he paints a self-portrait of pain and revulsion at his condition reminiscent of Ronsard's contemplations of his own disintegration.[86]" The spectral bride of "Youthful Sorrows" and the life-and-breath hungry Helen of the "Ollea" series turn into the pith-swilling "sable lady" (the second poem dedicated to "Lazarus"). In the following piece, the night thoughts of the pain-racked martyr are suspected of being once again "gods of ancient heathen worship," the same as the earlier "Gods of Greece,"

"Witzliputzli," Tannhäuser's Venus, etc. Spawned by "the horribly sweet Orgia" of nightly revels brought about by pain, opiates and the only faculty freely moving in Heine's body, his imagination, these "spooks" are what the poet tries to capture in words the following morning.

From the Mattress Grave (1855) contains Heine's last poems. They continue to explore the process of dying in the vein of the "Lazarus" poetry. A sonnet (poem number seven) reviews Heine's life. Starting in a sober, almost contented manner, it gradually reveals the terror produced by imminent personal extinction. The poet assesses the achievements of his life after a relatively painless day and a "happy night." The focus shifts from the assessment of one of his better days to a survey of the poet's past. He admits that in spite of his constant imaginary and real woes, disappointments and a longlasting terminal disease, this one day and night were in essence a rich life experience in which Heine had done exactly as he pleased regardless of the consequences, and had enjoyed a great deal of recognition. The second tercet presents an arresting image of the speed with which the realization that one should be, and indeed has been happy, turns into the vision of imminent death. "Morphia" (poem XIX) muses in a subdued manner at the kinship of sleep and death. The ancients symbolized them as "youthful figures:" Sleep (Hypnos) and Death (Thanatos), Hypnos's twin brother.[87] Heine finds the latter paler, sterner and almost nobler than his brother Sleep who, with the aid of morphine, "the poppy blossom wreath," gives only temporary respite from racking pain. Only the "sterner brother" can now cure the poet permanently. The last two verses of the poem

> For sleep is good, death is better, all
> considered,
> Though best would be to never have
> been born.

reflect the more pessimistic aspect of the Greek world view which lies below the surface of cheerful Olympian life affirmation.[88]

Poem number nine of "Lazarus" briefly summarizes the mystery that poses the understanding of the female psyche. Woman need not be represented as the quizzical sphinx; she is, essentially, a riddle even without the zoomorphic trappings of the Egyptian pantheon, in fact so much so that the continued smooth operation of the world as we know it depends on the female not finding the key to the essence of her being. And yet Heine's never-ceasing and certainly problematic involvement with the Eternal Feminine was to have one more, though purely spiritual, flare-up in the last agonizing days of his existence. Mathilde's intuitive wisdom and generosity tolerated Heine's almost childish infatuation with the enigmatic Camilla Selden, rechristened Mouche, "Fly," by the poet.[89] The romance ran its innocent and brief course terminating in Heine's death a few months after la Mouche's first visit.

"To Mouche," i.e., the "Fly Lady" contains Heine's last poems conceived in the vein of "Lazarus." Number XXVIII, considered his very last, echoes the Eros-Thanatos complex of Heine's poetic youth, as well as the universally-Romantic ambiguity of the couch-coffin symbol. More specifically, it evokes the concluding sections of Espronceda's Student of Salamanca, without the latter's danse macabre sequences and the metaphysical arrogance of don Félix that leads to the student's acceptance of the challenge by the skeletal specter of his mistress to physical communion.[90] The poem represents an unusual fusion of an objectively accurate account of the feeling of disintegration of the self and of that of a whole period of civilization, with a subjectively sensitive rendition of grieving over one's own demise. Around a sarcophagus containing a corpse untouched by decay which the poet recognizes as his own body[91] lie scattered in wild disarray the plastic beauties of Western civilization so dear to Heine. The poet chose to call them "glories of the Renaissance," apparently to portray the final demise of the latest form of the Hellenic spirit. This spirit had been revived first as the Renaissance experiment and again, in its latest avatar, as Romantic art. The challenge of a perishing individuality, flung in the face of eternity and the need for a belief in some kind of a transcendent order, has been seldom captured with greater pain and vividness than "the lovely column" staring upward "to the towering heavens,"

> As if the lightning's anger it were daring.

This is no "castle Romanticism," no quaint regionalism nor its caustic refutation, but the tragedy of man and of his dismal efforts to achieve immortality in this world by his art, vainly competing with eternal nature and cosmic forces. The motif of an equally eternal tension between the Greek materialism of the senses and Nazarene, other-worldly spirituality unfolds for the last time in this long, somber and majestic poem. The civilization which this tension helped to create continues to be torn between the "savage Pan" and the equally cruel anathemas hurled by Mosaic intransigence. Once more Heine seems to question Goethe's life and work as model of reconciled existential opposites of the greatest metaphysical relevance for the whole of Western civilization. What there is of a reconciliation in Heine's poem comes in the metamorphosis of the passion flower into a grieving female figure, a masterful embodiment of female intuitionism that recognizes the tragedy of the yearning for the Absolute.[92] Though Heine's conviction that the synthesis of Hellenism with Nazerenism will be the primary task of the coming age stands unassailed, the actual implementation of the task seems more remote than ever. Though in his last days he insisted: "Il y a pourtant un coin divin dans l'homme,[93]" suggesting a Platonic and indeed Nazarene openness to Divine Transcendence in man's psyche, the disconsolate ambience of the Mouche-poem casts doubt on this.

> And to no end will come this argument,
> For truth and beauty pull in two
> directions,
> Forever will the human host be rent
> Between the Hellene and barbarian
> factions.[94]

Unlike Goethe, Heine refused to come to terms with, and rise above his age, unable to "digest it," to use a Nietzschean term.95 Though only partially and often negatively, he did identify passionately with the self-lacerating Romanticism of his time. Like Heine himself, Romanticism could achieve a synthesis of its contradictory postulates only by paralyzing them in a realist compromise with the cosmos and human nature. Heine's twenty-nineth poem to "La Mouche" says it all, repeating once more a truth that never ceased to haunt him:

>The human lot -- what greatness wrought,
>What's good and fair, it must end badly.

Heine's life work and thought mirror the entire Romantic syndrome. This one ambiguous figure embodies it to a truer extent than any of the exclusively Romantic poets of Brentano's, Uhland's or Eichendorff's kind, simply because Heine never stopped trying, though to no avail, to transcend the movement's virtues and weaknesses. This effort alone puts him in a category by himself.

NOTES

[1] A term employed by Heine to describe Judeo-Christian spiritualism as a disease of healthy life forces. Cf. Max Brod, Heinrich Heine. The Artist in Revolt, trans. Joseph Witriol (London: Vallentine, Mitchell, 1956), 148 and passim.

[2] "About a Summer Night I lately Dreamed," from the cycle "To Mouche," Cf. XXVIII, Heinrich Heine. Werke, ed. Martin Greiner (Köln: Kiepenhauer und Witsch, 1962), I, 605 ff.

[3] A cult introduced by the Persian Manes, or Manichaeus, in the third century A.D. It is based on the eternal and never definitively resolved struggle between absolute good (Ormuzd) and absolute evil (Ahriman). It incorporated elements of Gnostic, Zoroastrian and other ancient cults, including some derived from Christianity.

[4] A term borrowed from Spanish literary criticism referring to neo-Baroque "shocker" novelism introduced by Camilo José Cela's Family of Pascual Duarte (1942).

[5] Gottfried August Bürger (1747-94), contemporary of Goethe. With Herder and Goethe he popularized the modern folk ballad. The seminal poem "Lenore" (1774) brought respectability to the folk motive of the specter bridegroom. Propounder of an unrestrained gratification of the senses in art, literature and life, he was Storm and Stress's arch-rebel against Neo-classical rationality.

[6] The eighth poem of the series enumerates historical and mythical robber captains that were household words in early nineteenth century Germany. Rinaldo Rinaldini (1797) is a robber novel by Goethe's brother-in-law Christian August Vulpius (1762-27). Its hero embodies the stock features of a popular folk hero. Orlandini is, apparently, a variant of the same name; Schinderhanno (or rather, Schinderhannes) (1783-03? 09?) was a historical

figure who operated in the Rhineland. Carlo Moor -- actually Karl von Moor -- is the hero of Schiller's play The Brigands (1782), a beau ténébreux (a beautiful but damned soul) who rebels against social injustice, a type of self-destructive avenger of mankind's ills so dear to the playwrights of the Storm and Stress period.

[7] The work of art... has its source not in the personal unconscious of the poet, but in a sphere of unconscious mythology whose primordial images are the common heritage of mankind. Cf. C.G. Jung, "On the Relation of Analytical Psychology to Poetry," The Collected Works of C.G. Jung, ed. H. Read, M. Fordham, G. Adler, trans, R.F.C. Hull (Princeton: Princeton University Press, 1975), XV, 80. Author's italics.

[8] Jung, "On the Psychology of the Unconscious," vii, The Archetypes of the Collective Unconscious," op. cit., VII, 94.

[9] Ibid., 93-94. My italics.

[10] Jung, "On the Psychology of the Unconscious," op. cit. VII, 149. My italics.

[11] Especially not exclusively to his Hamburg cousin (or cousins).

[12] Heinrich Heines lyrische Dichtung (Stuttgart: Ernst Klett, 1971), 29.

[13] The genre has been briefly discussed under II. FRIEDRICH SCHLEGEL'S VISION OF PROGRESSIVE PERFECTIBILITY THROUGH ROMANTIC CULTURE, note 12. The romance genre differs little from the ballad. Generally, it is the lyrical element that tends to dominate its epic aspects. Also, the stark terror of the Celtic, Germanic, Saxon, and Scandinavian balladry seems somewhat weakened by the sunnier, friendlier spirit of the romance, dominated by the courtly -- indeed "romantic" -- atmosphere, as it came down to us in the genuine romances of the Latin Southern and Slavic Eastern Europe. The birthplace

is multiple: the French Provence, Spanish Catalonia, Italy, Northern France and, of course, Castile, where it became codified, and enjoyed its greatest flowering. The ancient Castilian <u>cantares</u> or <u>canciones de gesta</u> like <u>El poema del mio Cid</u> (1140?) were written down in assonated verse ranging from six to sixteen syllables in length. According to Ramón Menéndez Pidal these long lines broke down into the eventually octosyllabic, still assonated verse of the <u>romance</u> genre in the fifteenth century, long before romances started to be written down during the reign of the Catholic Monarchs Isabel de Castilla and Fernando de Aragón (who reigned from 1469 to 1504, and to 1516, respectively). Ever since, the genre was imitated by the greatest poets of Spain and in the West down to our day. The most important subgenres of the Spanish folk tradition are <u>Historic Romances</u> dealing with the deeds and heroes of universal European tradition, Carolingian and Breton romances concentrating on the topics of the Old French Epic (<u>chansons de geste</u>), the <u>Frontier</u> and <u>Moorish Romances</u> that glorified a more historical past focusing on the last decades of the <u>Reconquest</u> of Spain from the Moors. There came down to us also the so-called <u>Fictional</u> (<u>novelesco</u>) and <u>Lyrical Romances</u> that deal with universal human themes of love, death, happiness and woe. In the late sixteenth and in the first half of the seventeenth century the <u>romance</u> was cultivated among others by Góngora, Lope de Vega and Quevedo. Even the Gallicizing eighteenth century of "enlightened" rationalism had writers of <u>romances</u> among which foremost figures Nicolás Ferdández de Moratín. With the advent of Romanticism, the <u>romance</u> enjoyed understandably immense popularity. Angel Saavedra and Zorrilla in Spain, much earlier Herder, Friedrich Schlegel, Tieck and especially Brentano (<u>The Romances of the Rosary</u>, Cf. V. EARLY ROMANTICISM, 3, "Brentano's Manifesto of the Romantic Ethos" in this volume), and Heine. Victor Hugo in France, Pushkin in Russia, F.L. Čelakovský and Julius Zeyer in Bohemia are just a random few Romantics and post-Romantics who tried their hand at reviving this most popular genre of the Late Middle Ages and the Renaissance. The greatest twentieth century collection of "artistic" <u>romances</u> is of course Federico García Lorca's <u>Gypsy Romancero</u> (1924-27). Among the non-Latin imitators, Heine's <u>romances</u> are unique in their mostly faithful preservation of the octosyllabic verse where the even lines (male or female) are rigorously assonated, the odd line remaining rhyme-free.

[14] Storz argues convincingly that the element of epically-oriented balladry that manifests itself throughout the "Youthful Sorrows" portion of the <u>Book of Songs</u> indicates Heine's progress toward a more realistically "objective" assessment of his own and the human condition in general. The earlier, often feigned "great sorrow" of unrequited love is replaced by the "reality of weighty gravity," traceable to a concretely experienced tragic sense of life. The "subjective confessions" of his earlier "songs" achieve in the ballad a "formally perfected (<u>durchformt</u>) containment." The poet "attempts to break out of the I-perspective." Cf. <u>Heinrich Heine's lyrische Dichtung</u>, 61-66.

[15] Among several poems directly dedicated to her the best and most typical of Heine's <u>matrolatry</u> and intimate familiarity with "the old lady" is a much later composition (1843) entitled "Night Thoughts" that appear in the cycle "Occasional Poems."

[16] "Will the heavenly replace the earthly Madonna for me? I want to drug my senses. Only in the infinite depths of mysticism can I cast off my infinite pain." The passage is excerpted from a letter to his Christian classmate Sethe. Cf. Brod, <u>op. cit.</u>, 52.

[17] Set to music by Robert Schumann in 1840 under the title "The Two Grenadiers."

[18] Written in "Spanish trochees," this romance maintains scrupulously female assonances in the even verse endings, a concession to Spanish metrics unknown to other German imitators of the Spanish <u>romance</u> genre, and abandoned by Heine only occasionally in his later years. Yet even Heine is not quite consistent in the assonance pattern; while a Spanish

poet would have maintained the same assonance pattern throughout the composition, or would have broken it up into sections each of which would have a consistently identical assonance pattern differing from every other section, Heine remains consistent in the first few stanzas only to introduce eventually a new assonance in each of the four-line stanzas. My translation renders fairly consistently this inconsistency. The "ardent-pardon," "marvel-under," "husband-nuptials," (ä or shwa assonance) changes to i-e in the following stanza ("bitter-smitten") only to return again to the original shwa pattern.

[19] Heine claims a Hebrew Passover hymn with the refrain "And it was at midnight" and the line "He who intoxicated himself drinking out of sacred vessels was slain that same night" inspired him as to topic, rhythm and sparse vocabulary. Cf. German Literature Since Goethe, ed. Ernst Feise and Harry Steinhauer (Boston: Houghton and Mifflin, 1958), 15.

[20] The octosyllabic base is gradually forced into crescendos in response to the growing tension pervading the poem through the introduction of a steadily growing number of dactyls. As the atmosphere of drunken boastfulness disintegrates into stark terror, the dactyls disappear, bringing a decrescendo in the general mood.

[21] Heine refers to them as the "dilettanti of revolution, with their physical-fitness clichés." Cf. Brod, op. cit., 94.

[22] A comparison with Goethe's poem "Welcome and Farewell" throws into relief some of the major differences between a fundamentally classical and Romantic treatment of the dashing lover theme. Although the Goethe poem belongs to the pre-classical Storm-and-Stress period it already features most of the traits of Goethe's realistic self-assessment and unabashed, healthy egoism. These qualities facilitated an honest subjectivism in the communication of his affective experiences, eliminating the need for the Romantic devices such as the Rollengedicht, the "role poem" fiction, behind which the pseudo-objec-

tive Romantic hides his feelings, pretending to be a hunter, sailor, troubadour, crusader, traveler, soldier of fortune, pirate, etc. Goethe's poem ends with a self-assured bantering declaraction of the independence of the self, aloof and detached from the emotional turmoil it causes in the heart of the beloved.

> I saw you and the look that glided
> To me was filled with gentle care:
> My heart with your emotion sided,
> For you I drew each breath of air.
> There glowed a rosy springtime weather
> Around her lovely face's curve,
> Her tender favors -- gods! -- to gather
> I hoped, but hardly did deserve!
>
> But, oh, the dawn sun barely rising
> With parting makes my heart grow tight,
> Your kisses, what bliss tantalizing!
> Your eyes, what sorrow in their sight!
> I went, you stood, your downcast glances
> Went with me with their humid pleas,
> But, being loved, what bliss one senses,
> And, oh, ye gods, to love what bliss!
>   (My translation).

[23] Namely in poem VIII of "Dream Images," XLII of "Homecoming," XXIX of "New Spring" (New Poems), and in the second part of "Jehuda ben Halevy" of the third book of the Romancero.

[24] Such as, respectively, the Heidelberg Tun, an immense wine cask with the capacity of 49,000 gallons, and the miracle-working image of Saint Christopher in the Cologne Cathedral.

[25] Ratcliff was never produced on the stage; the premiere of Almanzor was interrupted during the last scene when the irate audience was informed that the play's author was an "unpopular Brunswick Jewish money-changer named Heine." Cf. Brod, op. cit., 160.

[26] Heine compiled it by using the lyrics from his Travel Sketches, his first book of poems and the

"Lyrical Intermezzo" of the Tragedies and a Lyrical Intermezzo. The Book of Songs continues to be considered the crowning achievement of Heine's Muse to this day.

[27] Storz, op. cit., 69.

[28] "Either Caesar, or nothing!"

[29] Though only through translated texts.

[30] "Vasistha was a prominent sage among the brahmans. His name figures in both the Ramayana and Mahabharata." A.C. Bhaktivedanta Swami Prabhupada reports that according to legend "Vasistha could approach all the higher and lower planets.... There was a great tension between him and Visvamitra who wanted his kamadhenu, wish-fulfilling cow. Vasistha ... refused to spare his kamadhenu and for this Visvamitra killed his one hundred sons. Cf. "First Canto, Creation," Srimad-Bhagavatam (New York: The Bhaktivedanta Book Trust, 1972), Part II, Canto I, Chapter 9, 77.

[31] A topic treated as the struggle of good and evil over the poet's soul in the sixth poem of "Dream Images."

[32] The travel book on Italy launches in its last chapter "The Baths of Lucca" the earlier-mentioned unfortunate attack at Platen that initiated the notorious Heine-Platen feud, damaging and demeaning to both parties. The equally vicious satire on assimilated Jews at Lucca did little to endear Heine to many of his coreligionists. Perhaps the saddest thing about the Heine-Platen feud was the mutual incomprehension of their respective political and aesthetic principles which, in the final analysis, were almost identical.

[33] They are unrhymed verses of various lengths and irregular, though forcefully accentuated rhythmic patterns. Both length and pattern are regulated in each passage by an inner, emotive rhythm and affective intensity.

[34] Heinrich Heines lyrische Dichtung, 152.

[35] Brod, op. cit., 152.

[36] Heine's sojourns at the island of Nordeney off the coast of the North Sea in 1826 and 1827 was intended to cure frequent violent headaches, symptoms of a spinal disorder that was to paralyze him and, eventually, to kill him.

[37] The rhythmic pattern and free verse structure bear a heavy imprint of Goethe's poems from the latter's Storm and Stress period, namely of "Limits of the Human." Compared with the gods, Goethe's human falls woefully short of the Divine.

> Standing on bones which
> Sturdy are, pithy,
> Foursquare, firmly grounded by
> Earth the perennial,
> Short is his reach,
> Only with oak trees
> Or with the grapevine,
> Himself he'll measure.
>
> Gods from the humans
> How do they differ?
> Many a wave stalks
> Ahead of deities,
> An infinite stream.
> Us, up it carries,
> The wave us buries,
> And we have foundered. (My translation)

[38] Spawned by the mix of Ouranos' seed and sea foam.

[39] This aspect of Jupiter as "father-killer" is valid only by indirection. It was Cronos that mutilated his father Ouranos; Jupiter-Zeus merely forced his father Cronos to regurgitate Zeus' syblings.

[40] Brod, op. cit., 241.

[41] Heine gradually gave up on the idea of prac-

ticing law in Hamburg, getting an assistant professorship at Berlin through the influence of Rahel Varnhagen's husband, and, in Munich, through the good offices of the Bavarian Minister of the Interior. He was not even able to secure the post of Syndic with the Town Council of Hamburg.

[42] Forever searching for the *juste milieu*, the golden mean, and never finding it, Heine went through a brief period of adulation of père Enfantin's sexually "liberated" faction of the movement. Soon, Heine was deriding some of the more extreme measures advocated by Enfantin's followers who understood under the concept of "free woman" a "collective ownership of women." The actual founder of the movement Claude-Henri de Rouvroy, comte de Saint-Simon (1760-25) was already dead when Heine arrived in Paris. Saint-Simon advocated a state-directed economy of producers from which all idlers, whether due to laziness or affluence, would be excluded. The administrative and legislative power would go to "producers" (scientists, industrial executives, artists, inventors, workers) in direct proportion to their contribution to public welfare.

[43] Nerval translated some of Heine's poems into French. Théophile Gautier draws Heine's portrait as that of a god-like man, "mischievous like the devil," an extravagant spender, "more lavish still with the expenditure of esprit," i.e., with spirit and spirituality. Cf. Brod, *op. cit.*, 276.

[44] "Kant was our Robespierre." Brod. *op. cit.*, 217.

[45] Brod, *op. cit.*, 273.

[46] *Ibid.*, 216.

[47] Promulgated by Prussia in 1833, the Zollverein brought about an economic union of the German Lands under Prussian leadership, displacing the de facto political leadership of Austria. It eliminated interstate commerce barriers and unified all tariffs into a common tariff policy against non-German states.

[48] "A Lyrical Intermezzo," XI.

[49] Restating poetically the above-mentioned dictum "Kant was our Robespierre." Supra, note 44.

[50] Augustus, first emperor of Rome from 27 B.C. to 14 A.D., sent Publius Quintilius Varus with 20,000 troops to collect an increased tax burden from recently conquered German tribes east of the Rhine. The whole expeditionary force was annihilated by the Roman-educated Arminius. The victory put an end to the plan of gradual Romanization of Germanic Central Europe.

[51] Some of it Heine originally planned to publish as a second volume of the Book of Songs.

[52] Heinrich Heines lyrische Dichtung, 114-117.

[53] This sub-genre of exulting love lyrics renders a pleasant, immediate experience without the typically Heinesque dialectics of alternating joy-grief moods (with the latter inevitably winning out). As indicated above, it was initiated in the "Lyrical Intermezzo." The immediacy and unfeigned life affirmation makes these poems true Lieder, songs approximating young Goethe's nature, life and love intuitions. To this category belong the already commented titles "During the Splendid Month of May" of the "Intermezzo" and "You Are Just Like a Flower" in "Homecoming." These precious lyrical moments of brilliant vigor and happiness grow rarer with Heine's age and progressive paralysis.

[54] It echoes the "Lotus Flower" poem (number X of "A Lyrical Intermezzo").

[55] Spinoza views individual finiteness with equanimity inasmuch as sub specie aeternitatis, seen from the viewpoint of eternity, Being as universal substance is eternal.

[56] Storz, op. cit., 119-20.

[57] He calls this leveling of Heine's emotional

turmoil into a more objective, detached self-observation an "effect-oriented joy of engaging in persiflage and disillusionment." Cf. ibid., 121.

[58] Compare with Lamartine's "L'Occident," "Sunset" (1830) in the second part of this volume dealing with French Romantic poetry.

[59] Op. cit., 122. Storz also mentions the spade work done by Heine for the chanson genre developed in our century by "Brecht, Kästner and Tucholsky."

[60] supra, Head XVIII. The Venusberg of German legend is a mountain standing between Eisenach and Gotha (Thuringia). Travelers were allegedly lured to a cave below it where they were kept in eternal bondage to the charms of Venus.

[61] This process has been noted in the preceding discussion of the First cycle of the North Sea poems.

[62] The sixth and last series of New Poems.

[63] The word is a misspelled and truncated version of the Spanish olla podrida, "rotten pot," potpourri in French, meaning a "pottage" or medley of various motifs, songs and insights. Brod points out Heine's faulty and extremely limited knowledge of Hebrew (Cf. Heinrich Heine, 30). The same carelessness shows in Heine's imports from Spanish. A direct reference to olla podrida occurs in Atta Troll, Head XI, only this time Heine does not have in mind a medley but an actual Pyrenean dish. He is consistent in misspelling it as "Ollea-potrida."

[64] For Hölderlin see IV. TRANSITION FROM CLASSICISM TO ROMANTICISM. HÖLDERLIN'S MYTHIC POETRY, note 10, and Plato, The Banquet "What power has [Eros?]... To interpret and to ferry across to the gods things given by men, and to men things from the gods..."

[65] Aristotle refers to the experience of participatory immortalization as thinganein, "touching immortality." Cf. Metaphysics, 1072 b 18-31.

[66] It appeared for the first time in 1844 in Karl

Marx's Paris journal <u>Vorwärts!</u> (Onward!) It was republished later in the "Supplement" to the <u>New Poems</u>.

[67] The epos is written in scrupulously iambic octosyllables with no rhyme or assonance whatever.

[68] This right was criticized by most Romantics, namely Schelling and Novalis. See <u>supra</u>, 2. The Magic Idealism of Novalis, note 14.

[69] Feuerbach (1804-72) considered the idea of God no more than a projection of man's own noblest qualities. He insisted that theology and philosophy be converted into anthropology. Cf. <u>The Essence of Christianity</u> (1841). Bruno Bauer (1809-82) struggled for the dethronement not only of the transcendent Christian spirit but also of Hegel's theologizing atheism. He envisioned a reconciliation of reason with reality through a strictly personalized Being-through-oneself.

[70] Proudhon's principle "property is theft" was more than once ridiculed by Heine.

[71] Hamilcar Barca, generalissimo of Punic (Carthaginian) forces and archenemy of Rome made his son Hannibal (247 B.C. -83 B.C.) swear eternal enmity to Rome. Hannibal grew up to be Rome's nemesis when in the Second Punic War (218-01 B.C.) Hannibal led an expeditionary force across the Alps into Italy where he roamed virtually at will for some fifteen years, repeatedly defeating the armies of Rome.

[72] Heine's transcription of the Spanish female first name Urraca.

[73] The name does not seem to be Basque, although it could well be a variant to <u>euscaro</u>, the original Basque term for that language and nationality.

[74] The theme is all-pervasive in Heine's work but it becomes especially shrill in the earlier-commented "It's High Time Now That With Common Sense," poem XLIV of "Homecoming."

[75] The "revolutionary rationalist" and Romantic aesthete was not spared the final symbolic ignominy of his active life. During his last outing ever, he was caught in a street riot during the February Revolution of 1848 and had to hide in the Louvre where he collapsed at the feet of Venus de Milo. Henceforward he became confined to his "mattress grave" which allowed him some relief from constant pain and for a few years facilitated a limited writing activity. In the last seven years of his life, his creativity unabated, he could continue working only by making up and memorizing his verses during sleepless nights and then dictating them in the morning to his secretary.

[76] Heine plays havoc once more with taboos and puns drawn from German and French vocabulary. The name Crapülinski is contrived from the French cra-pule, blackguard; Waschlapski is a derivation from the German Waschlappen, wash-cloth, which in German has the additional connotation of limp will-lessness. The greetings "kokhan!" are derivatives of the verb "kochat," to like, love. "Shlakhtits" means nobleman in Polish. Jan Sobieski was king of Poland between 1674-96, a knight-errant idealist who saved Vienna from the Turkish siege of 1683 at great expense of men and equipment. Schelmufski is a current name derivative from the German Schelm, rogue, with the Slavic patronymic ending-ski tagged on; Uminski could be Heine's own compound with the Slavic noun um, meaning ability, art, artfulness, for base; Eskrokewitch has for base the French word escroc, swindler, cheat. Shubianski is a patronymic of Schubiak, a XVIIth century North German word meaning literally "scratch jack," scoundrel; Eselinski is derived from the German Esel, donkey.

[77] They are written again in unrhymed and unassonated "Spanish trochees."

[78] Juda Ha-Levi (1080-1140), poet and theologian of Toledo, was known to the Arabs as Abul-Hassan. He wrote both in Hebrew and Arabic. A treatise written in Arabic entitled Al Hazari presents arguments in favor of Judaism as a religion superior to

all others.

[79] Rudel flourished in the latter part of the twelfth century. He fell in love with the countess upon hearing pilgrims returning from Antioch praising her charms.

[80] Her real name was Crescentia Eugénie Mirat, but for Heine she was always "Mathilde." In 1841 when Heine was forced into fighting a duel, he legalized their relationship prior to the affair of honor in which he was nicked by the opponent's bullet. But even the marriage ceremony he had undergone for Mathilde's sake was not free of an ironic twist. Heine the rationalist Jew, for a while Teutonoman and Jacobin, then a non-practicing Protestant, was married according to the Catholic rite.

[81] It was held in Toledo during the reign of Pedro I (the Cruel), King of Castile from 1350 to 1369. Two eminently well trained representatives of the Catholic and Jewish faiths were allowed to argue the superiority of their respective theologies with the judgment awarded beforehand to Catholicism.

[82] A generic name used by the ancient Hebrews to include all gentiles. The poem was written in 1824.

[83] It is one of Gretchen's songs in *Faust* I.

>In Thule a king held power
>Whose troth went past the grave,
>His queen, in her dying hour,
>A golden cup him gave.
>
>...............................
>
>No prize he found more thrilling,
>Each feast from it he'd drink,
>And tears from his eyes went spilling
>His lips when touched its brink.
>
>...............................
>
>He sat, good cheer arousing
>For all his knights to see,
>In his sire's hall carousing,
>In the castle on the sea.

> The ancient drinker slowly
> Its life-blood's emptied the glow,
> Then threw the vessel holy
> Down to the flood below.
>
> He saw it falling, drinking,
> And sinking in the sea.
> His eyes, they too started sinking;
> No other drop drank he.

[84] Greek god of the north wind.

[85] "On the Psychology of the Unconscious," *Two Essays on Analytical Psychology*, vol. VII. 78 and 93.

[86] Pierre Ronsard (1524?-85) was the leading star of the sixteenth-century French Pléiade, a constellation of seven Renaissance poets intent on the revival of French poetry according to the principles of classical antiquity and on the propagation of the French language as peer to its Greco-Roman models. In addition to Ronsard, it included Jean Dorat (Ronsard's teacher), Joachim du Bellay, Jean Antoine de Baïf, Remi Bellau, Pontus de Tyard and Etienne Jodelle. They cultivated the ode, the sonnet and the alexandrine in preference to home-bred medieval poetic forms. There is a parallel between the first sonnet of Ronsard's Pièces posthumes; les derniers vers and Heine's "Lazarus" poems. Naturally, allowances have to be made for the differences in period and personality, but Ronsard and Heine share the same fascination with an objectively viewed drama of the disintegrating self. The following is the first quatrain of a Ronsard sonnet from the above-mentioned series.

> Nothing but bones a skeleton I resemble,
> Unmuscled and unnerved, untissued and
> unfleshed,
> On me death had its missile ruthlessly
> unlashed.
> I dare not see my arms for fear they'll
> start to tremble.

Cf. *Oeuvres complètes* (Paris: Gallimard, 1950), II,

634.

[87] Hypnos was represented with wings on the temples of his head and holding a poppy stalk with a sleep-dispensing horn; Thanatos, with wings on his back, and a downturned torch. Actually, Heine seems to be thinking of Morpheus (Dream), the son of Hypnos-Sleep, the former mentioned only by Ovid.

[88] It is also paraphrased by Calderón in the drama Life Is a Dream (1636) as "el delito mayor del hombre es haber nacido," "the greatest crime of man is having been born" (Act I, scene 2).

[89] Heine called her "Mouche" because she wore a signet ring with the engraving of a fly. At their first meeting, La Mouche was struck by Heine's "fascinating features," his "face of Christ with the smile of Mephistopheles." Cf. Brod, op. cit., 334. Details of her life are sketchy, even her real name and nationality have never been positively identified. When she met Heine she claimed to be twenty-five, an adopted child from a broken home, and tutor of German in Paris. She translated some of Heine's poems into French. Mathilde discreetly avoided her during the latter's regular visits at the poet's bedside.

[90] See the third part of this volume dedicated to Spanish Romanticism.

[91] As does too, in the time-honored fashion of Galician and Breton legends, don Félix de Montemar, the student of Salamanca.

[92] The only comic relief provides the inclusion of the proto-Romantic philosopher of enthusiastic intuitionism Johann Georg Hamann (Cf. IDEALISM IN THE ROMANTIC ERA of this volume) among the Old Testamental paladins and heroines. Actually, Hamann's inclusion is not accidental, his name occurs in the same verse with Esther and Holophernes. Heine is the punster to the end, confounding the German Hamann with the Hebrew Haman (with one n), villain in the Biblical Book of Esther.

[93] "And yet there is a divine corner in man." Cf. Brod, op. cit., 329.

[94] Subsuming both Christians and Jews under the title of barbarians does not in any way vitiate Heine's dedication to the Scriptural Judaism of his last years.

[95] Nietzsche's praise of Goethe as virtually the only superman of post-Renaissance Europe (except for Napoleon) is most instructive for the comprehension of Heine from whom, incidentally, Nietzsche had learned a great deal in terms of style and aphoristic thought structuring. According to Nietzsche, Goethe alone had been able to combine "reason, sensuality, feeling and will;" he alone "could dare to permit himself the whole scope and richness of naturalness" (i.e., of existential experience), "to whom nothing was forbidden except weakness." A truly "liberal spirit" like Goethe's "stands with a merry and confident fatalism in the midst of all, convinced that only what is particular is to be rejected and that, as a whole, the all redeems and affirms itself; he no longer denies." Cf. The Twilight of Idols, "Sallies of an Intempestive," 49. My translation.

2. Lenau, the Terminal Figure of German Romanticism.

Nikolaus Lenau (1802-50), actually by his full name Niembsch von Strehlenau, was an ethnic German born in Hungary of old German nobility which had some strains of Slavonic and Hungarian blood. In appearance and passionate temperament more Hungarian than German, he inherited a melancholy, restless nature from both parents and embarked early on a ceaseless and never-rewarded quest for beauty and happiness. Endowed with a genial sensibility for music, he was an aristocrat by blood and propensities, spoiled as a child by a mother who married again when widowed to provide the adolescent with some of the luxuries he never knew as a child. Uncertain whether to become a violinist or poet, Lenau drifted from the study of philosophy to agronomy, law and medicine at Vienna, Pressburg (Bratislava, now in Czechoslovakia) and Heidelberg. While in Vienna he frequented the Austrian poets Grillparzer and Zedlitz. In 1831 he moved to Stuttgart attaching himself to the Swabian School around Uhland. A legacy eased his economic situation; a book of verse (Poems, 1832) was an instant success and repeatedly republished.

On an impulse, he went to the U.S. in 1833 as "settler." Predictably, he became disillusioned with homesteading in Ohio and returned to Germany, only to move again to Austria. Back in Vienna, he fell in love with Sophie Löwenthal, a married woman of great insight and sensibility who stimulated his emotions and creativity without satisfying the need for a permanent relationship. The affair dragged on for a decade; these were Lenau's most productive but also most upsetting years. In 1838 he published Newer Poems. Faust (1836), a drama-epos, remained a fragment, as did Don Juan, (started in 1844, published posthumously in 1851). Two long epic poems Savonarola[1] (1837) and The Albigenses[2] (1842) deal with topics close to Lenau's elegiac nature: both show the hopelessness of Utopian schemes and charismatic movements that aspire to a radical reform of human affairs. Lenau was not an epic or dramatic poet per se, but his fundamental lyricism succeeds in breathing life into the haunted heroes of his dramatized narratives allowing their unfeigned Weltschmerz (spleen) to reach truly epic proportions. A similar mastery of mood Lenau achieves in two lyrico-epic poems dedicated to the Wandering Jew Ahasverus[3] and in a dirge on Héloïse's star-crossed love for Abélard.[4] As professor Johannes Klein points out, "Faust and Ahasverus are beset by spiritual suffering, whereas don Juan and Héloïse suffer the pangs of sensuality.[5]" Freeing himself at last from Sophie Löwenthal's spell, Lenau settled in 1843 once more in Swabia. He finally married a year later, but the mental disorders -- possibly a severe schizophrenia -- that have been plaguing him for years reached a state of crisis, culminating in a stroke and, eventually, insanity. He died a virtual vegetable in an asylum in Vienna in 1850.

The desperate search for some positive and lasting meaning of existence runs like a leitmotif through Lenau's epic and dramatic work. It originates in his radical alienation from an imperfect, insensitive world of banal realities and an irreconcilable tension between a will to believe and a repeatedly triumphant skepticism. A review of the topics that held attraction for Lenau reveals a great deal about his haunted psyche. He identifies with Faust the seeker of, first, absolute knowledge, and then, of the absolute human experience. As Klein points out Faust's world filled with "contradictions" turns in Lenau into an "existential void" (Leere des Daseins). What is left from Goethe's struggle for absolute individuation is the ghostly "Frau Sorge,[6]" Lady Care, who inspires worrisome concern about human affairs and poisons Faust's last moments. The searcher for an absolute self realizes too late that the struggle for any grand design can succeed only at the expense of true happiness which lies in simple, unpremeditated life-awareness. Ahasverus, condemned to an eternal pilgrimage without the reprieve of death, "had betrayed love, i.e., Christ," the same as don Juan[7] had degraded the act of love into a never-ending chase after the absolute possession of beauty. The drive to unattainable perfection leads to eternal restlessness; this restlessness causes existential fatigue, and fatigue, in turn, the suspicion of a metaphysical void behind the absurd phenomena of perpetual flux. Indeed, Lenau need not have read Schopenhauer, for the atmosphere of an existential letdown in the wake of the failure of French republicanism to transform the world, and the equally dismal outcome of the Napoleonic experiment were a universal phenomenon in the decades following Waterloo.

Klein contrasts Lenau's psychological landscapes with those of Eichendorff and Heine, and with the self-conscious but objectively detached classicism of von Platen who succeeded in effacing entirely his poetical personality from his work. Like Platen, Lenau wrote Songs of the Poles celebrating their struggle for independence, but the similarity ends there.[8] Like Heine, Lenau identifies his ego with his work and lets it speak through the landscape moods he conjurs; unlike Heine, there is no ambiguity or multivalence in Lenau's work, no satirical or cynical break in mood. What in Eichendorff was a mostly optimistic, though yearning-filled "ringing," is in Lenau "lament.[9]" But Lenau does not fully qualify for a nineteenth-century Gryphius[10] either, for the latter's threnodies on the "tears of the fatherland" shed amidst the horrors of the Thirty Years' War were a social, as well as a deeply personal statement. All things considered, Lenau had abandoned the pretense of singing with the voice of a folk poet; he was never attracted to the trappings of "Romantic mythology,[11]" i.e., to medievalism, castle Romanticism, the splendors of the Latin South, the mirages of the Orient, and Celtic and Nordic fogs. Virtually every Romantic can be accused at one time or another of striking the pose of the great sufferer, except Lenau, for he suffers from a genuine horror of "the abyss of an inexplicable metaphysical break[12]" in the fabric of existence. As far as his function in the process of phasing out Romanticism is concerned, he is not a transitional phenomenon like Heine. Though it would be unfair to equate Lenau with Heine's assessment of expiring Romanticism as a "trailing-off whimper" (Atta Troll, Head

XXVII), the movement simply passes on in Lenau's excruciatingly vivid analyses of flux and reflux of nature where there is no hope or hold for a sensitive seeker of beauty-in-permanence.

Professor Klein seems to value the short poems dedicated to Faust and Ahasverus much higher than most of the popular Reed Songs, Forest Songs, and the Voices, the usual fare[13] appreciated by the wide public. The allegorical representation of Faust as the carelessly venturesome creature in the short poem "Butterfly" is one avatar of Lenau's haunted self. Like all Romantic martyrs of the need for self-transcendence, Faust penetrates into the beyond only to find out that a return from this absolute experience is impossible. Once out of the meta-Platonic cave, he is barred from reentering it because of his greed for scientific (i.e., absolute) possession of the ultimate that surpasses the Platonic friendly exposure to it to the extent that befits and partially divinizes the finite individual. Faust's hybris as seen by Lenau helps to further refine the difference between Platonic classicism and Romanticism: the classicist leaves the reentry to finite existence open, a choice scornfully rejected by the Romantic. Faust's punishment is the discovery that although he had sacrificed his sanity to penetrate the beyond ahead of time for the sake of a live possession of the Absolute, the transcendent realm of spirituality refuses to communicate with him. The spirits whose dimension he had invaded may pity his plight, but "they must pass [him] by," pursuing "their course throughout eternity."

Two poems dedicated to Ahasverus ("Ahasverus, the Wandering Jew" and "The Wandering Jew") return to the already familiar motif of the haunted "chosen" sinner-martyr of existence who looks in vain for the release from life's inadequacies. As Klein points out, Lenau-Ahasverus realizes that "death would be the only hope to make life once again worth living.[14]" The second, longer poem of the two, shows a fairly staid, almost classical control of emotion in depicting the martyr of human hybris that bears resemblance to the suffering of Prometheus; yet the death wish of the life-weary searcher for the ultimate gains in poignancy through a contrast between turbulent content and impassive form. Lenau, the "intempestive" latecomer becomes an echo of a no longer fashionable Titanism nailed to a rock, "a furtive ray walled in a stony prison," a world too narrow for his flights and too adamant to forgive him for trying to break out of it.

"The Voice of the Rain" is a representative sample of the cyclus Voices. It introduces once more the figure of the outcast from the world of commonplace convention dressed in the role of a wanderer. But this is no playful, ironic role-poem in Eichendorff's style in which fiction and poet remain two separate, if closely communicating, entities. Lenau is the wanderer who contemplates, and quite objectively, the iron laws of flux, of a silence before the rainstorm, the thistles' rigid repose, disturbed only by the intrusion of human "clothing." The second quatrain of this sonnet introduces the mutual penetration of the gray rain skies and of an equally gray world in which for a brief moment the primeval oneness of man and world is reestablished, looming as an undifferentiated, pre-individual Universal Being in which the confidences of two equally life-weary creatures obliterate all difference between "my grief" and "yours." The two tercets carry the transformation of these soberly registered data into a most subjectively experienced feeling of overwhelming grief so powerful that the "ringing answer to a silent query," given by the crashing-down rain, and "the wind-lashed thistle's swish and humming," become too stark to be translated into humanly conceptualized language.

The excerpts from the Reed Songs (poems 1 and 5) included in this anthology are fairly typical of the tenor and form of the cyclus. They are impeccably sculpted consonated verses[15] that blend imperceptibly the keenly noted natural phenomena with the lethal spleen of the author.

The tone of the first Reed Song starts out again as a controlled and descriptive analysis of the sun's progress beyond the horizon. The third stanza once more converts these apparently indifferent data into an intimately experienced self-involvement. The "distance" corresponds, by its very nature of <u>extension</u>, to the poet's "deep, still woe."

Poem 5 repeats this emotional development of the author's empathy with the impassivity of existence. The setting shifts from that of a dying day to the dead of night. The first two stanzas are again a descriptive statement reminiscent of Eichendorff's nocturnes; the third introduces a "tearful" mood as the poet is overcome by the memory of his beloved whose absence blends perfectly with the peaceful indifference of nocturnal forest imagery.

"Lake and Waterfall" abandons the established octosyllabic meter[16] but not the stanzaic length and number. It is frankly normative in tone, postulating the classical balance between calm premeditation and precipitous action, once its course has been rationally determined. The allegory of the "deep, thoughtful lake" as opposed to the "noble daring" of the "thunderous waterfall" is not very original. Needless to say, in Lenau the execution of this ethical norm remains wishful thinking.

"Supplication" is directed to the "limitlessly gentle night," praised as "the stuff of dreams," and "serious" as well as "mild" in its quiet aloofness. This short poetic gem is a bid for self-transcendence, for a nobler level of awareness. Lenau's radical propensity to nocturnally conceived aloneness and existential uniqueness craves indeed the <u>Nachtseite</u>, night aspect, of a soul weary of the stark Apollonian clarity of daylight; it is, however, totally alien to the mystical or diabolic manipulations of the cryptic side of reality occurring in Novalis' or Hoffmann's visions.

"Autumn Lament" examines the downward cycle in the revolution of the seasons. Formally, it repeats the rhythm and rhyme pattern of the preceding poem.[17] Summer's demise is deplored as occurring all "too soon;" the advent of fall is heralded with the conventional apparatus of "mournful winds," "forest shudders" and "sighs of dying nature." The poet's intimate colloquy with the autumnal setting equates the season's gifts, the "dry leaves" as tokens of an inevitable passing, with "dry hopes" for happiness which return each year with the same, unerring regularity.

"Winter Night" is a haunting description of a landscape filled with air "stiff with winter's sting." In this silent, snowy life suspension the poet's drive to rush away from human inadequacy continues unabated; even the snow-laden tree limbs are seen as bowed "longingly to death." Here again Lenau-Ahasverus expects of death the self-transcendence he cannot otherwise achieve: he challenges the life-stifling frost to arrest his heart's "heat-churned recesses."

The four-line vignette poem "Question" redefines the foremost activity that Romantic sensibility made so much of: it is the act of aesthetic creation, spontaneous ("puzzlingly sired"), frail, transitory, and unrepeatably unique.

"Calm at Sea" unfolds another masterful contrast of formal metric regularity with an underlying, undefined metaphysical dread. The smoothly flowing trochees[18] reflect the imperceptible rhythm of the calmly indifferent sea. It is not the stormy sea that provokes the poet's spiritual unrest; a sea storm is no match for his spiritual turmoil, but the "ocean at rest," suggesting the classically ordered "music of the spheres" as taught by Pythagoras[19] has its echoes in the soul's dreams. However, the attunement to nature's calm is only superficial. Even though not articulated, the stirrings of the unconscious which hint at the unhealable rift between the World Ground and individuality produce a fear which "tightens its hold around "the holy, mute alliance" between the One and the All. This alliance, achievable in Goethean universalist classicism, only exacerbates the Romantic ego's impotence vis-à-vis the universe and the need for its concrete mastering.

"The Three Gypsies" from the cyclus *Figures* may well be Lenau's best known poem. This time, the lilting alternation of trochees and dactyls[20] stands in no contrast to an inner turmoil, but is a true reflection of the poet's love-hate relationship with a transcendence open to simple nature creatures like the carefree Gypsies. The image of the poet's coach "plodding" through a heath echoes his own vain quest for an existence less determined by human needs the absence of which the Gypsies seems to be so genuinely enjoying. He envies them their acceptance of the simplest phenomena of life: one fiddles for himself a fiery Hungarian air, obviously not haunted by Lenau's dilemna whether to be a violin virtuoso or poet; the second one contemplates, without philosophical hair-splitting, the curls of smoke rising from his pipe; the third is sleeping the day away while the wind, churning his dulcimer,[21] stirs dreams, probably quite pleasant ones, in the sleeper's soul. The Gypsies' threadbare and unkempt appearance reflects scorn for all the conventions of a society which Lenau cannot abide yet cannot live without, as his fiasco as settler in America had amply proved. He turns time and again after the Gypsies, longing for their insouciance imprinted in their outward appearance and even complexion, but knowing full well that their "triple way" of "scorning life" cannot be duplicated through premeditated imitation.

"The Distant One" is the briefest lyrical essay on the opposite of the proverb "absence makes the heart grow fonder." It is Heinean in theme, mood and even rhythm, one of those exuberant exclamations of unmixed joy over love and life, rare in both poets. The only hint of sadness is the underlying theme of the absence of the beloved, the same that pervades the first of the <u>Reed Songs</u>.

The title of "Arrival and Parting" sounds like a variant of Goethe's earlier-mentioned "Welcome and Farewell.[22]" Nothing could be farther from the truth; Goethe's healthy, erotic egoism has no place in this little dirge for the breakup of a love affair. The three stanzas elaborate, respectively, the arrival, the emotion-stirring words and the final farewell of a girl, identified by the poet with the last dream of his youth.

"The Night Wind At Last Suspended" develops the commonplaces of the Romantic forest song sub-genre.[23] The motifs of "peace," slumbering clusters of birds, the "whispering swells" of a well made louder by the universal silence bring nothing new. The third stanza, however, unfolds an original image of a spacially dialectic relationship between "nearness" turning into distance, and the nearing "memories." The theme recalls the first Reed Song which to a certain extent personifies "distance" as an empathizing force, "shining mild and bright" into the poet's "deep, still woe." The poem concludes with the restatement of the dilemna between rational acceptance of life's finiteness and its affective rejection.

"What Silence, What Discoloration[24]" fits well the tone and mood of the songs dedicated to reeds and forests. The poet's congenital melancholy identifies with the "tender expiration" of autumnal nature. The absence of birds and the skeletal-like presence of empty nests thrown into relief by the absence of leaves are accompanied by the muffled fall of those still remaining. The poem closes with what could well represent the fundamental essence of Lenau's lyrical being: a half-hearted acceptance of the fact

> That all this dying and decaying
> A secret joy is of becoming.

This then is Lenau's "last forest song of things Romantic:" the essential Romantic melancholy over the finiteness of life should be -- but hardly is -- tempered by the metaphysical insight that cosmic flux ought to be viewed as a passive exuberance of birth, death and change, a truly eternal becoming, permeation and rejuvenation of all finite things and events. But to accept this insight and to feel and think accordingly, is already the concern of Poetic Realism.

NOTES

[1] The Florentine Dominican Girolamo Savonarola (1452-98) was a radical reformer of monastic and social abuses. A fiery orator and fanatical ascetic, he led the Florentines on a Puritanic crusade that included book-and-art burning sprees and a restructuring of Florentine society along the lines of a fundamentalist Utopia which condemned the elegant trappings of Renaissance life as sinful vanities. Between 1494, when the popular faction expelled the ruling aristocratic Medici family, and 1497, Savonarola was a virtual dictator of a Florentine citizens' republic. His fulminations against the moral corruption of Pope Alexander VI's (Rodrigo Borgia's) court at Rome caused him to be excommunicated in 1497. A year later he lost face in an ordeal by fire the performance of which failed to materalize due to an opportune rainfall. Soon after he was accused of heresy, tortured and condemned to death by hanging and burning. An avowed enemy of Renaissance life exuberance, Savonarola was a despot in religious matters yet leaned in politics toward reliance on the spontaneous efficacy of the democratic process which could hardly function in the years of a ruthless power struggle between Italian city states and of French interventionism.

[2] With the city of Albi in Southern France as their center, the Albigenses flourished in the XIIth and XIIIth centuries. They were a fundamentalist Christian sect whose beliefs showed strong elements of Manichaean and Gnostic heresies. In 1208 Pope Innocent III (1198-16) called a crusade against them and the city of Toulouse. Their final defeat came in 1229 when Count Raymond XII ceded Toulouse to France. In subsequent years, papal inquistions managed to gradually root out the last remnants of the movement.

[3] The legend of the Wandering Jew goes back to a Leyden MS of 1602, supposedly written by Chrysostomus Dudulaeus of Westphalia. Within a decade the story of Ahasverus the "Eternal" Jew appeared in

Dutch, Flemish, French, Scandinavian and Czech translations. Ahasverus was condemned to wander about till the end of time for having taunted Christ on his way to Calvary by telling him to go quicker.

[4] Peter Abélard (1079-42), brilliant theologian, founder of philosophical conceptualism and professor at the Notre Dame Cathedral School in Paris was mutilated upon the orders of Canon Foulbert because of his love affair and secret marriage with Héloïse who was Foulbert's niece. The two lovers spent the rest of their lives in monastic seclusion. The famous correspondence between them dates from about 1125.

[5] Geschichte der deutschen Lyrik, 2nd ed. (Wiesbaden: Franz Steiner, 1960), 526-27.

[6] Op. cit., 527.

[7] Op. cit., 526.

[8] Op. cit., 527.

[9] Op. cit., 524.

[10] Andreas Gryphius (1616-64) was undoubtedly the greatest poet of reflective lyrical poetry in the Baroque era. As playwright, he was considered the "German Shakespeare" of Germany's and the world's tragic crises.

[11] Klein, op. cit., loc cit.

[12] Op. cit., 528.

[13] Op. cit., 533.

[14] Op. cit., 526.

[15] Most poems in this collection are written in octosyllabic trochees without a single deviation in rhythm and rhyme (female-male alternating rhyme endings of the ab ab pattern). Each poem consists of three four-line stanzas.

16 The poem foreshortens the meter to an alternating hexa-and heptasyllabic pattern of alternating male-female rhyme endings in the established ab ab sequence.

17 The number of stanzas grows from three to four.

18 This poem abandons the octo-and hepta-hexasyllabic rhythm pattern for a regularly alternating octosyllabic-pentasyllabic alternation. The rhyme alternation (female-male) and the four syllabic stanza structure remain unchanged.

19 Next to nothing is known of Pythagoras' person, life and only little of his philosophy. Even his birth and death dates are vague (585/65-495/75 B.C.). He set up a socio-political commune in Croton in Southern Italy for the training of men and women in wisdom and the art of living. His initiates were trained in the ascetic virtues, chief among them the maintenance of silence during a probationary period of five years. Pythagoras is the discoverer of the geometrical theorem named after him and of a mathematical, precisely calculable base of tones and accords. He read his discoveries in music into astronomy and metaphysics, speculating about an inaudible but real, mathematically provable "musical" harmony underlying the revolution of heavenly bodies, the so-called "harmony of the spheres." Like Plato later on, Pythagoras was able to reconcile rationalism and mysticism through the medium of the mathematical symbol.

20 The stanza count is expanded to seven four-liners with the odd octosyllabic verses ending in a male, and the even, heptasyllabic verses, in female rhymes.

21 The dulcimer is an instrument with metal strings which is played by striking the strings with two small hammers. It is an indispensable element of the Gypsy band. The image of its strings being ruffled by a wind gust recalls the Eolian harp (or lute, lyre, wind harp), an instrument dear to the

English Romantics. Like the dulcimer it consisted of a sounding box with strings, but it relied on the wind to produce sounds which was achieved by placing it in an open window. The instrument was named after Aeolus, god of the winds in Greek mythology. Coleridge has to his credit a poem entitled "The Eolian Harp."

[22] See VII, EXISTENTIAL COMPROMISE, 1. Heine the Exasperating Proteus, note 35, supra. The poem is built in three two-line stanzas consisting of decasyllabic couplets.

[23] This is again a four-stanzaic poem in the Heinean vein of alternating octo-and hexasyllabic female-male rhyme endings, each stanza consisting of four lines.

[24] The structure is basically the same as in the preceding poem except that the meter expands to nine syllables throughout, each verse ending in a female rhyme. This monotonous regularity enhances the sonorous gravity of the composition.

Marcus P. Bullock

ROMANTICISM AND MARXISM

The Philosophical Development of Literary Theory and Literary History in Walter Benjamin and Friedrich Schlegel

American University Studies: Series I (Germanic Languages and Literature). Vol. 51
ISBN 0-8204-0317-2   282 pages   hardback US $ 38.00*

*Recommended price - alterations reserved

Interest in Walter Benjamin's extraordinarily subtle, imaginative use of the materialist view of history has grown strongly in recent years. His interpretations of the changes in culture brought about by technological media of representation, reproduction and dissemination, and the intricate connections he explores between politics and the phenomena of literature and the arts, continue to be among the richest sources of thought we have on these questions. This book shows the relationship between his work and that of Friedrich Schlegel, whose ideas were the foundation of the European Romantic movement, and in many ways the basis of modern literary study. The scope of this investigation extends to such diverse phenomena in our century as surrealism and the philosophical contradictions of modern physics.

«*Not only does this original and imaginative book beautifully reinterpret both Benjamin and Schlegel for us, it should alter our idea of Marxism in a positive and fundamental way.*» (William H. Grass, Washington University)

Contents: Walter Benjamin - Friedrich Schlegel - Romantic and Marxist Literary Theory - The Philosophy of Science - 20th Century Studies.

PETER LANG PUBLISHING, INC.
62 West 45th Street
USA - New York, NY 10036